RUDGE-WHITWORTH

COVENTRY

No. 317.—" Acetyphote
Acetylene, **9/9** each.

Don't trudge it

RUDGE-WHITWORTH
COVENTRY

RUDGE it

Bryan Reynolds

Haynes

ISBN 0 85429 188 1

First published September 1977, reprinted June 1989

Published by
The Haynes Publishing Group
Sparkford Nr. Yeovil Somerset BA22 7JJ England

a FOULIS Motorcycling book

Library of Congress catalog card number
89-84783

Haynes Publications Inc.
861 Lawrence Drive
Newbury Park
California 91320
USA

Editor Jeff Clew
Design/Production Tim Parker
Jacket design Phill Jennings
Printed in England by J. H. Haynes and Co. Ltd.

CONTENTS

THE FOUNDERS

Dan Rudge

Charles H. Pugh

George Woodcock

FOREWORD

MANY marque books have already been written but until now none has been obtainable for one of the greatest of them all, Rudge.

Over the years this has been a cause of some anxiety to me as, with the passing of time, much original and first-hand information would inevitably be lost.

It was therefore with considerable relief and pleasure that I was informed by Bryan Reynolds that he had completed this history of the Rudge and invited me to write the foreword.

During the years in which I worked at Rudge, the late twenties to the mid thirties, I was keenly interested in the early history of the Company but could only obtain disjointed pieces of information from various and sometimes unreliable sources.

My desire for information was further whetted by an occasional sight of the many curious and assorted bicycles and tricycles which were at that time stored in a room above the offices in the Old House at the corner of Spon Street and Crow Lane. Several of these were reported to have been some of Dan Rudge's original experimental models.

Now however my anxieties have been put to rest and who better to tell the story of the Rudge than Bryan Reynolds.

Those of you who read this and are members of the Rudge Enthusiasts' Club will know of the years of concentrated and tireless effort which he has put into the Club and of the many Officies he has held, culminating in his present position of Spares Secretary.

In addition to the enormous amount of research that the preparation of this volume must have entailed, Bryan was far-sighted enough (and possibly luck too!) to obtain detailed records of every Rudge motorcycle ever produced at the final dissolution of the factory. This record is published as an appendix to the subject matter of the book and will be of inestimable value to the veteran and vintage enthusiast and to the restorer.

Quite apart from its historical value this book combines a nice balance between technical detail, competition results and a lively narrative which will I feel sure, commend itself to all its readers.

Tyrell Smith

H.G. Tyrell Smith
Solihull
West Midlands
15 June 1977

INTRODUCTION

THE origins of the Rudge organisation are to be found in the embryo cycle industry. The early days, including the involvement of Harry Lawson and George Woodcock are worthy of a book in their own right. However, the aim of this book is to follow the motorcycle side of the business, although the early cycle story is included briefly, to set the scene. The early development of the Company and the various takeovers established a conglomerate before this word had been invented. The move into motorcycles and other automotive areas such as wheels, was therefore a logical process.

To write the history of the resulting group would have been ideal but the size of volume would have been enormous. For example, although the motorcycle business is followed through into EMI and Norman Motorcycles, it would have been possible to follow the cycles through Raleigh Industries and into Tube Investments. As the group gradually broke up it would also have been possible to follow the development of the car wheel business through the Jaguar Car Company and then into BLMC, while the bearings factory eventually became part of Ransom Hoffman Pollard. Mention could also have been made of Senspray Carburettors and the Atco Lawnmower business, which eventually formed part of Qualcast.

Considerable space could have been devoted to writing about the men who made and rode the machines. The activities of the Pugh family, who built up the organisation, and Victor Holroyd, who put decisions into action. Later, this role was filled by George Hack who organised the greatest of the racing successes. More space could also have been allocated to the riders, many of whom became motorcycling legends. In particular, the road racing team of Ernie Nott, Tyrell Smith and Graham Walker could fill many pages as, not only were they excellent riders, but also raconteurs. There are many anecdotes told by and about this team which have been published in the past. Every effort has therefore been made to include in this book only those stories which have not previously been published. Many of the more popular stories may be found in the TT Special series published by G.S. Davison, which unfortunately are no longer in print.

To keep this history within reasonable limits therefore, the development of this motorcycle business forms the main theme, once production started in 1910.

In producing this record of a fallen giant, I must acknowledge the help and encouragement of two motorcycle experts who are no longer with us. First of all Jim Sheldon, who persuaded me to keep the factory records for posterity, and then Graham Walker, who commented on my first efforts to tell the story – more years ago than I like to admit.

Finally my thanks to all those Rudge Enthusiasts Club members who provided photographs of their machines which are included, and to Barbara, who typed the manuscript.

Bryan Reynolds
Potters Bar
Hertfordshire
June 1977

Chapter One

DAN RUDGE AND HIS LINE

IN the 1860's, Dan Rudge was the landlord of the Tiger's Head Inn at Wolverhampton. In addition, he was a skilled mechanic and became interested in cycles through Walter Phillips, shortly after R. B. Turner had brought from Paris (in 1868), the first velocipede to enter England. Walter Phillips had joined the youthful cycle industry and soon persuaded Dan Rudge to start making his own 'high bicycles'. These machines were to acquire the nickname of 'penny-farthing' and were of a very crude design, with plain bearings and direct drive between the pedals and the wheel. The first Rudge high bicycles were made in 1870 and in the next few years Dan produced a small number of machines of excellent quality. At the first cycle race meeting held in Wolverhampton in the summer of 1869, Dan himself won one of the races while others, mounted on his machines, also were successful.

Though at first the machines were very similar to those of other cycle makers, Dan Rudge was not content to accept design weaknesses and in 1873 he patented the famous Rudge adjustable bearing, British Patent 520. Initially, these were fitted to the high bicycles that he was making for racing. With so much less friction on the bearing surfaces, these machines soon established a reputation for fast starting and were handicapped by being required to start 20 yards behind the start-line. Further evidence of his forward thinking was contained in British Patent 3924, relating to a small wheeled safety cycle, one of the first of this design ever made. Unfortunately, no progress was made in this direction as Dan died on 26 June 1880. There the story might have ended.

The fact that he had established a name as a quality manufacturer is quite remarkable when it is remembered that he remained the landlord of the Tiger's Head Inn, having the machines manufactured in a small workshop behind the Inn. His manufacturing activities were really his hobby yet he managed to take out the first patent on adjustable ball pedals and adjustable ball-bearings within the hub of the wheel. Dan's widow continued the flourishing business which he had built up until November 1880, but sadly there was no designer to carry on where Dan had left off.

The House of Rudge Family Tree

Fortunately, however, George Woodcock, a wealthy Coventry solicitor, was taking an interest in the growing bicycle industry in the town. He had already acquired the firms of Smith & Starley and Haynes and Jefferis. At the suggestion of Walter Phillips, he purchased the patents and business from Dan's widow and then incorporated the well-known names of D. Rudge and Company and the Coventry Cycle Company in his new concern.

A complete book could be written about the companies that George Woodcock purchased to form the new group. Smith & Starley, for example, was founded by James Starley and Borthwick Smith in 1872, in Hales Street, Coventry, using a building known as the St. Agnes Works. This was later to become the centre of the Rudge-Whitworth organisation. Starley himself ultimately became known as 'The Father of the Bicycle'. The factory produced Europa sewing machines and bicycles, under the name of Ariel. As the sewing machines were selling well, the cycles were transferred to a new works in Spon Street, nearly opposite the site where the Rudge-Whitworth works were to be built later. In 1877, Smith & Starley moved the sewing machine works to Crow Lane, which also became part of the Rudge-Whitworth works.

Another business to hold a considerable influence in the new Company was Haynes and Jefferis, which George Woodcock had purchased in 1879. This was mainly an engineering firm, which James Starley had used as sub-contractors for many parts of his bicycles. The association was quite close so that when his nephew showed an interest in engineering and joined him in Coventry, he obtained employment with Haynes and Jefferis. The name of the nephew was James Kemp Starley, who joined the firm in 1877. Another employee of the firm, who was also to have a considerable, but not so beneficial an influence on the cycle industry, was James Henry Lawson, James Kemp Starley soon left the employment of the firm as he considered that it was rather conservative and not adventurous enough for him. A few years later he founded the Rover Cycle Company and designed the first successful safety cycle. Lawson himself later claimed that he was the originator of the safety cycle and it is true that the machine he designed in 1879 was several years ahead of Starley's. The story of that machine appears later in this book but the conflicting claims may be resolved by saying that whilst Lawson was first to design a safety cycle, James Kemp Starley was the first to produce a commercially successful version.

With Haynes and Jefferis, George Woodcock had purchased the tools for the manufacture of an unusual tricycle and from Smith & Starley he obtained the rights to produce this machine, which was then called the *Coventry Lever Tricycle.* This machine, which first came onto the market in January 1877, had a large driving wheel on the left side of the rider and two smaller ones in line with each other, on the right. The smaller wheels were controlled by tiller steering, while two levers drove the larger wheel, the rider sitting astride the cross-bar in the centre. This tricycle later became the *Coventry Rotary,* when pedals replaced the levers under British Patent 972 of 1877. The original tiller steering was replaced by a rack and pinion arrangement under British Patent 520 of 1878, in which form the machine became quite popular. A slightly wider version was also marketed, on which two riders could sit, side by side.

With the amalgamation of these companies, the works were thoroughly reorganised. The old Spon Street works of Haynes and Jefferis and Smith & Starley were given up and the business was concentrated in Crow Lane, which was fitted up with new machinery. At the same time the name was changed to the Tangent & Coventry Tricycle Company. George Woodcock was an excellent organiser and business man and as a result, the business prospered. The Ariel trade name was dropped and the company concentrated on the production of six models, three high bicycles, the *Special Tangent Bicycle,* the

Tangent Bicycle and the *Swiftsure,* two tricycles, the *Coventry Lever Tricycle* and *Coventry Rotary Tricycle* and the *Bicyclette* rear-driven safety cycle. The *Swiftsure* was, in fact, a cheaper version of the *Tangent Bicycle* which, with crossed spokes, had been the first of this type to be built, in 1877.

With the arrival of the Dan Rudge employees in 1880, this name was used for the better quality high bicycles and the tricycle was renamed the *Rudge Rotary Tricycle.* With the change of name came improvements, particularly the steering handle by a rack and pinion device. The high bicycles were soon selling well, but this was not true of the *Bicyclette.* It had been introduced in September 1879 under British Patent 3934 and was very similar to the later safety cycles but was not popular with the cycle buying public even though it was well advertised at the third Stanley Show in Holborn Town Hall in 1880. It was considered too advanced in design by the somewhat conservative prospective buyer. With this machine the Company added the word bicyclette to the French language as they were just opening up a sales depot in Paris. There was no equivalent in the French language for safety bicycle, so the firm coined and registered the word *Bicyclette.* This is the name by which any cycle is now known in France. The machine was greeted with much ridicule by other cycle makers, who nicknamed it *the Crocodile,* little suspecting that it would eventually replace the ordinary bicycle. The machine came to be known as the *Woodcock* in this country, the name *Ariel* being allowed to lapse. This was later admitted by the Company to be one of their major mistakes.

Lawson himself had designed the *Bicyclette,* which was originally called *Lawson's Safety Bicycle.* The machine was far from perfect and had one very serious fault. To obtain a reasonable gear ratio with a small rear wheel, the pedal sprocket was enlarged and the cranks were of the long penny-farthing type. This brought them alongside the front wheel, making it impossible to turn out of the straight by more than a few inches. Lawson rather foolishly persuaded Mr. Woodcock to try the prototype and the latter is reported by eye-witnesses to have come a fearful cropper. It is also reported that he rose from the ground using language that only a naval lieutenant would employ. George Woodcock had been a naval lieutenant in his younger days. It is suggested that this accident, plus the fact that Mr. Woodcock would have to pay for many hundreds of sets of stampings which were valueless, caused a break with Lawson. J. Newton, who had joined the Company as the office boy in that year, wrote the following verse to commemorate the event:

"We only sold one crocodile
and that one went to Spain.
It is just as well for this fair isle
it ne'er came back again".

A more interesting development occurred in 1880 which is more in keeping with the motorcycle story. This was Lawson's first motorcycle patent, British Patent 3913/1880, which related to a two wheeled machine driven by compressed gas. There is no record that this machine was ever assembled and run, which was perhaps not a bad thing when considering the claims made by Lawson for the later Pennington design.

The high bicycle was still in great demand, particularly for racing. By 1882, the racing Rudge cycle, with 58 inch wheels, weighed no more than 21½lb. It could be said that Lawson was one of the first rider manufacturers, as he and Richard Howell both gained world championships on Rudges. These successes and the improved quality brought about by the influx of the former Rudge employees, resulted in an immense

THE KING OF THE ROAD.

impetus to the business and the works were enlarged. To keep up with demand for the high bicycles, the *Bicyclette* was withdrawn in 1881.

From 1881 to 1884 the works continued to produce ever increasing numbers of high bicycles and rotary tricycles but the safety cycle was not being ignored. British Patent 13078 of 1884 covered a much advanced safety cycle, developed from the *Bicyclette*. The prototype was ridden around Coventry by enthusiasts from the works and caused a good deal of favourable comment from other riders. The improved *Bicyclette* was introduced in 1885 and sold well.

In 1885, George Woodcock decided to form the concern into a private limited liability company, to be known as D. Rudge & Company Limited. Twenty-six of his business friends in Birmingham and Coventry subscribed. This increase of capital brought about an expansion of trade, causing yet another enlargement of the premises.

The expansion of the business was due more to the opening of new markets than an increase in sales within the United Kingdom. Many bicycles were being exported to the United States of America, France and Germany and during the year, others were shipped to Denmark for the first time.

Although business was booming, the Company still found time to make unusual devices that utilised cycle parts. One that provided great entertainment was a cycle boat, to seat three, which was taken many times to be tested on the nearby canal. The first three to propel this unusual contraption were R. W. Smith, S. F. Edge and F. Cooper, all to become well-known in the cycle and motor world. While the boat was on the canal it was usual for someone to cycle along the bank to keep an eye on the boat. On one occasion it is recorded that this task fell to Charlie Mann who, being engrossed with the progress of the boat, rode off the tow-path and into the canal but managed, by a piece of gymnastics, to drop on the bank. To the regret of those at the works, the boat was soon claimed by its new owner, who took it away for use on the Thames.

Whereas the boat allowed the cyclist to practice on water, the works also produced a cycle which would allow an oarsman to practice on the road. This 'road-sculler' was a tricycle, which could be propelled by pulling two handles towards the rider, using exactly the same movement as rowing. These were, however, some of the less usual items emerging from a factory which was coming near to producing 100 bicycles a week. Production consisted mainly of the ordinary bicycle and the safety cycle, although the rotary tricycle and a quadricycle were still selling quite well. In 1887, George Woodcock was persuaded by Lawson to enlarge the shareholding of the Company and this was carried out on 4 August 1887, when the name was changed to the Rudge Cycle Company Limited. This was one of the first occasions when Lawson offered shares of a cycle company to the public and fortunately the amount of capitalisation was fairly modest. Lawson later went on to even greater 'successes', netting large amounts of money from shareholders. This enlargement of capital in many cases was not upheld by an increase in production and when the companies could not pay dividends, they went into liquidation. These problems were to come to the fore during the slump which took place in the early 1890's.

A series of depots, owned by the Company, were set up in Great Britain and abroad to sell the Company's products direct to the customer. Although initially they did much to promote the sale of Rudge bicycles, they were later to cause considerable ill-feeling in the trade, and lead to litigation. There had been a shop in Queen Victoria Street, London for some years before 1880, that originally sold ecclesiastical brasswear on the behalf of an art metal manufacturer by the name of Hodgkinson. The proprietor was George Woodcock and it was the success of the sale of Rudge bicycles from these premises that led to the development of the depot system.

One of the earliest depots was established in Paris and a high point in the Company's progress was reached in 1889 when the Company was awarded an International Gold Medal at the Great Exhibition.

In 1890 the first storm clouds appeared on the horizon, as the American market disappeared. After importing bicycles from England, the Americans copied the machines and by introducing mass production techniques, undercut the English cycle prices and closed the market. The Company's attention was therefore turned again to France, where exports had been good since the Exhibition success. Unfortunately this was not enough, as there was a slump in the United Kingdom market at the end of the year. The situation demanded all George Woodcock's financial ability, but he was already a sick man and he

Rudge-Whitworth
Britain's Best Bicycle

The Rudge-Wedge No. 70 Gent's Roadster.

This excellent popular-priced machine is built on Standard lines, its parts being interchangeable with the parts regularly kept in stock by Cycle Agents generally. It is a soundly-constructed machine in every respect. It is exceedingly well finished and equipped and is fully guaranteed for 12 months. The price both by easy terms and for cash is most moderate, and there is no other machine of such good value at anything like the price.

Frame. [illegible] 19 in., 21 in., 23 in. and 25 in. (see page 33), highest quality steel tubing throughout with All Steel Joints, no malleable castings used.
Wheels. 28 in. with 21 in., 23 in. and 25 in. frames; 26 in. with 19 in. frame; finest high tension spokes.
Hubs. All-Steel, dust proof and oil retaining.
Rims. Nickel plated, Cold rolled Steel, with Tubular Edges.
Tyres. 1½ in. Waverley Wired on.
Handlebar. Flat.
Brakes. Back and Front Rim, operated by independent rolling levers. New Popular design, with Patent Adjustment to Back Brake.
Free Wheel. Silent Frictionless Ball bearing.
Cranks. 7 in.
Pedals. [illegible] in. Solid Rubber.
Gear. 68 in. (44 x 18).
Mudguards. Arch Section. Beaded Edge.
Saddle. No. 111.
Finish. Frame, Forks and Mudguards, Black Enamel, lined red and green; usual parts heavily Nickel plated.
Equipment. Pump, Pump Clips, Tool Bag, Spanner and Oil can.
Option without extra charge: Edinburgh instead of Waverley Tyres.

No.	DESCRIPTION	PRICE £ s d	Payable by 12 Monthly Payments of s d	Cash Price (10% deducted) £ s d
70	As above Specification	6 - 0 - 0	10 - 0	5 - 8 - 0
7041	As No. 70 but with Coaster Hub Brake instead of Back Rim Brake	6 - 10 - 0	10 - 10	5 - 17 - 0
7042	As No. 70 but with Two Speed Gear (80 & 61)	6 - 16 - 6	11 - 4	6 - 3 - 0
7043	As No. 70 but with Three Speed Gear (89, 68 & 52)	7 - 10 - 0	12 - 6	6 - 15 - 0
7044	As No. 70 but with Three Speed Coaster Hub instead of Back Rim Brake	7 - 19 - 0	13 - 3	7 - 3 - 0

died in May 1891. Like Dan Rudge, George Woodcock also died on licenced premises, in this case the Kings Head in Coventry, which he also owned. Although his name is not very well known, he was the real founder of the Company in the last of his three separate careers. As a young man he had served in the Royal Navy and, on his discharge,, he had qualified as a solicitor and had much success in this sphere. He had then built up the cycle company from approximately 200 employees in 1879 to over a 1000 by his death, manufacturing products that were known world-wide.

Although paternalism in management is now out of fashion, he ran the Company firmly but fairly. It was not all work either. In the late 1880s he maintained a home at Brighton and each year he would invite employees down for a week's holiday. W. H. Nelson, who later became Assistant Works Manager, wrote of the period "during the early days we used to make the most of life and did not by any means neglect our pleasures. In this respect a great event of the year was the annual trip to Brighton, where the late Mr. George Woodcock had a house. The firm then, as now, used to contribute to the expense so that for a very small sum we were able to spend four or five days in Brighton in quite Royal fashion. We used to arrive there early in the morning, about 300 or 400 in number and, headed by the town band, would march to breakfast in the Town Hall, with colours flying in brave style. One item on the programme was a sea trip to Shoreham, which we made in a ship that had been to the bottom some six or seven times".

One of the reasons for the success of the Company, was the ability of George Woodcock to pick the right man for the job. For example, when W. H. Nelson knocked on the door of the Rudge works in Crow Lane in 1883, the doorman threatened to call the police to remove him for loitering. Fortunately, George Woodcock saw him and took him on the next day. Within three years he became the chargehand working on the *Bicyclette* and he later recalled that in those days there was no drawing office. Every foreman had to originate his own designs, make patterns and get materials. When more than one foreman worked on the same pattern, it was a case of each fighting for his share when the castings came in.

George Woodcock was not averse to recruiting staff from business acquaintances. Amongst those who later reached senior management were his bank clerk and his solicitors clerk. The latter was J. Newton who was taken on by the Company in 1879, as a shorthand writer. He joined a sales office which consisted of four employees, including himself, under the control of 'Black' Draper, the Works Manager, who got his name from his dark complexion and not his disposition.

The Assistant Works Manager was R. W. Smith, who gradually established a name for himself as a designer. He designed the first Rudge tandem in 1886 and many cycle accessories. As the Rudge Company had expanded during the 1880s it had been their practice to manufacture parts for other concerns. One of these was Perry & Company and R. W. Smith designed many of their accessories, which were produced in the Rudge factory. The Manager of the Perry Cycle Department was Albert Eadie and in 1893 R. W. Smith left the Rudge Company to become a founder of the Eadie Manufacturing Company and the Enfield Cycle Company.

Before this however, in 1887, R. W. Smith had designed the *Olympia* tricycle tandem for Marriott & Cooper. Marriott & Cooper were former associates of Thomas Humber who, when the association was dissolved, retained the joint right to use the Humber trademark. Through the connection with Smith, all Marriott & Cooper Cycles were manufactured by the Rudge Company under the name M. & C. Humber.

The prototype *Olympia* tandem was used by S. F. Edge and G. L. Morris to establish a new record for 100 miles on the road by completing the journey in 6 hours 57 minutes 32 seconds. Using a later *Olympia* tandem, S. F. Edge and J. E. Bates reduced this record to 5 hours 30 minutes 31 seconds, and this was to stand for the next thirty-four years. In addition to M. & C. Humber tandems, the Rudge Company was producing its own tandems and these proved very successful in competitive events. These were developed even further by Smith, who was able to produce 'quads' and 'quints', four and five-man tandems, which were used for pacing on the cycle tracks. Later, these were to be replaced by motorcycles, after the turn of the century.

A less happy connection with the Humber concern occurred in 1893, when the General Manager, Walter Phillips, left to join this competitor. He took with him the M. & C. connection, which was later integrated with the main Humber Company. Thus, at a time when the Company was facing a slump, it had lost three key men, Walter Phillips, R. W. Smith and George Woodcock, the founder.

The Company was now in serious difficulties, and the management was reorganised, but it did not have the same paternal approach as that of its predecessors. Cost clerks were put in to try and save the Company but immediately prior to the Cycle Show, all the foremen and chargehands left.

Early in 1894, it was decided to make the *Giraffe* Cycle under licence. This was a very tall safety cycle, which was advertised as 'Keeping the rider clear of mud and road dirt'. It was found, however, that other manufacturers were copying the design without paying royalties, so the project was dropped. It was now quite obvious that the Company was in severe difficulties and the only alternative to liquidation was a merger with another company which had more successful management.

Chapter Two
THE PUGH FAMILY

ALTHOUGH the history of a company should be presented in chronological order, whenever possible, the origins of the Rudge Company are such that it is necessary to go back from time to time to bring the threads of the story together.

While the Rudge Company struggled for its existence in the early 1890's, a new cycle firm had been founded in Birmingham. This was the Whitworth Cycle Company, which was set up in June 1891 by Messrs. Pugh and Sons, an old established firm. The Works Manager of the new firm was John V. Pugh, a young and energetic engineer. Using new plant and new methods, the Company was a success from the start, and within six months, larger works had to be acquired in Rea Street. By 1893, expansion demanded further capital and a private company was set up, the Whitworth Cycle Company Limited. Increased sales demanded further expansion and negotiations were opened with the directors of the Rudge Company, with a view to amalgamation. These took nearly a year to complete and, in October 1894, the companies merged to form Rudge-Whitworth Limited.

In 1893, the Rudge Company had set up a Drawing Office and also it was quite apparent that its sales organisation was superior to that of the Whitworth Company. As a result, in December 1895, the offices and staff of the latter company were moved from Birmingham to Coventry, leaving the chief component cycle parts to be made at Birmingham. The following two years were boom years in the cycle trade and many companies expanded rapidly. With the merger of the two companies only just achieved, the new organisation was more restrained, particularly as the directors felt that the boom could not last. Even so, the production of cycles increased from 9,000 in 1895, to 18,000 in 1896 and 25,000 in 1897.

The integration of staff at Coventry, although not affecting the work-force, caused problems with duplication of management. Fortunately, the number of depots was being increased throughout the country and managers on the sales side soon found new locations. The management at the works, however, remained a little over-crowded, the Works Manager at the time of the amalgamation being Mr. J. Davidson.

Davidson had travelled extensively in China and Japan and was really a structural engineer. It was suggested by his deputy, W. H. Nelson, that his ideal bicycle was something like the Menai suspension bridge and weighed about 100lb. In fact, he did have a quadracycle made on these principles, complete with tie-rods etc. Fortunately, he was a good manager and was able to complete the integration of the production of both companies before his death in 1896.

Although John Pugh had the title of Works Manager, he had little to do with the day to day running of the machine shops. This was taken over by Victor A. Holroyd who, until 1896, had been given the title Works Superintendent.

C. Vernon Pugh, who had founded the Whitworth Cycle Company in 1891, was appointed Managing Director on the formation of the new company and J. Wallis, formerly a Rudge company man, was appointed Chairman. A former Whitworth Cycle Company director, J. S. Taylor, became Vice-Chairman.

Another asset of the new Company was the Registered Trade Mark of the Whitworth concern, No. 156,827. This took the form of a raised hand superimposed on a bicycle wheel, a trademark which was soon to become synonymous with the name Rudge.

The merging of the two companies saw the phasing out of a bicycle which had been in production as long as the Company, the *Rudge Rotary*. It went out on a high note, however, as one of the last was fitted with pneumatic tyres and sold to Princess, later Queen Alexandra.

John Pugh, being a bachelor, moved with the office staff to Coventry, where he took up residence in a small flat over the works in Spon Street. By 1897 the Coventry cycle industry was in serious difficulties and he was fully engaged in saving the Company. Initially the slump came about through the activities of Henry Lawson and Terrah Hooley. Together, they had floated a large number of cycle companies, over-capitalising and making large profits out of the share issue, which the public rushed to buy. As competition became fierce, profits could not be maintained and as a result dividends were passed up. Into this troubled situation came the first foreign competition, which was to sorely test the English companies. It was the practice at that time to quote cycle prices relating to a frame and a few basic parts and then charge extra for a majority of the fittings. Thus a bicycle that might appear to cost £15 could well total £30 by the time it was fully equipped for the road. The American manufacturers, having satisfied their home market, turned to England and started exporting mass-produced cycles, which were complete yet cost only two-thirds of the price of an English cycle. This was the challenge which faced John Pugh and the Board of Directors at a time when the factory had managed to produce a total of 1,216 bicycles in one week. His answer was simple and effective. He standardised on a small range and slashed the price of the Standard bicycle from £20 to £12 12s and that of the Special bicycle from £30 to £16 16s. These cuts proved very effective in keeping up the production of cycles and were followed in 1898 by further price cuts, at which time the Standard machine was listed at £10 10s. These prices were not, of course, popular in the trade but most other manufacturers were forced to follow suit. The reduced prices made the imported American cycles less attractive and their mass importation soon ceased.

At this time the Company introduced the easy payment system, whereby anyone could cycle away with a new bicycle, having paid one guinea and signed an undertaking to make eleven other monthly payments of the same amount. This early system of hire purchase proved very popular and helped increase the production of cycles so that larger premises became a necessity. On 27 May 1898, 380 machines were completed in the one day and by 1900 this number per day was commonplace. A new building was therefore commissioned in Crow Lane and was ready for occupation early in 1901. Meanwhile the Board had rewarded John Pugh for his handling of the business by appointing him Works Director during October 1900.

Less rewarding for him was a downpour in the Coventry area on 31 December 1900, which caused the Sherbourne, a small stream alongside the works, to rise and flood the surrounding area, including the Rudge works. First thing in the morning the works were waist deep in water and much of the new stock of machines was spoilt, as they were all on the ground floor. As the water subsided, a pathway of planks was laid down through the centre of the works, so that the management could come and inspect the damage. The planks extended to the end of the building, where the lift had been raised to the first floor, out of the water. John Pugh walked to the end of the planks to view the situation, but unfortunately, a further plank had drifted in the water to the end of the line and when he trod on it, he disappeared into ten feet of water in the lift well. There is no record of his comments when he surfaced!

Following this disaster, the Dispatch Department was relocated on the first floor of the new building, to avoid a recurrence of this flooding damage.

The Company's first involvement with the motorcycle market came at the turn of the century. The Werner Company in Paris had been producing motorcycles for several years and was looking for export markets. The Rudge Company, with a depot in Paris and a direct sales organisation throughout Europe and the Empire, was ideally placed to market their machines. The Werner Company already had representatives in Great Britain but the Rudge organisation in South Africa had the only well organised European outlet. The initial approach came from the depot manager in Johannesburg, who asked whether he might have an agency to sell Werner motorcycles. Charles V. Pugh therefore entered into negotiations with Werner Motors Limited, who had secured the manufacturers rights from Werner Freres of Paris for the United Kingdom and the British Colonies.

Following negotiations, Rudge-Whitworth Limited entered into an agreement with Werner Motors Limited whereby they became the sole agents in South Africa for Werner motorcycles at the 'lowest price' of £33 7s per machine. Thirty-six machines were purchased and offered for sale.

All went well for a while until the Johannesburg depot discovered that Werner machines were being sold by other firms in South Africa for £28 7s, undercutting them by £5 per machine. On receiving this news, Charles Pugh was most upset and refused to pay to Werner Motors Limited the £378, which represented the balance of the account. Werner Motors Limited were not prepared to let the matter rest and on 17 November 1903 the case was heard in the King's Bench Division before the Lord Chief Justice. Mr. J. Eldon Bankes, KC appeared for Werners while Mr. C. A. Russell, KC, counterclaimed on the behalf of Rudge-Whitworth for breach of contract to the amount of £1500. Mr. Pugh was first to give evidence, supported by Mr. Telford, the depot manager in Johannesburg. Under cross-examination he was unable to say whether the twelve machines had been sent to South Africa before or after he had signed the agreement with Werner Motors Limited. On their part, Werner Motors Limited claimed that if the machines had been sent after the agreement had been signed, they must have been sent by Werner Freres of Paris, even though the latter denied taking such action.

At this point it was agreed that some documents would have to be produced showing the date of delivery of the twelve machines which were being offered in competition with the Rudge Werners. The Lord Chief Justice therefore suggested a postponement and the two parties settled their differences out of court.

In consequence, the Rudge-Whitworth Board was rather prejudiced against the embryo motorcycle market. No further attempt was made to market a motorcycle of their own, especially as the factory was now fully engaged in what was to be known as the Society boom.

Cycling had been very much a middle-class pursuit during the 1880's but it had been largely ignored by the upper-classes. Although Queen Victoria had taken delivery of a *Royal Salvo* from James Starley in 1881, and had granted Starley Brothers the Royal Warrant, the upper-classes did not take to cycling in any number. By the turn of the century however, quite a number of machines had been delivered to the Royal household and were used by Queen Victoria's children. This sparked off a boom which was to go on for several years and the Rudge-Whitworth Company was fully engaged in expanding output. By 1906 this had reached 75,000 cycles a year.

The Rudge-Whitworth Company had also adopted a little 'badge engineering'. The Rudge-Whitworth name was associated with quality and keen prices. The up-to-date machinery had enabled the company to streamline production to the new factory. In addition, the Company made a practice of employing a large number of female employees. They proved to be most skillful in cycle assembly, yet were paid less than their male counterparts. It was therefore possible to market a very cheap cycle although the Board felt that this cut-price version should not bear the name Rudge. As a result, after 1894, the *Crescent* cycle was launched and sold at the very low price of £6 15s. This helped to bring the cycle within the reach of the working man. The Crescent name had been used before on cycles and tricycles exported to America, particularly the early three wheel tandem.

Another forward step came in 1902 when H. L. Heathcote was appointed to head the Chemical and Physical Laboratory, which nowadays would be called the Research Department. Once established, this laboratory conducted research into new materials and tested existing parts. For example, Aero Special cranks were tested to 600lb and cycle chain to 1300lb breaking strain.

At the same time however, the Company again became involved in the motorcycle market through the family of Dan Rudge. When Dan's widow sold the business to George Woodcock, she received a cash sum plus a regular pension. This arrangement was carried on by the Rudge-Whitworth Company. Dan's son Harry inherited his father's interest in cycles and went into business in 1891 with Charles Arthur Wedge, to produce the Rudge-Wedge cycle. In 1902 they became interested in the motorcycle market. Early in 1903 this Wolverhampton firm produced their prototypes, which were displayed on the stand of H. M. Hobson at the Crystal Palace Show in February 1904. The machine was fitted with a Minerva engine clipped to the front down tube. The most unusual feature was the frame, which represented an early attempt at sprung suspension. There were in fact two frames, with only the steering head common to both. The saddle, handlebars and pedals were mounted on one frame while the wheels and engine were mounted on the other. The two were attached at four points by springs and the front forks were solid.

A contemporary magazine stated that "This machine should be completely insulated from road shocks as there are no less than four different sets of springs provided to render it independent of the inequalities of the road surface". Unfortunately, the springs were not damped in any way so that the rider stood a considerable risk of becoming seasick. Furthermore, this additional movement did nothing to help the road-holding of a machine that was higher than usual.

The make of engine used in the later models is open to doubt, as H. M. Hobson were sole British agents for the French Peugeot. Also, as Charles Hamilton had an interest in the firm, he may have fitted one of his own engines.

Unfortunately for the Rudge-Wedge concern, 1904 saw the start of a four year slump in the motorcycle industry. This placed the firm in financial difficulties as the cycle side was not large enough to compete with the major manufacturers. Harry therefore turned to the Rudge factory, which had looked after his family so well over the years, and his firm was taken over. The Wedge name lived on, and joined that of the Crescent, as one of the cheaper Rudge cycles. With memories of the Werner litigation of 1903 and in view of the motorcycle slump, no action was taken to continue manufacture of the Rudge-Wedge motorcycle, and, as far as is known, none has survived to this day.

Far more exciting, as far as the Company was concerned, was a development at the Regent Street depot, which had been opened by the Company in April 1894. A gentleman approached the manager, E. M. Mayes, and asked whether the company rented cycles or alternatively allowed them out on approval. The Company did not normally allow either but when Mr. Mayes discovered that the gentleman was an equerry to His Royal Highness, The Prince of Wales, he was given a tricycle to ride to Buckingham Palace so that the residents could try it out. The equerry returned the following day to say that the machine had proved a great success. At this, Mr. Mayes arranged for the delivery of a range of cycles, and this was followed almost immediately with an order from Her Royal Highness, Princess Henry of Battenburg and others of the Royal Family. The Company subsequently received the Royal Warrant, which was proudly displayed on all cycles and motorcycles for many years.

The increase in production necessitated additional factory space, which was constructed in Spon Street, Coventry between 1905 and 1906. On 31 July 1905, 1,369 cycles were produced in one day, a greater number than the record for a week set in 1897. As production increased so did the range and at the peak of cycle production in 1908, the catalogue listed 75 models, each of which was offered with a ten-year guarantee.

During this period of growth, the trade had become increasingly critical of the Rudge depot system. This was seen as direct trading, which undermined the position of the local cycle dealer. The magazine *The Cycle Trader* had been particularly vocal in its criticism, and by early 1908 the Rudge-Whitworth Company issued a writ against the magazine on 15 April. The case came before High Court in January 1909 but did not proceed as the magazine apologised and withdrew all statements published between 1904 and 1908. The magazine had little option as, on 24 September 1908, the Company had been appointed a member of the Cycle and Allied Trades Association, following acceptance by that body that the depot system did not constitute unfair competition.

In the general area of competition the Company was doing well. A wheel building side of the business had developed from cycle wheels into the realm of proprietary detachable car wheels. Following the success of S. F. Edge and his Napier at Brooklands, using these wheels, they were fitted to a large number of racing cars. In the 1908 TT, for example, twenty-one out of the thirty-five starters used Rudge wheels and only one finisher did not have them fitted.

As might be expected in a large cycle factory, a Rudge-Whitworth Cycling Club had been formed and this too provided publicity for the Company through record attempts. On 10 June 1908, G. A. Olleys rode from Lands End to John O'Groats in three days five hours and twenty minutes, reducing the existing record by two hours forty-four minutes. His machine was a No. 5 Rudge Speed Iron, which weighed only 22lb. On 5 September, the Company claimed first, second and third in the Tandem Race at the Canning Town Track, while T. A. Fisher set a new 1000 miles cycle record in three days nineteen hours and one minute.

DON'T TRUDGE IT, RUDGE IT

Although John Pugh led a fairly tough management team, every effort was made to keep staff and works relations at a good level. In June 1908 he introduced a house journal called *The Rudge Record*, to keep everyone informed of the Company's progress. This form of publication was fairly rare in 1908 and is not particularly common in factories even now. As the Company had its own printing press to print catalogues, the journal was produced by the Advertising Department and J. F. Tidswell became the editor. It was he who coined the catch phrase of "The Temple of the Open Hand" for the works. Early editions of this journal reveal a wide range of social activities, in addition to the very successful Cycling Club. Apart from football, shooting and other sporting activities, the Pugh family arranged a number of social functions. It was usual for Mr. Vernon Pugh, the Chairman, and Mrs. Pugh, to throw a garden party in June at their home at Radford. In 1908, some four hundred and thirty staff and works employees enjoyed their hospitality. The managers of the various departments and of the depots throughout Great Britain were regularly entertained to dinner, in addition to the barge trips and other similar outings.

More unusual were the competitions in *The Rudge Record*, in which employees could win cycles by suggesting improvements in the Company's products. Cycles could also be won by constructive criticism of the previous year's range and also of the catalogue.

At the Annual General Meeting held on 2 November 1908, Vernon Pugh announced a profit of £15,860, which was down on the previous year, but the Company's assets had increased to £401,506, not counting goodwill, and there was a total reserve of £94,054 on a share capital of £200,000. This was accepted with satisfaction by the shareholders, who were informed that the Regent Street depot had been transferred to 230 Tottenham Court Road, which is quite near to Warren Street which was becoming the centre of automotive activity in London.

The production of machines continued unabated into 1909, the only major change being the replacement of the arch section mudguards by those of a new V section. This was to be a notable Rudge feature for many years to come. The year also saw the first exports to Japan, through Nichibei Shoten of Tokyo, although the Japanese were soon to follow America by manufacturing their own machines and closing the market.

Among the racing successes, the most outstanding was recorded on 3 July 1909, when J. H. Bishop completed 513 miles 1430 yards in the 24 Hour Race for the Dispatch Cup. This beat the previous record by 37 miles. The third, fourth and fifth riders home were all mounted on Rudge cycles.

On the manufacturing side, the various divisions were now in full production. Hubs, nuts, pedals and tools were made at the Birmingham Works in Rae Street, ball bearings in Reddings Lane, Birmingham, and wheels and other cycle parts, including cycle assembly, at Spon Street, Coventry.

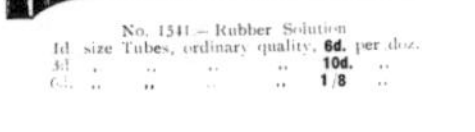

No. 1541 – Rubber Solution
1d size Tubes, ordinary quality, 6d. per doz.
3d .. .. 10d. ..
6d .. .. 1/8 ..

Chapter Three
A NEW ERA BEGINS

IN 1909, the Rudge-Whitworth Company made its third move towards the motorcycle market. The name Rudge was already fully established as a quality bicycle and over 1500 a week were leaving the Coventry works. It was decided that a new motorcycle would be produced entirely within the factory. During 1909, much experimental work was carried out as secretly as possible. Although the products of other manufacturers were examined, the designers began to break fresh ground and were granted a number of new patents which were to remain in force for many years. One feature, which was to last until motor cycle production ceased in 1939, was the one-piece front fork shackle, British Patent 546796 of 1909. This, together with enclosed front fork spring, which also continued until 1939, did much to establish a reputation for good handling.

Other design features were aimed at providing a rider with ease of servicing. On the water-bound road surfaces of the day, punctures were frequent, so most journeys of any length involved at least one removal of the rear wheel. To facilitate this, British Patent 567465 covered a hinged rear mudguard flap. Although this particular feature was dropped when the Multi went out of production thirteen years later, succeeding models incorporated rear mudguard fixings which could be removed easily. On the last machines to be produced, the whole of the rear mudguard (apart from a small section behind the gearbox) could be removed by undoing two nuts and two bolts.

The majority of motor cycle engines produced in 1909 were of side-valve design. One or two overhead valve engines had been produced but these were not popular, due to valve breakages. On a side valve engine, a broken valve meant little more than the engine ceased to run, whereas on an overhead valve design, the broken head would fall onto the crown of the piston and frequently cause expensive damage. The Rudge designers therefore adopted a compromise layout in the form of the 'F' head. In this design, the inlet valve is located immediately over the exhaust valve, to the side of the cylinder. The machine therefore had an overhead inlet valve and a side valve exhaust.

Although the layout was tried by other motor cycle manufacturers, including Villiers, none achieved the success of the Rudge engine, which was produced in a number of capacities for the next thirteen years.

The first machine was assembled in the factory on 27 July 1910, from blueprints completed on 18 July – no time lost here! Although the engineering practice of the day was to cast the cylinder head and barrel in one piece, on the Rudge the head was separate from the barrel, the two parts being held together by three bolts which screwed into the crankcase. The valve chest was positioned to the front right-hand side of the cylinder and the exhaust valve and guide were mounted in a plate bolted to the bottom of this chest, with the inlet valve mounted in a similar manner on the top. Over the inlet valve was a cap held by a central nut through which passed a short pushrod from the overhead rocker. The magneto was mounted on a platform in front of the engine and was chain driven at half engine speed from a sprocket on the camshaft actuating both valves from one cam. The valve lifter operated from inside the timing cover, working on the cam follower. The 'V' pulley on the engine shaft was connected by a belt directly to the pulley on the rear wheel, although the factory was at that time in the process of patenting a multi-plate clutch, British Patent 26634-1910.

Two more machines were built from these blueprints, one on the 19 August which was registered DU 4219 and another on 27 August, DU 4916. These numbers cannot be taken as an absolute guide however, as it was the practice of most companies to use the same registration number on different machines. Those who have read the Brough Superior story will know that George Brough continued this practice long after it had been given up by most other manufacturers.

One of the problems that had not been solved in 1910 was an efficient method of sealing a joint between two metal surfaces under compression. As the original engine had a separate cylinder head, it was necessary to tighten the three head bolts extremely tightly, even though the engines were of relatively low compression. The shape of the cylinder head and the position of the valve chest to one side precluded the use of more than three bolts and as a result it distorted, leading to an even greater gas sealing problem. The cylinder head was therefore redesigned on 1 September 1910 and strengthening bars were added to it, between the retaining studs, to resist distortion. To make room for the additional metal, the priming tap had to be moved across the head to the near-side, the furthest possible point from the sparking plug. Two more machines with the new design of engine were produced on 29 September 1910 and taken out for testing. The registration numbers of these machines? Yes, you've guessed it, DU 4916 and DU 4219! Unfortunately the cylinder heads on these machines proved no more successful than the originals so it was back to the drawing board again.

The engine designed at the end of September 1910 had the inlet valve mounting and head cast in one piece. This detachable part of the head consisted of little more than the inlet valve and manifold. The priming tap was moved back to a more central position in the fixed part of the head and the inlet valve was now operated by a rocker bearing directly on the valve, in place of the complicated cap and short push-rod of the earlier engines. The magneto and camshaft were gear driven and each valve was operated by its own cam, on a single camshaft. The valve lifter remained within the timing cover, operating directly onto the cam follower. A considerable amount of tidying up had taken place generally, the oil drain plug, for example, having been moved from underneath the crankcase to the right-hand side.

In the early days of the cycle industry, Dan Rudge had established his name through successes in sport. This was also to be the policy for the Company's motor cycles as the machine assembled from the third blueprint was to be a competition model. It was

No. 1554.—Tricycles for Boys only : 12in. front wheel, **14/-** ; 14in., **15/-** ; 16in., **16/3** ; 18in., **17/3** ; 20in., **18/6** ; 23in., **19/6** ; 25in., **20/9** each.

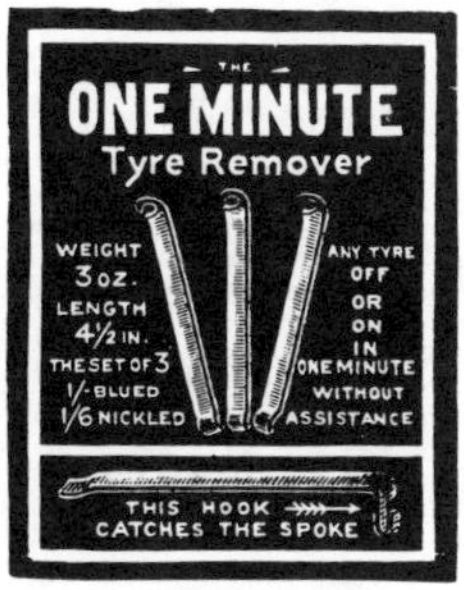

No. 1552.—Tyre Levers, "One Minute." (Set of three) blued, **7/-** per doz.

No. 1553.
Tyre Stopping.
6d. tubes.
3/- per doz.
1/- tubes, **6/-** doz.

No. 1555.—Tricycles, superior finish, with plated parts and best saddle, suitable for either boy or girl : With 16in., 18in., and 20in. side wheels, **30/-** ; 22in., **31/6** ; 24in., **35/-** each.

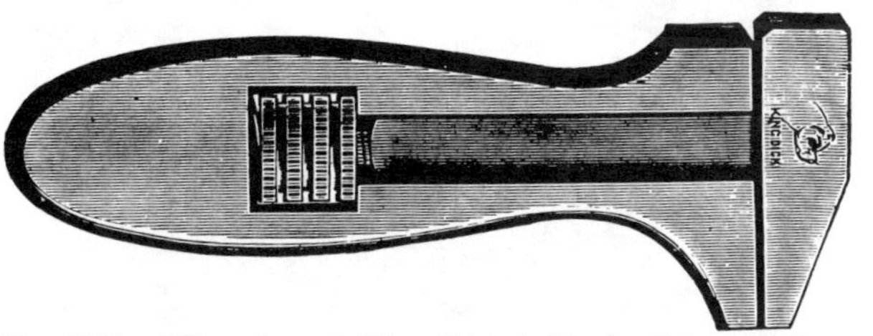

No. 1556.—Wrenches, "King Dick," black, **20/-** per doz.

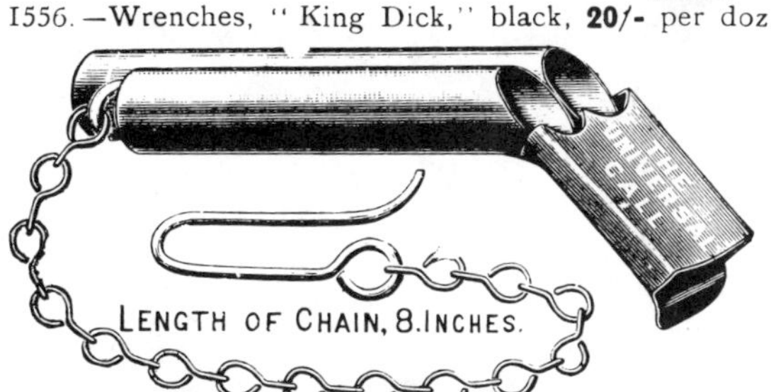

No. 1557.—Whistles, "Universal." Small, **2/6** per doz. ; medium, **2/10** per doz. ; large, **3/4** per doz.

No. 1558.
Varnish, Transfer.
Small bottles, ~~4/-~~ 6/-
Large ,, ~~8/-~~ 12/-
per doz.

By Special Appointment to H.M. King George V

Rudge-Whitworth
Britain's Best Bicycle

Rudge-Whitworth Coventry

The Rudge-Whitworth Engine

The Rudge-Whitworth Engine has been evolved after a long and exhaustive series of practical experiments, and is now a model of power, reliability, and easy working. As will be seen from the illustration the cylinder is set vertically in the frame, and is provided with ample radiating surface, which is largest on the combustion head where most heat is generated. The piston has one ring at each end, this being found in practice to give most power; it also conduces to even wear on the cylinder walls, and properly regulates lubrication. The fly wheels have been designed with the same regard for efficiency, being very heavy, with the weight massed in the rim. Special attention has been given to the valves, and exhaust valve trouble, so common on many other designs, is unknown on the Rudge-Whitworth Engine.

The inlet valve is of the overhead type, actuated by a rocking lever, with external spring on the tappet. The advantage of this is that the spring remains cool, and the exhaust valve, being immediately underneath the inlet, is kept cool by the incoming gases. The inlet valve can easily be adjusted without disturbing any part of the engine, but should it be desired to examine either of the valves, they can be taken out in a few moments without removing the cylinder. The exhaust valve and pipe, and the silencer, are all very large, providing an easy escape for the exhaust gases.

The cylinder can be removed from the crank-case by taking off four nuts, and without disturbing the carburetter and valves; and the whole engine can be removed from the frame by taking out four bolts.

Full specification and further details of the construction of this machine, together with particulars of the Rudge-Whitworth Motor Bicycle Guarantee, are given in the special Motor Bicycle Catalogue, sent post free on application.

Constructional Details.

Light Weight with Great Strength.

Continuous experiments in the Laboratory and on the Road with all varieties of Steel and other materials enable us to build our machines much lighter, but of greater strength and durability than any other make. Rudge-Whitworths are produced at weights from 10% to 20% less than the average of other makes. The saving of effort to the rider, resulting from being relieved of so much useless dead weight, is very important, and is one of the chief causes of the remarkable easy running of our machines.

Patent Fork Crown.

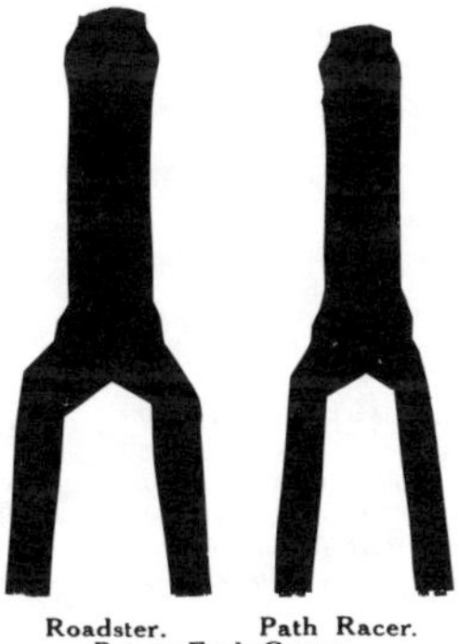

Roadster. Path Racer.
Patent Fork Crown.

The crown is perhaps the most vital point in the construction of a bicycle, for, as the one unsupported junction of parts in a machine, practically all vibration is concentrated there. A breakage at the crown is the most dangerous that can occur, as it is always sudden and complete, owing to the crown being the sole connection between the front wheel and the rest of the machine. In an ordinary crown the vibration is concentrated in the angle formed by the flat crown-top and the ball-head; consequently the metal frequently crystallizes at that point, and fractures are common. In the Rudge-Whitworth design all sharp angles are avoided, and the metal of the crown passes for 2 inches right up the fork stem. This construction distributes the vibration, thus diminishing the tendency to crystallize, and completely abolishing the danger of the machine breaking in two. Another advantage of the Rudge-Whitworth design is that its sloping shoulders and absence of angles allow dust and mud to fall away instead of accumulating and clogging up the brake and steering.

Patent Crank Bracket Mechanism.

This universally admired feature of the Rudge-Whitworth differs totally from, and is far superior to, all others. The bracket shell is itself part of the steel flush-joint frame. The axle and cranks are formed of but two pieces of high-carbon steel, connected by the ingenious patent serrated joint (with its spaces for future adjustment), which does away with the objectionable cotter pins, washers and nuts, by which in other makes the cranks are wedged on to the axle. The chain wheel, embodying the well-known Open Hand Trade Mark, is formed of hard cold-rolled steel, and is attached to the axle by the same patent joint which connects the cranks. This joint is strictly concentric, and retains this quality however frequently it may be operated. The cranks, axle and chain wheel, therefore, consist of but 4 parts, which can be dismounted or put together by loosening or tightening one small flat nut at the right-hand end of the axle. In the Rudge-Whitworth system the number of parts in the group embracing axle, cranks and chain wheel is but 4, as against a minimum of 10 parts in any other system. The bearings of the bracket have an absolutely concentric adjustment of great simplicity and reliability, and are so scientifically designed that the ball pressure on the bearing surfaces is little more than half that on other makes. In other bicycles the adjustment is effected by wedging the bearing cup with a cotter pin, which frequently squeezes it out of truth.

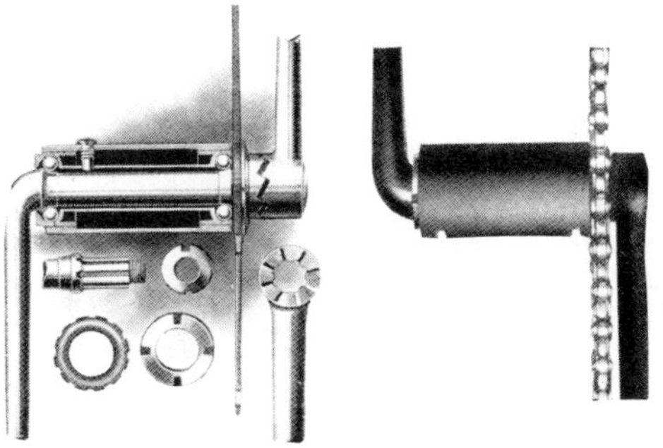

Roadster. Path Racer.
Patent Cranks and Gears.

Chain Wheel.

All Steel Flush-Joint Frames.

This unique feature of the Rudge-Whitworth is of the greatest importance. The ordinary bicycle has its frame built up of a combination of steel tubes with cast-iron joints, the latter being the well-known swellings seen at the angles of such frames. The only advantage of the use of cast-iron is that it is much cheaper, both as a material and in working up. The disadvantages of the cast-iron joints are the inferior strength of the material—to overcome which greater weight is necessary—the inevitable weakening of the steel tubes where they enter the cast-iron lugs, the uncouth

By Special Appointment to H.M. King George V

Rudge-Whitworth
Britain's Best Bicycle

Rudge-Whitworth Coventry

Constructional Details—continued.

appearance of the finished frame, and the tendency of the enamel to crack at the ridges where the cast-iron and steel meet. The Rudge-Whitworth flush-joint frame is made throughout of high quality cold-rolled steel. It is thus uniform in material throughout, a fact which greatly increases its strength and its life. The surface of the frame is uniform and free from ridges and surface joints. It is also much lighter than the ordinary frame owing to the total absence of so weak a material as cast-iron and the exclusive use of high grade cold-rolled steel, which, in its absolute uniformity and freedom from hidden flaws, stands without rival as the most reliable material in the world.

The Standard sizes of frames in which the various models can be had are set out in the specification of each machine. The following table will be useful to guide purchasers in selecting the suitable size of frame :—

19in. Frames suit Riders from	...	4ft. 4in. to 4ft. 10in.
21in. Frames suit Riders from	...	4ft. 10in. to 5ft. 3in.
23in. Frames suit Riders from	...	5ft. 3in. to 5ft. 7in.
25in. Frames suit Riders from	...	5ft. 7in. to 5ft. 11in.
27in. Frames suit Riders over	...	5ft. 11in.

The illustration below shows how the steel joints of the Rudge-Whitworth frame are reinforced at every point by internal webs and liners, and indicates the reason for the great strength of this frame.

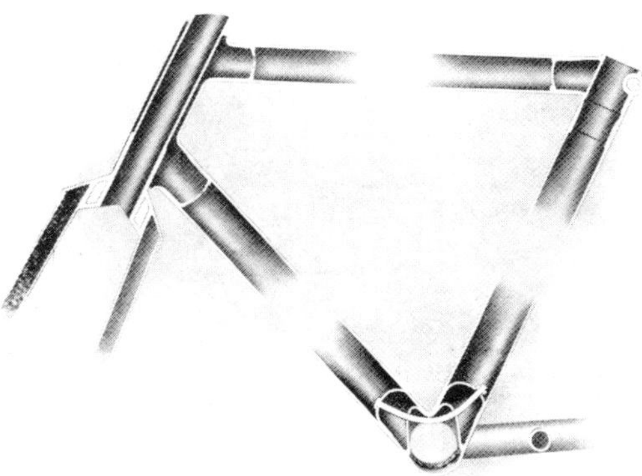

Section of All Steel Flush-Joint Frame.
(For Sizes of Frames see above.)

Rudge-Whitworth Patent Wheels.

In every detail Rudge-Whitworth wheels differ from all others, and surpass them in liveliness, rigidity and strength. The hubs are built up of cold-rolled steel of great toughness, while the bearings are of first grade high carboned tool steel.

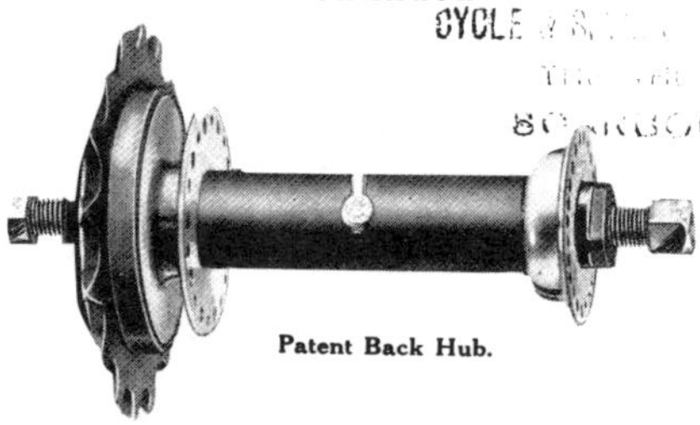

Patent Back Hub.

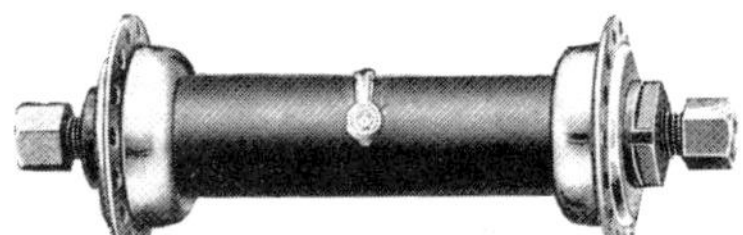

Patent Front Hub.

This system of building up instead of making in one piece permits the most suitable material to be used in each point instead of a heavy mass of uniform character, which at some points is eminently unsuitable for the work it has to do. The great width of the spoke flanges of the hubs of Rudge-Whitworth wheels, and especially the width gained by the dishing of the back wheel, are some of the reasons for their great strength. It is only necessary to apply pressure sideways to the hub of an ordinary wheel, while holding the rim firmly, to see how inferior it is to a Rudge-Whitworth Wheel.

Rear View of Dished Back Wheel.

Handlebar and Head Adjustment.

Section of Handlebar Adjustment.

The ordinary practice is to control these two adjustments by one clamp screwed up by a bolt, with the result that the handlebar cannot be raised or lowered without disturbing the head adjustment and vice versa. Moreover, the effect of the clamping arrangement is to squeeze together the head tube, which frequently distorts the bearings and stiffens the steering. In the Rudge-Whitworth the two adjustments are absolutely independent of each other. There is no clamping, both adjustments being strictly concentric, consequently there is no distortion of the head bearings. The handlebar is secured in its place by a robust internal cone which is drawn up by a bolt whose head appears on the top of the handlebar lug.

produced on 18 October 1910 and weighed 104lb. This compared favourably with its two predecessors, which weighed 208lb each. The machine was entered immediately for the A-CU Round Midlands Tour, in which it proved a satisfactory if not spectacular performer. The three machines were then displayed at the Olympia Cycle and Motor Cycle Show towards the end of November, before the sports machine was sent to the Dublin Depot for promotional purposes. Back at the factory however the mediocre performance of the competition model was not really acceptable and so a fourth engine design was devised.

Even at this early stage, the importance of good engine breathing was apparent to the designer, with the result that the new engine had an enlarged inlet port. The petrol tank followed the long slim lines of the period, and had a separate half a gallon oil section at the front. Lubrication was by means of a hand-pump mounted in the top of the tank. The rear section of the tank had a petrol capacity of 1.35 gallons and there were two petrol taps. One supplied the carburettor while the other allowed petrol to be fed into the priming tap on the cylinder head for cold starting. The most distinguishing feature of the tank was a vertical tube which passed through the tank, immediately over the inlet valve. This made it possible to grind in both valves, after they had been mounted in position – a practice that is rather questionable. The tube was later used to mount a small oil gun so that oil could be dripped onto the inlet valve while in motion.

The inlet dome was spigotted into the barrel and the inlet stub threaded so that the pipe could be securely fixed. Unlike the earlier designs which had vertical fins, the head was bare, apart from the priming tap which was over the centre of the bore.

John Pugh was very much a rider manufacturer, testing out the new machines himself. The earliest known photograph of one of the prototype machines was taken at a social occasion. It was the practice of the various departmental managers at the factory to hire a narrow boat and go for a weekend cruise on the nearby canals. In September 1910 one of these trips had been arranged on the Ashby de la Zouch canal, but due to business commitments John Pugh was unable to join the boat when it sailed on the Friday night. On the Saturday afternoon he arrived on the new machine, and caught up with the boat by riding along the towpath. The photograph was taken when the machine was being loaded aboard the boat, as he joined the party. This was later printed in *The Rudge Record*, the Company's house magazine.

When the new fourth design appeared, it looked similar to the third, but much had been done inside the engine. Plain bearings had been replaced by rollers in both the big and small end bearings and this had necessitated a new connecting rod and crankpin. The valve lifter had been moved from inside the timing case to work on the valve itself, being attached to one of the cylinder barrel securing bolts. The magneto platform was now horizontal and the overhead rocker pillar had been strengthened. The exhaust port was enlarged so that the exhaust pipe located inside it, dispensing with the threaded stub and gland nut used previously. As it was necessary to recast the timing side crankcase, the opportunity was taken to incorporate the word Rudge below the timing cover and this was retained for the next four years. The drawings had been completed by 2 November, and the first of the new machines was produced on 19 November 1910. Six more were produced during December of that year. Although three of these were fitted with clutches, the standard production model was offered for sale with a fixed engine, as the machines fitted with clutches were all works competition machines. The standard production model weighed 177lb while the works machines, with clutches, weighed 182lb.

Probably the most notable of these machines was the one assembled on 12 December 1910. C. S. Burney took it to Brooklands on 17 January 1911 where it successfully climbed the Test Hill, with its average slope of 1 in 5, breasting the top at 15mph. On 30 January 1911, again ridden by C. S. Burney, the machine was recorded in the acceleration test as having a rate of 4.99ft per second over 187 yards. Four days earlier however, V. J. Surridge claimed world records when he completed fourteen laps at an average speed of 61.39mph, with a record lap of 62.71. The care that had gone into the early design of the engine had provided quick rewards.

Production of machines to sell to the general public commenced on 11 January 1911 but one lucky buyer was supplied with one of the prototypes. He was B. Alan Hill, who was provided with a fixed engine model so that he could compete in the Exeter Run.

As mentioned earlier, one of the features of the Rudge Company's sales policy was a chain of depots throughout the country and the Empire, which sold direct to the general public. The first production machines were therefore dispatched to these depots together with copies of the first motor cycle catalogue, which was also produced during December 1910.

What did the motorcyclist find in the Rudge depot window when the local manager had received his machine? The answer was something fairly conventional, when compared to the other machines of the day. Although a quite satisfactory clutch had been tried out on one or two of the prototypes, the first production run provided no such refinement and the machines all had a single fixed gear.

The 499cc single-cylinder engine was mounted vertically in a diamond frame just in front of the bottom bracket. The pedals were connected by a chain to the rear wheel sprocket which incorporated a free wheel so that the pedals could be used as footrests when the engine was running. The main footrests were, however, set well forward in front of the engine, to avoid interference with pedal starting. Later on, the pedals were redesigned so that the left crank could be kicked backwards, to drop down into a similar position to the right-hand crank, thus providing alternative rear-set footrests.

Above the engine, the petrol tank followed contemporary practice with an oil compartment from which oil was fed to the engine by means of a hand pump. Soldered to the left-hand side of the tank was the advance and retard lever, connected by rod to the magneto. The rear brake was a vee block, which was forced into the rear wheel belt pulley by a left-hand foot pedal. The front brake was a fairly flimsy stirrup type, operated by cable from a lever on the right-hand side of the handlebars.

As the engine had no clutch, the machine needed to have a valve lifter which was operated by a lever mounted on the left-hand side of the handlebars. The only other controls were two carburettor control levers mounted on the right-hand side of the handlebars. The earlier models were all fitted with a Brown & Barlow carburettor which the factory proudly announced was made to a special Rudge-Whitworth design. Transmission was by means of a 7/8in rubber vee belt, which provided a fixed gear ratio of 6 to 1.

Having established a name for quality cycles, a number of desirable features were incorporated into the new project to maintain the good name of the company. For example, the handlebars and hub centres were celluloid covered, a fact much appreciated by those who disliked the constant need to clean nickel plating. The wheels were 26in by 2¼in, with a choice of either wired or beaded edge tyres.

The specification was not one to cause a great stir in the motorcycling world because of its revolutionary features but it did have one asset which was to stand in good stead for many years – reliability. In addition, the factory had paid attention to the many minor points that caused difficulties to motorcyclists of the day and where possible effected some improvement. After the initial batch of machines had been despatched, between 11 and 20 January 1911, some extra thought was given to the problem of punctures. The substantial rear-stand and hinged mudguard flap made puncture mending much easier in the case of the rear wheel, but to deal with the front wheel it was necessary to find a brick or a piece of timber to wedge under the crankcase, in order to raise the wheel off the ground. As these items were not necessarily available at the spot where a puncture occurred, a front wheel stand was added to the specification on 23 January 1911.

Although the initial batch of production models followed a common specification, it was possible for a customer to specify variations to suit his own requirements. The first recorded modification occurred on 24 January, when a Mr. Greenwood of Muirkirk had a machine supplied with a nickel plated belt rim. By the end of January, production had reached the rate of six machines a day and a clutch was now available as an optional extra. For those with a fixed gear model, the engine pulley could now be pre-set to provide a gear ratio within the range of 4 and 6 to 1. Even so, the last word had not been said on the subject of gearing as, from the beginning of February, it was possible to obtain from the factory either the fixed or the free engine model fitted with an NSU 2-speed gear. It was with these four variations on a basic theme that the company joined the motor cycle market as a major manufacturer.

The successes of C. S. Burney and V. J. Surridge at Brooklands in January had already encouraged thoughts on the production of a sports model. The first two TT models were produced on 1 March 1911, even though no Rudge had ever entered for this event! The machines were stripped down versions of the normal production models, without pedals and with smaller rear belt rims, to give a slightly higher gearing. The two machines were sent to the Dublin depot for testing, as the constabulary there were less interested in speeding machines than those in the vicinity of Coventry. The following report was subsequently received from Dublin.

> "With regard to hill climbing. I was out on Saturday evening with Mr. Healey and Mr. Kerr, Mr. Fitzherbert, an old Brooklands rider, who has a four-cylinder (famous make), and a captain of the barracks here who has (another famous make), and they went specially to test a hill in the Wicklow mountains, with a very big bend. Healey rode it four times in succession in good style. Kerr was stuck for the first time with his TT Rudge-Whitworth, his gear ratio being 4½ to 1 while Healey's was 5 to 1. They reduced the gear to 5 to 1 on the second TT model and mounted the hill in good style but neither Mr. Fitzherbert nor the captain could climb the hill, try as they might. I had the captain in here on Monday and he said that he intended to give us an order for a machine about the 1st of next month, remarking that our machines were "devils to go".
>
> "Healey and Kerr told me that they ran their machines up to 60mph on one or two occasions".

This test report was unofficial, but at Brooklands the machines were making quite a mark for themselves. On 12 May 1911 Victor Surridge claimed three world records for the flying kilometre in 34 seconds, the flying mile in 54.4 seconds (66mph) and 5 miles in 4 minutes 36 seconds (65.5mph). On 25 May he claimed a record for which he will always be remembered. His machine completed 60 miles 783 yards in an hour, to be the first machine of under 500cc to achieve over 60 miles in one hour. In those days, 60mph with indifferent steering and insufficient brakes was regarded with as much respect as 100mph is today.

Although the TT model was soon introduced into the catalogue, sporting

Rudge-Whitworth
Britain's Best Bicycle

RUDGE WHITWORTH COVENTRY

Bicycles for Boys and Girls.

Bicycles for Boys and Girls are too often mere toys badly designed and most dangerous to ride. Rudge Whitworth Boys' and Girls' Bicycles correspond in design, materials, manufacture and reliability with full-sized Rudge-Whitworths and, consequently, are perfectly safe and can be ridden without interfering with proper growth and development. These perfect models were selected by His late Majesty King Edward the Seventh for presentation to his grandchildren, Princes Henry, George and John, and Princess Mary, the photographs of the Royal children on these bicycles were taken at Balmoral, in September, 1910, and specially published by the gracious permission of King George.

No. 56. For Boys of 5 to 9 years. **(3-ft. 6-in. to 3-ft. 10-in. in height.)**

Frame.—Flush-joint 15½-in.
Wheels.—20-in.
Rims.—Nickel-plated Steel, with Tubular Edges.
Tyres.—1¼-in.
Handlebar.—No. 91, Upturned.
Brake.—Rolling Lever Front Rim.
Free Wheel.
Cranks.—5-in.
Pedals.—3½-in. Solid Rubber.
Gear.—40-in. (32 × 16).
Mudguards. Steel.
Saddle. No. 114.
Finish.—Frame and Forks, finest black enamel; usual parts first quality Nickel-plate.
Equipment. 10-in. Celluloid Pump, Pump Clips, No. 739 Tool Bag, with Spanner and Oil-can.

No. 53. For Boys of 9 to 12 years **(3-ft. 10-in. to 4-ft. 4-in.)**

As No. 56, but with
Frame.—18-in.
Wheels.—24-in.
Gear.—48-in. (32 × 16).

No. 57. For Girls of 5 to 9 years **(3-ft. 6-in. to 3-ft. 10-in.)**

As No. 56, but with Loop Frame.

No. 54. For Girls of 9 to 12 years **(3-ft. 10-in. to 4-ft. 4-in.)**

As No. 57, but with
Frame.—18-in.
Wheels.—24-in.
Gear.—48-in. (32 × 16).

Boys and Girls over 4-ft. 4-in. in height should ride the smallest size adult bicycle, with 19-in. Frame.

No.	DESCRIPTION.	PRICE. £ s. d.	Payable by 12 Monthly Payments of s. d.	Cash Price (10% deducted). £ s. d.
56 & 57	As above Specification	5 - 0 - 0	8 - 4	4 - 10 - 0
53 & 54	As above Specification	5 - 15 - 0	9 - 7	5 - 3 - 6

EXTRAS.—Back Rim Brake complete in addition to Front Rim Brake, **7/6**
Chain Cover (for Girls), **5/6**
Black Laced Dressguard (for Girls), **2/6**

activities were not confined to racing, as much publicity could be achieved through the local long distance sporting trials. B. Alan Hill and C. S. Burney were the most successful, gaining non-stop awards in the A-CU Winter, Spring and Summer Quarterly Trials. The former also scored a first for heavyweight machines at Sutton Bank in April but was not the first Rudge to make the climb, as the *Leeds Mercury* recorded on 31 March 1911.

> "Any motorcyclist who has climbed Sutton Bank has done something that we can pardon him for being proud of, but it seemed madness for anyone on a 3½ horsepower single-geared motor bicycle to dream of getting up this precipitous hill last weekend, when the surface was nothing else but a succession of patches of greasy slimy mud and loose stones.
>
> "There was one motorcyclist who knew he could do it and his name is J. A. Prendergast, and his 3½ horsepower Rudge-Whitworth (without pedals) in its fullest touring equipment hot from a run of nearly 50 miles and without any preliminary tuning up, made four perfectly clean ascents of Sutton Bank which includes a bad hairpin bend and a gradient of 1 in 3.9 in places. Two of the tests were from the bridge and two starting on the steepest part of the hill, and all four tests were made from standing starts.

Rudge-Whitworth
Britain's Best Bicycle

Rudge-Whitworth Motor Bicycle.

The Rudge-Whitworth Motor Bicycle embodies the latest and best experience in Motor Cycle construction. It includes many new features, which after exhaustive tests have proved to be very great improvements. Among these features are the special design of frame, affording a very low seat and comfortable riding position; a new and particularly effective spring fork, and a very economical Carburetter, which allows of a great range of running speeds. Special attention has also been given to the accessibility and easy manipulation of all parts, in which direction the rider will find a general all-round advance upon previous practice.

Engine. 3½ h.p. single cylinder, 85 m/m bore × 88 m/m stroke. Volume 499 C.C.
Carburetter. Special Rudge-Whitworth design, handlebar control.
Ignition. High-tension Magneto.
Valves. Mechanically operated; inlet by overhead lever, exhaust of special large diameter.
Silencer. Large and unusually efficient, with cut out.
Transmission. [illegible] in. rubber belt.
Gear. Can be altered from 4 to 1 to 6 to 1 by means of Rudge-Whitworth Adjustable Pulley.

Frame. Rudge-Whitworth special design, affording low and comfortable riding position.
Spring Forks. Rudge-Whitworth special design. The most effective design for absorbing road shock.
Handlebars. Special New Rudge-Whitworth pattern, very long.
Tanks. 22 gauge tinned steel-plate. Oil capacity, 1 quart; Petrol capacity, 1½ gallons.
Foot Rests and Pedals. Foot Rests carried well forward. Pedal gear fitted; pedals may also be used as foot rests.

Brakes. Front Rim operated from handlebar, and Foot Brake acting on Belt rim.
Tyres. 26 in. × 2¼ in. Beaded Edge Dunlop Non-Slipping.
Mudguards. 4 in. wide with patent back guard hinged on Carrier, registered No. 56740.
Saddle. Large size Motor Cycle.
Stand. Spring operated, picks up automatically when cycle is moved.
Accessories. Tool Bag of special registered design No. 570581 with Oil can and Canvas Roll, containing full necessary equipment of tools.

DESCRIPTION	PRICE £ s. d.
As above Specification	48 - 15 - 0
As above Specification, but with addition of Free Engine Clutch	55 - 0 - 0

For detailed Specification, Guarantee, and Terms of Business, see special Motor Cycle Catalogue, post free on application.

"Each attempt was successful and there was not the slightest suspicion of knocking in the running of the engine.

"One thing we are certain of, judging by what we have actually seen and by what we have heard, is, that Rudge-Whitworth's will prove to be most formidable competitors in this season's organised hill climbing contests."

In April 1911 G. T. Gray and W. G. Elce joined B. Alan Hill to gain Gold Medals in the Land's End run, in which C. S. Burney also gained his Silver Medal.

In addition to the NSU 2-speed, a number of purchasers were specifying the Phillipson adjustable pulley or two-speed rear hubs, although unknown to them another more interesting variant was being tried at the factory. This was the Mabon variable gear, which was fitted to a number of machines from the end of March 1911. This consisted of a pulley on a countershaft, which expanded and contracted when a tank lever was moved. The countershaft moved in an arc round the mainshaft so that the belt remained at constant tension. Below the lowest gear, the lever moved the countershaft to a position where the belt was slack, thus giving a free engine position. The quadrant had seven positions, free plus six forward gears and was known as the six notch multi. Although only a dozen or so were made, they were only one step from one of the most famous of

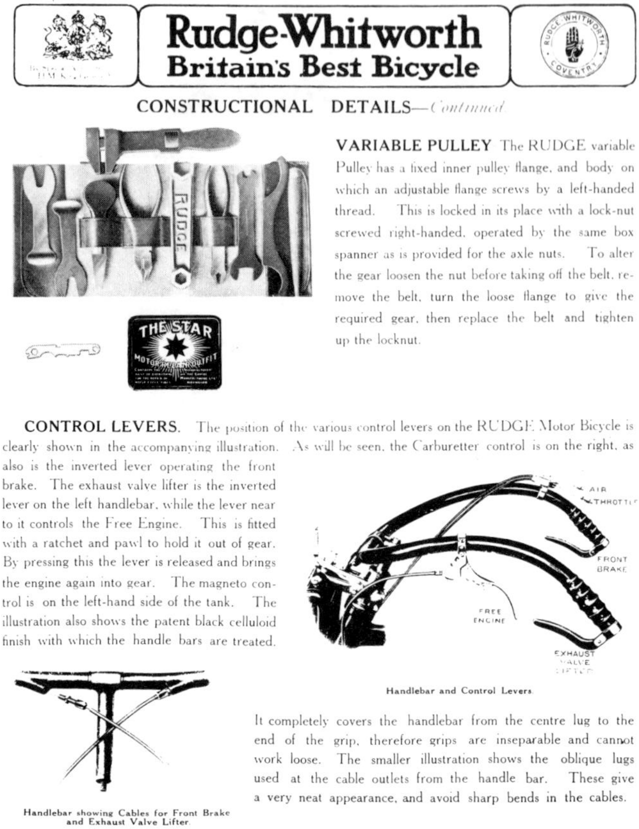

Rudge-Whitworth
Britain's Best Bicycle

CONSTRUCTIONAL DETAILS—*Continued*

VARIABLE PULLEY The RUDGE variable Pulley has a fixed inner pulley flange, and body on which an adjustable flange screws by a left-handed thread. This is locked in its place with a lock-nut screwed right-handed, operated by the same box spanner as is provided for the axle nuts. To alter the gear loosen the nut before taking off the belt, remove the belt, turn the loose flange to give the required gear, then replace the belt and tighten up the locknut.

CONTROL LEVERS. The position of the various control levers on the RUDGE Motor Bicycle is clearly shown in the accompanying illustration. As will be seen, the Carburetter control is on the right, as also is the inverted lever operating the front brake. The exhaust valve lifter is the inverted lever on the left handlebar, while the lever near to it controls the Free Engine. This is fitted with a ratchet and pawl to hold it out of gear. By pressing this the lever is released and brings the engine again into gear. The magneto control is on the left-hand side of the tank. The illustration also shows the patent black celluloid finish with which the handle bars are treated.

Handlebar and Control Levers.

It completely covers the handlebar from the centre lug to the end of the grip, therefore grips are inseparable and cannot work loose. The smaller illustration shows the oblique lugs used at the cable outlets from the handle bar. These give a very neat appearance, and avoid sharp bends in the cables.

Handlebar showing Cables for Front Brake and Exhaust Valve Lifter.

all machines – the Rudge Multi. This step was still nearly a year away however, but first there was the 1911 TT.

Six riders had been entered on Rudges for the race but only four started. One of those who failed to start was Victor Surridge, who had put up such successful performances at Brooklands during the preceding months. Regrettably, he crashed during practice at Glen Helen and died as a result of the injuries he sustained. He had the sad distinction of being the first fatality in the Isle of Man TT races.

Of the four Rudges which started, one was ridden by J. A. Prendergast who had been so successful at Sutton Bank. Unfortunately, this was not repeated in the Isle of Man, where he was forced to retire, as was A. J. Sproston.

The first Rudge to finish was ridden into 21st place by J. Stanhope Spencer, while J. Gibson followed him home 22nd. Two modest positions, which gave no hint of TT successes yet to come.

Back on the mainland however, the factory was able to claim greater success in the London to Edinburgh Run, as the nine Rudges that started the outward journey all finished the course. On the return journey, all seven of those that started successfully completed the double journey. It is interesting to note that A. Mabon himself was one of the Rudge riders.

By August the association of the Rudge name with speed was re-established when Stanhope Spencer completed the Flying Mile in 49.3/5th seconds (72½mph) at the Clipstone Speed Trials, to establish a new world record. At the same time, Rudge riders were competing in the A-CU Six Days Trial, in which B. Alan Hill, Basil H. Davies and G. T. Gray achieved Gold Medals and C. S. Burney and A. J. Sproston Silver Medals.

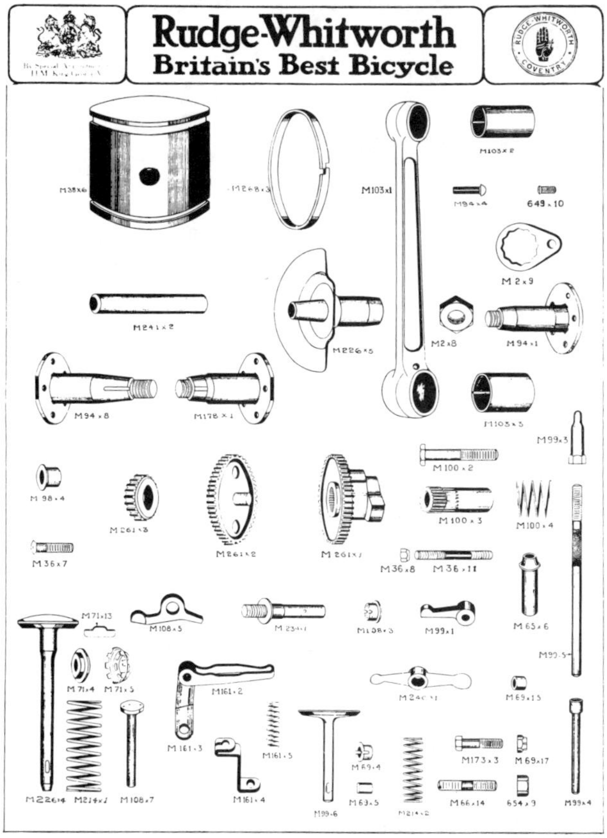

Although sport was establishing a name for the company, it was John Pugh's aim to provide as wide a range of machines as possible. Early in April 1911 he broke fresh ground by adding four sidecars to the catalogue. These were not, at first, produced by the Rudge company but were proprietary sidecars, two from Mills Fulford, and two from Montgomery. One of each make was of the cheap but popular wicker work type. The Mills Fulford better quality sidecar specified a sprung wheel and had a cane body that was upholstered in red or green Pegamoid. The Montgomery alternative, also had a spring frame and offered a coach built body, with upholstery in red, green or tan for an all-in price of £16 10s 0d. Each sidecar was fitted with a 26in x 2¼in wheel, the same as that of the motorcycle, so that one spare outer cover would fit all three wheels.

By May 1911, the advantages of the clutch had become so apparent that the fixed engine model was dropped from production, although it could still be obtained by special order. With the introduction of the clutch, it now became unnecessary to get the machine in motion before the engine could be started. As a result, the pedal starter was redesigned, so that the machine could be started on its stand. A sprocket, which incorporated a free wheel, was attached to the idler gear between the mainshaft gear and the camshaft gear wheels. The pedals remained in the same position at the foot of the seat tube, behind the engine, and the chain from the pedal gear connected directly with the engine. It was therefore possible to start the engine with the clutch disengaged, the free wheel device preventing the pedals from rotating dangerously. Even so, they could still inflict a painful blow if the engine backfired!

Rudge-Whitworth
Britain's Best Bicycle

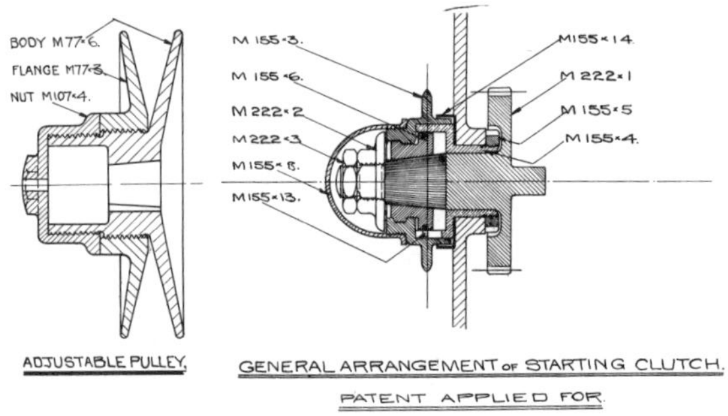

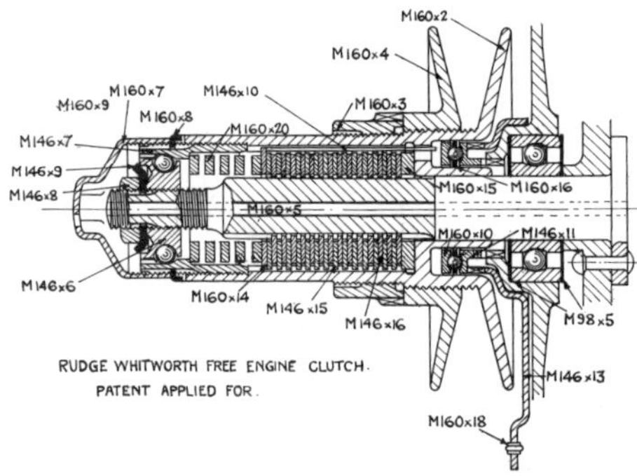

With John Pugh's fertile mind thinking up fresh ideas for machines and modifications almost daily, Holroyd and his experimental team were kept busy. Later, during May 1911, a ladies model was produced. Many factories had already gone into production with a model of this type and the Rudge was similar to most, with the top tube dropping down to a lug half-way down the seat tube, to allow a lady to ride whilst wearing a long skirt, with an element of decorum, without the risk of her breaking her neck when mounting or dismounting. Only one prototype was produced and the project was dropped in view of the difficulties caused by the height of the engine as a result of the overhead inlet valve. In 1911 the Rudge was very much a man's machine.

After the TT the variable gear experiments continued but the range for 1912 had to be considered. Although modifications were introduced as soon as they proved effective, models for the following year had to be designed and built before the Motorcycle Show in November. At the Olympia Show, the factory exhibited four machines. The first had the latest version of the variable gear and was fitted with a sidecar. The second was a TT model with fixed engine and the other two standard roadsters with clutches. The two latter machines had slightly different engines in that a new type of cylinder barrel was being tried out. When looking down from the head of the original engine, the valve chest was almost circular so that the chest and cylinder barrel were in the shape of a figure eight. The new cylinder barrel had extended fins around the chest, to produce an overall oval effect. As this did not appear to give any appreciable difference to the performance or improve the cooling, it was later dropped. One change to remain however, was the increase in the width of the mudguards, from 3½in to 4in and the addition of a large mudflap to the front mudguard.

As a prelude to the Show at Brooklands on 3 October, Stanhope Spencer completed 65 miles and 803 yards in the hour and went on to complete 122 miles 210 yards in two hours, both of which were World Records. The following day the *Daily Telegraph* carried the following report:

Motor Cycling Records

Riding in a strong wind at Brooklands yesterday, Stanhope Spencer on a 3½ horsepower Rudge beat the Class C Motor Cycle records from 50 miles to two hours. Class C is for the popular type of machine as exemplified by the 3½ horsepower single cylinder engined bicycle. The records which he beat in the first half of his ride were of recent accomplishment, but the figures for two hours had stood for nearly a couple of years. Spencer's records, together with the previous bests were as follows:

	NEW RECORD	OLD RECORD
50 miles	*45 min 34.1/5 sec*	*47 min 24.3/5 sec*
1 hour	*65 miles 803 yd*	*63 miles 194 yd*
100 miles	*1 hr 34 min 8 sec*	*1 hr 37 min 52.2/5 sec*
2 hours	*122 miles 210 yd*	*108 miles 1367 yd*

The old 50 miles, 1 hour and 100 miles were held by J. R. Haswell (3½hp Triumph) and the previous 2 hour records stood to the credit of G. Leigh Evans (single cylinder engine). Mr. A. V. Ebblewhite, of the Auto-Cycle Union, timed the attempts.

Stanhope Spencer also beat the five miles record covering the distance in 4 minutes 33.3/5 seconds, as against the 4 minutes 36 seconds by the late Victor Surridge during the previous May.

A sidecar record was also established by F. E. Pither who, riding a similar machine and with a 10 stone passenger in the sidecar, covered 40 miles 1667 yards in an hour.

The machines were claimed by the factory to be absolutely standard, except for the carburettors being provided with larger jets and chokes but perhaps it might be more accurate to say that they were standard TT models. Stanhope Spencer returned to Brooklands on 6 November to take further records for 150 miles, 200 miles and 3 hours.

It was quite obvious that the new engine was capable of high performance yet it had something which was still fairly rare at that time of motorcycling development – reliability. The 3½hp Triumph had proved very reliable at the same time but the Rudge had the advantage of added speed. In addition, Rudge had taken the top sidecar awards in the Leeds to London and back reliability trial and also in the MCC 100 miles Reliability Trial, invading a field formerly dominated by the 1000cc vee twins. All this had been achieved in their first year of manufacture.

An early purchaser of one of these machines was a young man called Bernard Montgomery, who later confirmed that it had been his first mechanically propelled vehicle. This early customer was later to become Field Marshal Lord Montgomery of Alamein.

P. C. Dewhurst on the Rudge outfit which he rode in the North-West London MCC London to Coventry Reliability Competition on May 18, 1912. He successfully completed the course and was awarded a silver cup. Later he went into business in Cricklewood with Ray Abbott and assisted the latter with the machine on which he came second in the 1913 TT

Chapter Four
THE BIRTH OF A CLASSIC MACHINE

BY the end of 1911, the majority of the machines produced by the Rudge factory were fitted with a clutch but had only a single gear. The NSU two-speed gear was frequently requested as an optional extra and one or two machines fitted with the Mabon gear had been sold to the general public. The 1911 TT, which was the first over the mountain circuit, had proved the need for a gear capable of wider variation. Although the Mabon gear had partly filled the gap, it proved difficult to de-clutch quickly and the moving parts wore rather rapidly. Whilst the standard variable gear machine was on display at Olympia, John Pugh was producing another version to which he gave a name destined to go down in motorcycling history -- the Multi gear.

The machine was fitted with the normal Rudge engine-shaft clutch, but the engine pulley was made in two separate parts. The outer part was attached to the clutch but the inner was controlled by a tank mounted lever which, when moved, engaged with ramps on the outside of the crankcase. As the lever was pushed forward, the inner half of the pulley ran up the ramp, which pushed it outwards towards the clutch, thus reducing the space between the two sides of the pulley. The belt, running in this space, was therefore forced outwards and turned through a larger diameter.

The lever was also attached by a rod to a bellcrank lever at the centre of the rear wheel spindle. This operated a short push-rod which closed the rear wheel pulley as the front pulley was opened and vice-versa. This took care of belt tension, which remained constant. To prevent the outer rear wheel flange turning in relation to the inner wheel flange, the two parts were interlocked by the 76 spokes built into the wheel. This gear provided ratios ranging from 3½ to 7 to 1, although higher gears could be obtained by using a rear wheel with a smaller belt rim.

The new gear was tested throughout the remainder of November and into December, without any major problems arising. The necessary tooling up was completed early in 1912 and the first two production models were released from the factory on 3 February 1912. No-one could then have foreseen that the Multi gear would remain in production for ten years, to become the classic feature of the Rudge Multi motorcycle.

The January 1912 catalogue announced the Multi in a very low key. The standard fixed engine machine was illustrated, even though very few of these were being sold. The model fitted with a clutch was offered as an optional extra and beneath this, for an extra £5, it was mentioned that the Multi speed gear version could be obtained. Given equal prominence in the catalogue to the fixed engine machine, was the TT model, although success in this event was yet to come. The Publicity Department was not slow to take advantage of successes in other areas as the model was described as 'stripped for Brooklands'. This machine could be purchased, ready to race, for £47 15s 0d, Racing number plates cost five shillings extra.

The Rudge-Whitworth Company was not the only business absorbing the energies of the Pugh family. A new carburettor had been designed, based on the principle of the scent spray. The petrol jet was mounted in the centre of the inlet pipe and this was attached directly to the float chamber. The inlet pipe round the jet rotated around a horizontal spindle, so that it could move to a position at right angles to the pipe, thus cutting off the air-flow. As the throttle lever was opened, the carburettor body rotated so that at full throttle the pipe was straight through. The prototypes were tested on Rudge machines at the end of 1911 and the carburetter, known as the Senspray, was fitted as standard to all Rudge models by the end of January 1912.

At this time the company decided that the machine was good enough to bear its name and this was added to the tank transfer. During 1911, the machines had carried three small transfers, which could not be read at any distance. The first proclaimed that Rudge-Whitworth was Britain's best bicycle. The second was the Royal cipher and the third proclaimed that machines had been supplied by appointment to H.M. the King. The latter did not, of course, refer to the motorcycles but to a cycling Royal Family who used Rudge bicycles at Sandringham.

With so many changes it was quite obvious that a revised catalogue was required so in May a new version was issued. The 499cc Rudge Multi was now featured more prominently, with the free-engine and fixed gear models offered as optional extras. More interesting, however, was the fact that the TT model was now entirely different from the Brooklands model. The latter continued in production without mudguards, the only other modification, apart from the carburettor, being the substitution of a straight through exhaust pipe for the perforated expansion box used previously. The TT model now sported mudguards, toolboxes and all the other fitments that the speed merchant of the day might require. Although it had not been named as such, the Replica had arrived! The price, including all the additional fittings was still £48 15s 0d, but the range of optional extras had now increased. For the serious racer, a larger tank with quick fillers could be obtained, with an increased oil capacity of four pints and capable of carrying two gallons of petrol. Knee grips were available for 6s 6d and a cable operated magneto control on the handlebars cost an additional 10 shillings.

As the rear wheel pulley now opened and closed, it was no longer possible for a vee block brake to be used. The ramps on the crankcase had moved the belt pulley out from the engine, and the rear pulley had also been moved outwards, leaving a flat surface between the belt rim and the wheel rim. The rear brake was therefore changed to a curved shoe, which pressed on the outside of this rim. Until June 1912, it was possible to specify either beaded or wired edge rims, as both were available. But from the middle of that month, beaded edge tyres were fitted as standard.

During the summer of 1912, the factory was producing between 12 and 15 machines each day, the majority of which were Multis. These were proving to be very popular, particularly in solo form. The picture was not so rosy in the very lucrative

The Rudge
Motor Bicycle.

BROOKLANDS RACER.

Rudge Motor Bicycle.

The RUDGE Motor Bicycle has been designed and made by a firm who have for many years been in the closest possible touch with Cycle construction and with Motor Car Racing, and whose technical staff numbers many expert Motor Cyclists. Naturally the products and experience of such a firm embody such features and workmanship as place it in the front rank of Motor Bicycles, a position which its Brooklands performances confirm. Among these it will be remembered that the late Mr. Victor J. Surridge, on May 25th, 1911, rode 60 miles 783 yards in the hour. This was the first time that any machine of 500 c.c. capacity covered 60 miles in the hour. On October 3rd of the same year Mr. Stanhope Spencer rode no less than 65 miles 803 yards in the hour, and 122 miles 210 yards in two hours, being a two hours' run at a little more than the rate attained bv Mr Victor J. Surridge in his earlier 1 hour record. The machines in both cases were absolutely standard, except that the carburettors were provided with large jets and unusually large air-openings. All experienced Motor Cyclists will agree that there is no more gruelling test than Brooklands racing and record breaking.

2

The Rudge Motor Bicycle.

By Special Appointment to H.M. King George.

CONSTRUCTIONAL DETAILS—*Continued.*

Free Engine Clutch, showing Cover removed.

When pressed together by the powerful spring, the discs cannot slip past each other and the clutch drives solid. The pressure is relieved by the handlebar control, the plates are then free to slip past each other and the engine is free. The plates are oiled automatically through the centre hole of the axle. It will be perceived that a high speed clutch of this type can be slipped almost indefinitely without damage.

It is hand-operated, thus leaving both feet free for balancing—a great advantage when using the Clutch either for starting or stopping.

THE RUDGE MULTI-SPEED GEAR (Pat. Nos. 14663/11–22400/11) gives a gear ratio of from $3\frac{1}{2}$ to 1 to $7\frac{1}{2}$ to 1 by a series of indefinitely small gradations.

It has the following advantages over all other variable gears :—

(1.) It is provided with the RUDGE patent plate clutch, which is available at all gears, and obviates the slipping of the belt as a clutch, the

The Multi-speed Gear (Pat. No. 22400/11) **Lever Celluloid Covered.**

Back Wheel Pulley and Brake Drum.
(Pat. No. 14336/11).

The Rudge Motor Bicycle.

By Special Appointment to H.M. King George.

CONSTRUCTIONAL DETAILS—*Continued.*

HIGH TENSION MAGNETO. — Owing to the special form of armature winding the Magneto though smaller is not less efficient than other larger designs, and a saving in weight of from 3 to 4-lbs. is effected. The contact breaker cover is well designed and quite water-tight, it is retained with a strong spring, and the platinum points are very substantial. Teeth cut on the armature shaft fit inside the pinion, which again fits inside the cam. The number of teeth inside the cam differ in number from the teeth on the axle, consequently giving a Vernier adjustment of less than $\frac{1}{400}$ of a revolution. This feature secures exceedingly fine adjustment without the slightest liability of slipping, which liability is inseparable from cone drives, and which have been eliminated from the RUDGE magnetos by extending the armature shaft.

1913 Magneto.
Rudge Magneto Cover (Reg. design No 578324/11)

SPRING FORKS.—The fork consists, as will be seen from the illustration, of two members connected on either side to the Ball-head by solid stamped steel shackles. The advantage of a pair of shackles as compared with four unconnected links from the point of view of rigidity and fine steering and stability in grease will at once be obvious to the expert. The large spiral spring of high tension steel wire is anchored to the ball head spring bracket at the top and the fork bridge at the bottom, taking up the road shocks by compression, and affording a damping action by extension. This spring is contained in a telescopic sheath filled with grease, and the combination is strikingly neat and efficient. It has shown no sign of weakness in the severest test on the road or at Brooklands. For steady steering at all speeds it is without a rival.

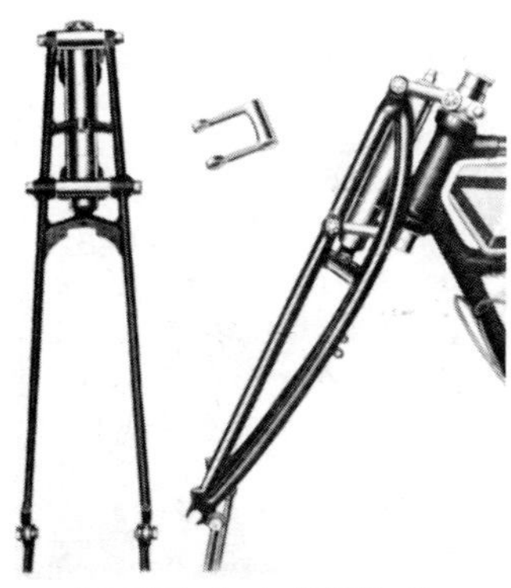

Spring Forks showing Rigid Shackle.
Reg. No. 546796/09.

10

sidecar market however, as the machines were at a disadvantage when compared to the 1000cc vee twins being offered by other manufacturers – even though the Multi gear provided greater flexibility. The answer was more power. How could this be achieved without producing an entirely new vee twin engine? The answer was one which has been used many times, before and since – enlarge the existing engine. On 5 September 1912 a new Multi was assembled. The cubic capacity had been increased to 750cc, by lengthening the stroke from 88mm to 132mm. This had been achieved by nothing more than fitting a longer connecting rod and cylinder barrel! This created at least one major problem, as the longer rod fouled the crankcase mouth, but the latter was then chamfered to permit the necessary clearance. Heavier flywheels were also fitted, and it was necessary to enlarge the cut-out in the tank, to accommodate the projecting inlet valve.

Meanwhile, the standard production machines were being given their face lift, ready to be introduced as 1913 models. The most noticeable change for 1913 was the new Senspray carburettor, which had a separate float chamber. Another change at this time was an export only development. 50% of the year's production had been sent abroad, a large number of which had been sent to Johannesburg. The South African roads were almost non-existent and this resulted in a number of frame breakages. From September onwards, a heavier frame was produced for export, which was fitted to what was designated the Colonial model.

The Rudge organisation in general, and John Pugh in particular, were always looking for new areas into which the organisation could expand. Wheels, carburettors, cycles, motorcycles and sidecars were already being manufactured. What was more natural than to look at the expanding cycle-car market? John Pugh and Frank Pountney therefore spent the summer of 1912 producing a Rudge prototype, which incorporated many of the motorcycle parts currently in manufacture. It was an open secret in Coventry that a prototype cycle-car was being built in the factory and in October the model was wheeled to the door. Unfortunately the door proved too small and part of the wall had to be removed before the car could see the light of day. It was described as a remarkable machine, combining lightness with simplicity, and having great powers of acceleration – according to the few that saw it on its early morning runs (to avoid prying eyes of the competition and the attention of the local constabulary). A 750cc single cylinder engine was mounted between the front wheels, which were widely splayed. These were, of course, standard motorcycle front wheels and two Multi rear wheels were fitted to the rear. The usual Rudge clutch was fitted to the engine shaft and from this power was transmitted, by means of an enclosed belt, to a countershaft mounted across the frame, under the driving seat. At the ends of this shaft were mounted belt pulleys and each drove a rear wheel by external belt. The belt rim on the rear wheels opened and closed in the same manner as the normal Multi gear, but the pulleys on the countershafts were fixed. The pulleys were eccentric to the centre of the shaft and could be moved in an arc to take up the slack in the driving belts when the belt pulleys were opened. This arrangement gave a gear ratio which could be varied between 3 7/8 to 1 and 9 to 1. The complete vehicle weighed only 4½cwt, the body forming part of the chassis, which is a quite modern feature. Petrol and oil were contained in a motorcycle tank mounted over the engine, which formed the top of the bonnet. To start the engine, a handle was mounted on the offside of the bonnet and was geared to the camshaft in such a way that only one turn was necessary when cranking, (or so the report says) if care was taken with the decompressor! With a width of 4ft the car was very stable, even when driven at its maximum speed of eighty mph and its cooling was better than that of most contemporary cycle-cars. Stability was aided by the use of rack and pinion steering, the front part of the cycle-car being underslung on semi-elliptical springs of considerable length. The rear of the vehicle was suspended on quarter elliptic springs.

In October 1912 the cycle-car was tried out by a journalist from *Motor Cycling,* who recorded its performance in glowing terms, particularly its ability to climb hills at speed and its smooth acceleration.

A more stylish 500cc version was produced early in 1913, with the engine enclosed by a panel on each side, immediately below the petrol tank, and a false radiator. Unfortunately, neither of the cycle-cars was put into production. One interesting feature was however retained, the introduction of a decompressor valve into the cylinder head to assist with starting. Turning the engine over by hand on full compression was extremely difficult and it was not possible to operate a valve lifter when standing outside the car. Although a decompressor valve was not used on any production machine, the idea was not forgotten and it reappeared as a 'pip' on the camshaft to assist starting on the later four-valve engines.

The 500cc version of the Rudge Cyclecar. The top of the bonnet is a normal motorcycle petrol tank

An early export to Australia, this 3½hp Multi was photographed in 1913. The pillion appears to be well suited for the roads that would have been experienced 'out-back'

An early example of a Rudge in a military role. This photograph of Trooper May was taken at TA Camp in 1913. The machine is the fixed engine (no clutch or gears) Brooklands model to which road going equipment has been added

Chapter Five
THE YEAR THAT NEARLY WAS

IN the history of motorcycling there have been many instances where, but for a twist of fate, disaster might have been averted at a later date if one had the gift of foresight. 1913 might well be described as such a year as far as the Rudge factory was concerned, although the effects were not to be felt for another twelve years.

The year started well with the production of machines running at about fifteen a day, of which four or five were fitted with the enlarged 750cc single cylinder engine. The majority were Multis, of which approximately 1800 had been made in the previous year. The catalogue was very similar to the 1912 edition, with pride of place given to the Brooklands Racer on which so many world records had been established during the previous year. The TT model was still listed without Multi gear, although this device was beginning to make itself felt in competition. The standard road-going 499cc machine, with fixed engine, sold at £48 14s 0d, but had very few takers. With single speed, but with the multiplate clutch, it cost £55 and these models were still selling at the rate of perhaps one or two a week. Pride of place went to the machine with both Multi gear and multiplate clutch at £60. At the top end of the range, the 750 with larger tank was available for £70. Easy terms were available, and it is interesting that these, or alternatively, part-exchange with an existing machine, added an extra 10% to the purchase price.

At the end of November 1912 a development started which was to extend the factory beyond the production of motorcycles. On 28 November 1912, a sidecar chassis was produced and sent to Brooklands for testing. The chassis was underslung, the main tubes being about 4in below the wheel centres and, in addition to the two cross-members, a diagonal tube ran from just in front of the sidecar wheel to the foot of the front fixing. The wheel itself was not interchangeable with those fitted to the Rudge motorcycle, and was of the detachable car wheel type, similar to those being produced at the factory for cycle-cars. The rim size was, however, the same as that of the motorcycle, so that one spare outer cover would fit all three wheels of the outfit. The sidecar itself was suspended on coil springs, two at the front and two at the rear, the latter having swinging shackles.

After testing the first chassis at Brooklands, a second was produced on 7 December 1912, together with a prototype sidecar body. This did not follow the normal practice of the day, which was a form of construction akin to that of a wickerwork bath-chair. The sidecar in general outline can be best compared to a fairground swing boat. The shape was formed by an ash framework, to which were attached aluminium panels. The dipping curve of the nose was designed for wind cutting, to throw the air currents clear of the passenger's head. In the absence of a windscreen, it was provided with a large storm apron. Access was by means of a small door and the sidecar and chassis, complete with fibre footmat, could be purchased for 16 guineas. A bracket was provided for a sidecar light, but this necessity came as an optional extra, for a further 21 shillings. The sidecar was finished in green to match the colour of the motorcycle tank, with similar black lining. By the beginning of 1913 production was in full swing and during February, sidecars of this design were being produced at the rate of approximately five a day.

The first event at Brooklands in 1913 was the BARC meeting, held on Easter Monday, 24 March. The Rudge team was under the direction of F. Clark, the foreman tester, but more nerve racking for the riders, was the attendance of John V. Pugh himself. His appearance must have spurred them to greater efforts, for they took the first four places in the long handicap of 8½ miles. The order was C. G. Pullin, F. Bateman, L. Hill and S. Heales. A very pleasing start for the factory team.

Rudge riders were also successful at the BMCRC meeting on Wednesday, 2 April, taking first and second places in the 500cc handicap and second and third places in the 500cc scratch race. L. Hill, riding a 500cc Rudge and sidecar, recorded the first successes for the 100% Rudge racing combination, by achieving third place in the scratch race and second in the handicap, losing first place in the latter race by a second or two. This was an unfortunate omen of disappointments yet to come.

Happier however, was the victory of P. F. Glover, who won the three-lap 1000cc handicap, as this was the first Brooklands win of a Rudge using the Multi-gear. Because it was seldom necessary to use anything other than top gear when racing at Brooklands, it was the usual practice of Rudge riders to race with a fixed gear and no clutch, to save weight.

At the Whitsun BARC meeting held on 12 May, Rudges claimed both the short and long handicap races, with A. J. McDonagh easily taking the first and F. Bateman the second. As he was to compete on his Multi in the TT, Frank Bateman took the machine back to the track on 17 May and recorded a flying start kilometer at 74.57mph and the flying start mile at 73.47mph. Unfortunately he suffered tyre trouble in the following Senior Brooklands TT race, and failed to finish.

On 24 May at the Essex MCC meeting the Rudge sidecar scored again when G. T. Gray won the two sidecar races, the open and members' handicaps.

While these successes were being recorded at Brooklands, the factory was not resting on its laurels. F. A. (Rowley) Rowlandson, the Competitions Manager, was well aware that the Isle of Man would offer a much greater test than the comparatively smooth Brooklands circuit. The team therefore engaged on a number of gruelling overseas events. The first, on 26 and 27 April, was the 638 mile International Road Race around the River Po. Although the route passed through Turin, Brescia and Bologna, the main part consisted of dusty tracks, with many hairpin corners, over which the riders were required to maintain a scheduled speed of 25mph. In addition to the official Rudge team of Rowlandson, Scott and Newman, there were Italian teams of Rudges, as Italy was a major export market for the company. At the end of the first day, from Milan to Turin and Bologna, Rowlandson led with Vailati, also on a Rudge, in third place. For the return trip the riders left at 4am in the morning, there only being twenty survivors out of the sixty who had originally started. Five hours later at Levvo, Rowlandson crashed, but managed to finish in second place, even though his wheels were afterwards found to be 8in out of track! Before the crash, Rowlandson had won the Aprica hill climb, in which he was 1½ minutes faster than any other rider. Only fourteen competitors survived to the finish, where Vailati became the overall winner, averaging 30mph and finishing an hour ahead of Rowlandson, who was some way ahead of the third rider.

Back in England, over slightly better roads, in the MCC London-Edinburgh-London Trial, ten Rudge riders completed the 800 mile course to obtain their Gold Medals. Rowlandson, however, had remained in Italy, to take part in a race on the Cremonese circuit on 18 May. The race comprised three laps, 65 miles long, running through the villages of St. Giovanni and Piadenna. Rowlandson later commented that the aim of the race seemed to be the wholesale slaughter of fowls, which strayed onto the roads to be caught unawares by the motorcyclists racing through at about 50mph. Rowlandson averaged about 55mph, to win the 500cc class. With Vailati and Fossati, he took the Manufacturers Team Prize.

With all these successes, the outlook for the Tourist Trophy Races in the Isle of Man looked very good indeed. A very strong team was entered and the factory had high hopes of winning. If the race was won by a Rudge it was considered that the financial boost through increased sales, might well influence the subsequent outlook of the Company.

There was no doubt that a Tourist Trophy win would have considerable effect upon the sales of machines for the rest of the year. The 1913 race was unique in that it was the only TT held over two days, the 5th and 6th June, the first day being a qualifying three lap event, with the main four lap race for the survivors on the second day. There were a hundred entries for the Senior class, of which twelve were Rudges, the largest entry of any one make. Favourites to win were either the eight Indians, the make that won in 1911, or the four Scotts, one of which had won the previous year's race. Rudges were not unfancied, however, in view of their performance in the sporting field during previous months.

Frank Appleby, on his Scott, was the first man away, followed 20 seconds later by Frank Bateman on a Rudge. The first surprise came at Ballacraine, where Frank Bateman passed Frank Appleby, to lead on the road.

At the end of the first lap, Rudges occupied the first four places followed by two Indians, a Matchless and a Scott. The fancied Scotts were not doing so well, as they were suffering from persistent sparking plug troubles. At the end of lap two however, Tim Wood forced his Scott up into second place, amongst the leading Rudges. At the end of the third lap, which concluded the preliminary race, the flying Scott had taken the lead, to be followed home by Frank Bateman, and the Rudge and Indian teams. The Scott was the only one of this make to survive the first day and there was a total of fifty retirements. The Friday race started with only half the original entry.

In 1913 the Mountain course was much closer to being a dusty cart-track than the tarmacadamed circuit we know today. On the first lap of the Friday race, a stone thrown up from another rider's rear tyre pierced a hose on the Scott radiator, causing Tim Wood to stop and make hasty repairs. Frank Bateman then swept back into the lead at the end of the first lap, followed by Alexander on his Indian and Ray Abbott on another Rudge. On the second lap Alexander took the lead but this was soon regained by Frank Bateman, in the climb over the Mountain. Coming down the Mountain the first disaster struck the Rudge team, when Frank Bateman got caught in a rut at the side of

The Rudge Motor Bicycle.

By Special Appointment to H.M. King George.

$3\frac{1}{2}$ H.P. (499 c.c.) Rudge Motor Bicycle.

SPECIFICATION.

Engine.—$3\frac{1}{2}$ h.p. single cylinder, 85 m.m. bore, and 88 m.m. stroke. Volume 499 c.c. Cylinder set vertically in the frame, and provided with ample radiating surface. The Piston has one ring on each end; crank shaft mounted on ball bearings; fly wheels are solid steel stampings with exceptional weight massed in the rims and carefully balanced.

Wheels.—Specially strong tubular edge steel rims for beaded-edge tyres. Hub Centres celluloid covered. The ball bearings are exceptionally large, easy running, weather proof and wear resisting. Back wheel easily detachable by removing belt and unscrewing 2 nuts, the work of but a few minutes.

Carburetter.—"Senspray," efficient and flexible; handlebar control, very economical, running evenly over a wide range of speeds.

Ignition.—High-tension Magneto.

Valves.—Pat. Nos. 25474/10, 22399/11. Mechanically operated, of specially large diameter, over-head inlet with adjustable tappets.

Silencer.—Large, with very simple foot operated cut-out. Seven inches clear from the ground.

Transmission.—$\frac{7}{8}$-in. rubber belt.

Frame.—Rudge special design, affording low and comfortable riding position.

Spring Forks.—(Regd. No. 546796/09). Complete insulation from road vibration, perfect steering at all speeds.

Handlebars.—No. 100 (see page 15), with celluloid covering and grips. Very long, to suit backward position. Well dropped to afford an easy wrist action.

Tank.—Made from tinned steel plate with solid drawn ends, and extra large oil and petrol fillers, with splash proof caps. Oil capacity $\frac{1}{2}$ gallon. Petrol capacity $1\frac{1}{4}$ gallons. All fittings on left side to facilitate easy removal from frame. Petrol feed to compression tap, to ensure easy starting.

Foot-rests and Pedals.—Pat. No. 29979/10 Rubber rests carried well forward. The pedals by a special device can both be kept down after starting. The resulting position is extraordinarily comfortable, comparable only to the perfect seat on horseback, with the further advantage that the feet are close to the ground for instant support. The pedals can instantly be restored to the starting position. The foot-rests are quite independent of the engine attachments, and can be removed without disturbing same.

Brakes.—Front rim operated from handlebar, and foot-brake acting on belt rim.
(Reg. No. 573749).
(Clip Reg. No. 573750).
(Brazed on Fulcrum stud Reg. No 571107), and with perfectly straight rod, giving direct pull. Mounted independently of foot-rest.

Tyres.—26-in × $2\frac{1}{4}$-in. Beaded-edge, Dunlop.

Mudguards.—With patent combined number plate, and back-guard hinged on Carrier (Registered Design No. 567465, Pat. No. 17975/10). Metal shields combined with front guard.

Saddle.—Brooks' Large motor saddle, pan seat, or XL'ALL Saddle, No. 11, **5/-** extra.

Stand.—Spring operated; lowered by the foot automatically picks up immediately cycle is moved. Front wheel stand also fitted.

Foot Pump.—Powerful Celluloid Foot Pump with long rubber connection.

Accessories.—Two armoured tool kit bags (Registered No. 570581/10) with full necessary equipment of tools. See page 12.

	Cash Price.	Credit or Exchange Price.
As specification above, with Fixed Engine & Pedal Engine Starter	**£48 15 0**	**£54 0 0**
Ditto, but with Free Engine multi-plate clutch and pedal engine starter	**£55 0 0**	**£61 0 0**
Ditto, with Free Engine multi-plate clutch pedal engine starter, and multi-speed gear	**£60 0 0**	**£66 0 0**
4 Extra for 750 c.c. Engine and Large Tank,	**£10 0 0**	**£11 0 0**

the road at approximately 70mph, which caused him to strike the bank and sustain injuries from which he subsequently died. This left Alexander on the Indian in the lead, but carburettor trouble slowed him down and Ray Abbott became the new race leader at the end of lap two.

Coming over the Mountain for the last time, Abbott held a lead of four minutes but this was being rapidly whittled down by Tim Wood. Fate again intervened for whereas both riders ran off the course on the last lap, Tim Wood managed to keep his engine running, whilst that of Ray Abbott stalled. The former won by five seconds.

Rudge Side-car.

WHEEL.—The spoking is of the dished type, now so familiar on the Rudge Detachable Motor Car Wheels.

The flat side of the spokes is towards the car. The outer spokes are inclined outwards at a considerable angle to give greater lateral stability.

The Hub Flanges are flared outwards to throw off mud and water from entering the bearings.

At the back of the hub a dust cap is fitted to make it oil retaining and dust proof,

MUDGUARD.—The attachments of the mudguard are well thought out. They comprise tubular stays fore and aft, coupling the two bottom ends directly to the side tube, while the centre of the guard is supported by a duplex steel member embracing the crown of the mudguard both inside and out and rivetted through. This member rises from a pad brazed on to the side tube in the same manner as the spring supports. This makes an absolutely rigid job, extremely unlikely to break, but at the same time the guard can readily be detached without disturbing the wheel.

CHASSIS.—The Chassis is under-slung. The main tubes being about 4 inches below the wheel centre. In addition to the side-tubes and two cross members, there is a diagonal tube connecting the left outside tube with the right inside tube, thus equalising the pull between the outside and inside tubes and reducing the liability of breakage to a minimum.

METHOD OF ATTACHMENTS TO THE MOTOR CYCLE.—The front diagonal stay is united to the side-car tube with a telescopic clip. The top stay bolt has a taper seating in the lug, which is snugly ensconced in the angle between the bottom tube and the lower frame tube. Additional security is given by a steel clip attached to the foot-rest bar.

The Telescopic Seat Stay is short and rigid. It is attached to a swivelling bolt on the cross lug of the chassis and to the cycle by an eyed seat bolt.

The rear clips are of substantial design bolted on the chain stay, and the chassis has an extension resembling an axle passing through this lug and held up by a massive nut and lock nut. This thread provides for any lateral adjustment which may be needed in fitting the side-car to standard Rudge models.

SPRINGS.—These have coils at both ends and the back coils have also swinging shackles (which undoubtedly afford luxurious riding) for the attachment to the car.

THE CAR,—in general design resembles a swing boat. The exceptionally clean lines of the back will be appreciated, while the curves in front are accurately designed for wind cutting and to throw the wind currents clear of the passenger's head.

The price of the Rudge side-car as above, complete with Storm Apron, is **£16 16 0.** **13**

Ray Abbott described his ride as "a glorious blind, never enjoyed anything so much in my life!", but he must have been very disappointed at losing the race by such a narrow margin. At the time some commentators described the error on the last corner as going too fast to get round, and others stated that he lost his way. I spoke to Ray Abbott many years later and he provided a slightly different explanation. At the time of the mistake, he had already been in the saddle for 2½ hours on a rigid frame machine, driving over appalling surfaces at speeds up to 70mph. By the time he reached the corner he was physically and mentally exhausted and just failed to react when he should have turned. With the Multi gear in top instead of bottom position, the engine stalled, and the time taken to restart it was well in excess of the five seconds by which the race was lost.

These were probably the most expensive five seconds in the history of the Company. A local man, who did know the way but was on a slower Rudge machine, came home in sixth place. He was later to go on to become the first Manx rider to win a Tourist Trophy, when he was mounted on a Douglas. This was, of course, T. M. Sheard. The other Rudge entries were not so successful however, and all retired, none because of mechanical failure. An additional hazard this year was glass spread over the course by suffragettes. One item that was taken to be a contributory factor to failure was the hand-operated oil pump. This required the rider to let go of the handlebars at least once every five miles, to ensure adequate lubrication. On the uncertain surfaces of the day, and with the Multi gear to operate with the same hand, the strain on the rider was considerably increased. Something had to be done and the problem was solved by the inventive mind of John Pugh. When examining the work allocated to each hand and foot when riding the Rudge Multi, it became obvious that the right foot had nothing to do other than sit on the footrest! It therefore made sense to design a foot operated oil pump and this was done. The pedal was attached to a separate oil tank underneath the saddle by means of a Bowden cable. Inside the oil tank was a tube and plunger, very similar to a tyre pump. The plunger was kept at the bottom of the tube by a heavy spring which, together with a ball valve, prevented the oil running down into the crankcase all at one time. When the pedal was depressed, the plunger slid up the tube, compressing the spring and allowing oil to run beneath it. When the pedal was released the spring forced the plunger down and a charge of oil into the rear of the crankcase. After testing the device on competition machines, it was incorporated into the production models for the 1914 season.

After the disappointment of the TT Rowlandson took the Rudge team over to France for the Grand Prix at the Circuit de Picardie, held on 13 July. It followed the car Grand Prix at which, incidentally, a large number of the entrants had used Rudge spoked wheels.

Tommy Greene, who was forced to retire in the TT, took the lead at half distance and held it to the finish. There were only twelve finishers out of the thirty-six entrants and these included Ray Abbott in seventh place and Rowlandson in eighth.

Although this was Tommy Greene's first international success on a Rudge, he had already made a name for himself in Ireland, in speed trials and long distance events. Immediately after the TT he had established a record time of 56 minutes 2 seconds for the 50 mile speed trial on Portmarnock Sands. In April he had embarked on a more unusual feat, by riding from one end of Ireland to the other. He took ten hours 38 minutes to cover the 396 miles from Rock Island Coast Guard's Station to Ballyvoy, beating the previous record by 2 hours 12 minutes. The *Irish Cyclist* commented that he must have had a constitution of iron to withstand such a strain.

News of Rudge successes continued to reach the factory throughout the rest of the sporting season until, in November, it was possible to boast that the marque had achieved over 300 first places during the year. Most British events were contested but opportunities to score in export markets were not overlooked. The most important of these were outright wins in the Grand Prix of Denmark, the Championship of Russia, the South Africa Continental Cup and the Open Championship of Belgium. John Pugh lost no opportunity of bringing the name Rudge to the attention of potential buyers. On August Bank Holiday the second International Motorcycle Trial between England and Holland was held, in which Ray Abbott was a member of the British Team. Two Dutch riders,

Citroen and Neurdenburg, were also Rudge mounted. In fact N. Citroen was awarded the prize for the best performance by a Dutch private owner. The day after the trial the Rudge management entertained both teams to a dinner at the factory. Part of the running shed was suitably decorated and approximately 100 guests were entertained, followed by a conducted tour through the remainder of the factory. The Dutch guests were given souvenirs in the shape of a buttonhole badge and cigarette case each, bearing the Rudge motif.

At Brooklands, Cyril Pullin was establishing a name for himself with the Rudges he tuned. He won the motorcycle race at the BARC meeting held on 4 October and on 18 October he established a record that was to stand for many years. A well-known rider of solo motorcycles, he took out a 499cc Rudge and sidecar in the one hour race and won his class by completing 52 miles 764 yards, at an average speed of 52.43mph. Switching back to his more usual solo machine, he won the Senior 1 Hour A-CU Championship Race for the *Motor Cycle* Challenge Cup, completing 64 miles 294 yards in the time allocated. In this race Tommy Greene was third and the two were selected to attack the major long distance records. The record attempt took place on 20 November, when the two riders broke the following records.

Rudge Records
Passed by the Auto Cycle Union

In class C cylinder capacity not exceeding 499cc and
In class D cylinder capacity not exceeding 750cc

The 499cc Rudge holds

Distance	**Speed**
250 miles	*59.57 miles per hour*
300 miles	*59.72 miles per hour*
350 miles	*59.72 miles per hour*
400 miles	*59.79 miles per hour*
Duration	
5 hours	*59.71 miles per hour*
6 hours	*59.77 miles per hour*
7 hours	*59.92 miles per hour*

(ridden by C. G. Pullin and T. E. Greene)
In class E cylinder capacity not exceeding 1,100cc

The 499cc Rudge holds

Distance	**Speed**
400 miles	*59.79 miles per hour*
Duration	
7 hours	*59.92 miles per hour*
8 hours	*52.42 miles per hour*
9 hours	*46.60 miles per hour*
10 hours	*41.94 miles per hour*

(ridden by C. G. Pullin and T. E. Greene)

These records were to stand for many years. 1913 ended with great expectations for the competition season yet to come. This anticipation appeared justified early in 1914, when B. Adams won the Durban-Johannesburg race in 11hrs 30mins and 19secs, a time that was to stand until 1921.

An 'on the road' posed photograph prior to the 1914 TT

A carefully posed photograph which forms one of a series taken for the Company during the 1914 TT series. Cyril Pullen is seated on the box on the right with the piston in his hand. The machine must be the only 500cc single entered in the races which had two complete cylinder barrels!

Chapter Six
SUCCESS TOO LATE

IN 1914 the Rudge Company had its first TT win when Cyril Pullin took first place after the previous year's winner, Tim Wood, had set a record lap, but failed to complete the course. As far as the Company were concerned, the win was commercially too late for the clouds of war were already gathering and the successful sales that would normally follow such a victory, were soon to be denied the Company. Nevertheless, this did not detract from the victory itself, which is best described by Cyril himself when he wrote a report of the race for the *Rudge Enthusiasts Journal* in 1963.

"When late in 1913 'Rowly' Rowlandson, the Competition Manager of Rudge-Whitworth Limited, suggested that I should ride in the 1914 Senior TT Race, I had some misgivings. My previous experience on Rudge machines had been confined to records and races on Brooklands track, and although the single gear belt drive, together with a frame that gave perfect steering combined with the ideal riding position for minimum wind resistance, I had the feeling that I should like to get more into the heart of the structure to give a lower centre of gravity and better control generally for high-speed cornering. To substantiate this, my observations in the 1913 TT showed the Rudges to be very fast, almost too fast for the course, which resulted in a most regrettable accident. I also realised certain other requirements, as the result of my ride in the 1913 Junior TT on a Veloce, the forerunner of the Velocette, when I finished just in time to qualify for an award. Having given the matter full consideration, I told Rowly I would ride if a machine could be built to my requirements.

"A mock-up frame was constructed in my workshop in Vauxhall Bridge Road, London SW, and a specification drawn up covering the main essentials. Rudge-Whitworth Limited, also very enterprising, lost no time in building some machines incorporating the then famous Multi gear. Tests at Brooklands and on the road were most gratifying and the TT Rudge Multi turned out to be the best steering motorcycle I have had or have ever ridden.

"As regards the engine, I already had two machines capable of lapping Brooklands at 72mph, with a maximum of 80mph, so in conjunction with the Multi gear, the chance of holding the Scott, Matchless and Indian were quite reasonable. Actually, the machine I rode in the race clocked Brooklands consistently at 75mph, with a maximum over the half mile of 83mph, this, with the large section low-pressure Dunlop tyres that I had under test on the track and the road.

"Tuning and adjusting the Multi gear was well worthwhile, but the principle and the mechanism had to be fully understood before any worthwhile adjustments could be made. Belts – well, the John Bull gave wonderful results and I used the same belt first stretched in practice and left hanging in the cellar with a 56lb weight attached, throughout the race. Belt adjustment on the Multi could be accomplished by a small handscrew at the end of the rear wheel spindle. This meant getting off the machine to take up the unwanted stretch. I fitted a small spike to the end of the crank lever that permitted the inside of one's boot heel to effect adjustment and quite effective it proved to be.

"I must mention belt fasteners. What a mess these could be. However, we had some made out of the solid and fitted with punch-screws. It needed a lot of skill to make a reliable job but I had very little trouble in practice and the one used in the race was as good when I finished as at the start. Of course, a spare belt was carried round the waist. It fitted nicely then – but now the machine would require a longer wheel base for my bodily comfort.

"Special features of the Rudge included large diameter petrol and oil filler caps, the oil being carried in a separate tank and the oil feed pump operated by a conventional heel pedal. A shoe-type brake worked on the flat section of the rear wheel belt rim, not too bad when properly adjusted and the usual cycle type front rim brake. The rear mudguard hinged just below the carrier and the tool bags, to permit easy removal of the rear wheel. No tummy rests were used but knee grips strapped to the tank gave considerable help. I discarded mine and had pads fitted inside the special black leather riding suit I had made, modelled on a conventional boiler suit, incidentally a size too small so as to give a pretty neat fit to cut down windage. The handlebars, nicely finished with black celluloid covering, were just pliable enough to allow cold setting to requirements, this of course within reason. The spring fork was excellent but could perhaps have been improved by a damper of sorts, but at this juncture they were not even thought of in the minds of the riders, nor steering dampers for that matter. The engine exhaust discharged into a silencer, or container, mounted in just the wrong place, i.e. in front of the engine crankcase, and a plurality of small pipes discharged tangentially from the casing of the silencer. The engine compression ratio, as measured, worked out at 3½ to 1 and I believe the fuel used, standard brands of petrol, had a specific gravity of 0.680. A three point spark plug seemed to give good results but as the lowest useful gear was 7 to 1 it was necessary to use the ignition lever mounted on the tank to help the engine round the Ramsey corners and the Gooseneck.

"The Rudges were splendidly finished and beautifully equipped, especially the spares pack which included three jets, a complete magneto contact breaker, high tension brush etc., and the usual toolkit with tyre levers and puncture outfit. Oh yes – a butted end inner tube – but this was carried round the waist.

"In April 1914 Rowly, Tommy Greene and myself went to Italy for the Giro d'Italia – a road race round Italy. Road race is hardly an apt description. Reasonable roads were few and far between, even the railroad track gave a welcome break. Five days of this, under appalling conditions of heat, wind, mountain storms etc., served as good training for the TT and when I returned to England and the Isle of Man, my first practice

Timing side of the 1914 3½hp Multi engine. The word Rudge cast into the crankcase was dropped after the First World War. Above the pedal starter on the timing chest can be seen the cap covering the Vernier timing adjustment for the magneto. The pedal immediately behind the footrest operates the oil pump in the oil tank

ride, even on the course as it was in those days, seemed like Brooklands. We had a very happy camp, all the Rudge riders, including Tommy Greene, 'Milky' Abbott, Adamson etc., being well satisfied with their mounts and full of confidence. I found in practice I could hold any of the dangerous rivals, so my programme was set to ride as fast as I could, come hell or high water.

"The great day arrived, warm, with brilliant sunshine. My number being 57 left me among the last to start. This I thought might be a good thing, but I had not reckoned with the dust, especially along the Ramsey straight. The little but necessary foot slogging around the Gooseneck, coupled with my tight-fitting leather suit, raised the internal body temperature to such an extent that it took some ten miles to cool off again. On the third lap the engine began to dry up and cough but thanks to the adjustable jet I had fitted, a few turns and it sent her off as before. Choked jet no doubt, or it may have been a hot plug as I had been steadily pushing up the revs, thanks to the Multi gear.

"I had no idea of my position, but concluded that the misguided people at the pits wished to convey something to me, although their antics were most unconvincing. It then occurred to me that I might have reached a promising position so proceeding to coax the last rev from the motor and making the fullest use of the gear, also to put a little more energy into the foot slogging at the Gooseneck, I sighted the rear view of one of the Collier boys prior to entering the Ramsey straight and should have caught him at Ramsey. When I failed to do so I concluded that either I was not travelling fast enough or he must have retired. One more lap to go with the wick turned up to smoking point. My goggles had been smashed by flying stones half-way through the race and the dust, apart from reducing visibility to an awkward degree, played havoc with the eyes which must be kept open most of the time if one wished to follow the road; which was my intention. Well here we are, Ramsey again and the Gooseneck. How I hated that bend with its towering foot slog, the Mountain and the dash down to the finish. What a thirst – what a crowd, can't hear them, only the echo of the old Rudge that gave me a lovely ride throughout. Thanks to all the helpers then off to tea, but first to the doctor who removed thirty-six pieces of Manx road from my eyes.

"As to the speed, just under 50mph – 49.7 if I remember – not much really but what a fine sport."

There was no doubt that Cyril Pullin's machine was much faster than the other Rudges in the race, as the next Rudge rider home was again Tim Sheard, this time thirtieth place. J. W. Adamson, who held second place at the end of the first lap, dropped back to forty-first, to be beaten by J. McMeekin, in thirty-eighth place, while P. H. A. Matthews finished in forty-third place. Unlike 1913, when ten of the twelve entries had retired, five of the six Rudge riders completed the course. This established a name for reliability which was well earned when one considers the state of the roads in the Island in 1914. When the winning machine was stripped it was found to be in excellent condition, much to the surprise of the examiners. In fact, 'Rowley' Rowlandson was very keen to get the engine back to Coventry, to see just why it was faster than the other factory machines. Cyril Pullin, however, took the machine back to Brooklands to preserve his secrets of tuning. Nevertheless, the new frame with the lower riding position was retained on the Works machines and later introduced for the road-going range.

The one retirement was T. E. Greene, when his machine caught fire at Quarter Bridge after the petrol tank had split. J. W. Adamson might well have given Cyril Pullin a much closer race, but he was delayed by a horseshoe which lodged in his tyre. This was an ever present problem for the riders of that era that does not occur today!

No. 1641.—Brazing Compo, 1 lb. tins, 6/- per doz.

Chapter Seven
LIGHTWEIGHT NEAR MISS

THE Company had commenced motorcycle production with a range of 500cc models. They were later followed by a 750 single, to cope with sidecar work. Although the standard 500 weighed little over 200lb, a number of experiments were conducted in the under 300cc class. The first of the prototypes appeared in April 1914 and was remarkable for its ingenuity. The single cylinder overhead valve engine was of 275cc and was fitted with an outside flywheel. The cam wheel was mounted on a massive shaft in front of the engine, to which was attached the driving pulley. The most unusual feature, however, was the method of operating the overhead valves. A beam was mounted over the valves and this was pivotted from the centre of the cylinder head. The cam follower was the shape of a large C, positioned round the single lobe camshaft. As a result, the camshaft raised and lowered the push-rod according to the position of the cam. When the push-rod was raised, the rocking beam depressed the inlet valve and when the cam was at the bottom of its turning circle, the exhaust valve was depressed by its return.

Had the push-rod been in one piece, the engine might have been successful. Unfortunately, to allow for expansion, the push-rod had a normal tappet. To allow the exhaust valve to be depressed, a spring was mounted on the push-rod to force it down. This meant that on the inlet stroke, the camshaft had to depress two springs, and the rate of wear on this component can well be imagined.

Later in the month the engine was redesigned with the normal Rudge mode of valve operation, namely a side exhaust and an overhead inlet. Strangely enough this engine had a remarkable resemblance to the engine produced by Villiers at the same time, except that the latter incorporated a two-speed gear. Unfortunately neither went into production, so it is not possible to make a more direct comparison between the two.

A machine that did go into production in fairly large numbers was a model fitted with a Sturmey Archer 3-speed hub gear. This was introduced in March 1914 and during the year approximately 100 were produced. It was fitted to both the 500cc and 750cc models, but as far as is known none has survived to this day. The Sturmey Archer advertisement of the time stated that the 3-speed hub gear would be the one place where a rider would find no trouble, but in fact, from experience on other machines, it was virtually a constant source of trouble. No doubt this is why these machines have proved so hard to find!

The name Rudge has always been synonymous with big singles but this period saw the birth of a Rudge parallel twin. Although a 750 single was produced for sidecar work, the majority of manufacturers produced a 1000 vee twin for the same purpose.

During 1913, whilst the 750 single was being produced, John Pugh was still looking at the big twin market. Manufacturing capacity was fully engaged in producing the existing range, so no time could be spared to produce a prototype. This was no problem to a man of his ingenuity. He came up with the obvious answer – just bolt two 500cc engines together! A standard 500cc Multi with sidecar attached was used, having the engine in its normal place. The extra engine was added to the timing side, by attaching extra frame tubes from the steering head and the saddle lug. The second engine had a timing side mainshaft on both sides and that on the driving side was attached to the timing side of the first engine by a splined driving sleeve. By this means it was possible to couple the cranks at any desired angle to each other – very simple but very effective. The only modification to the first engine was the removal of a small part of the timing cover, to accommodate the coupling sleeve. The pedal starters were also removed, so that bump starting, using the valve lifters, was the order of the day. Each engine had its own magneto and, although a single carburettor was tried, twin carburettors provided better performance. The rider was able to cut out one engine and control the machine with the other when cornering or slowing down, as each carburettor had separate levers on the right-hand side of the handlebar. The two engines were held rigid by a cast distance piece, which also protected the sleeve coupling.

A journalist from *Motor Cycling* was given a ride in the sidecar and he reported that "those who know the capabilities of the 3½hp (500cc) Rudge will guess that a sidecar outfit fitted with two of these engines can travel at a great speed and this was certainly the case". A normal Multi has a top gear ratio of 3½ to 1 and can reach about 70mph. This outfit had a top gear ratio of 2 3/8 to 1, so the speed potential was quite considerable.

Nothing is known of the experimental machine's later history, although it was a factory practice to restore experimental models to standard specification and then sell them off. The registration number was DU 2562, although, as previously mentioned, these numbers tended to be shared by many different factory-owned machines.

Even if the original version was not the first parallel twin, it was certainly one of the first to have two engines in a single motorcycle. In recording this I am, of course, mindful of the fact that the earlier Quadrant was a tricar and not a motorcycle.

Just to make sure that the experiments with twin cylinder engines covered the widest possible scope, another parallel twin was produced, this time using two 750cc engines. This was known as the 10hp Twin and the tester reported that he could have driven it up the side of a house without any difficulty. The big problem with these engines, however, was the width, and the outrigger engine to the right of the machine did nothing to help roadholding on the narrow tyres of the day.

Much useful data was collected during the year that the machine was tested and there shortly appeared on the market a 1000 Multwin, which was really two Multi engines on a common crankcase, this time in the normal vee position, the parallel twin layout having been abandoned. The prototype was wheeled into the running shed on 2 September 1914. It was a 60 degree twin, having cylinders with the normal Rudge inlet over exhaust valve layout. The frame was longer than that of single cylinder models, but otherwise the cycle parts were identical with those used for the 750 single. The machine was fitted with a Multi gear although, as on the parallel twins, the amount of power now available caused more belt slip than had been experienced on the single cylinder models.

A second prototype with a Multi gear was produced on 3 November 1914 and a third on 21 November in the same year. Experiments continued during the winter until a fourth prototype was assembled on 6 January 1915.

In later years, a considerable amount of publicity material drew attention to the fact that Rudge motorcycles had four-speed gearboxes. Because of this publicity it is often assumed that the first four-speed gearboxes were fitted in 1923. This is not so as the first machine with a four-speed gearbox was the fourth experimental vee twin, produced in January 1915. This was fitted with a proprietary Jardine gearbox, driven through an engine shaft clutch by chain, while the final drive to the rear wheel was by belt.

The machine featured in the Company's catalogue of that year, but production of civilian machines was on the decline and in the end only twelve were made. The engine shaft clutch tended to be rather harsh on the gearbox and as a result a fair amount of trouble was experienced with it.

The 1914 TT was held in May and the factory looked forward to building on this success. The 1915 models were to be introduced in July, as it was the Company's usual practice to commence the new range in the middle of the year. However, between the TT and 1 July, Archduke Ferdinand and his wife were assassinated in Sarajevo, sparking off the First World War.

The sales disaster was not immediately apparent, as motorcycle production continued much as before. Earlier in 1914, production had reached twenty motorcycles a day, of which approximately five were 750cc models. Of these, at least half were exported to Europe and the colonies. A large number went to the Rudge depots in Johannesburg and Port Elizabeth in South Africa and others to Australia and New Zealand. In Europe, the biggest customer was Veladini in Milan, Italy, but there were also plenty of customers in Austria, France, Latvia and Russia. Once the war had started, the Austrian sales were lost, but the good name of the Company in Russia stood the sales effort in good stead. A large order was received for dispatch rider's machines, which were the standard 3½hp Multi painted drab green. The late 'Griff' Griffiths remembered the order very well when I spoke to him a few years ago. The daily production rate of twenty machines would not have been enough to satisfy the initial demand, which had to be met in a hurry. As a result, every unsold machine in and around the factory was gathered in, even some that had been made several years earlier and had been returned to the factory in part exchange for newer models. These were given new engines and the whole batch stood in a corner of the factory. The conversion to military use consisted of hosing down the batch with green paint until everything, including the tyres, had been covered. The machines were then shipped off, post haste, to their new owners. A second order for four hundred machines was received from the Belgium Army and this order was completed early in 1915. Hopes of a contract for the British Army were dashed when the order was placed with the Triumph Cycle Company instead, but a small order was received from the Admiralty, to supply Royal Naval shore establishments.

Quite a number of Rudges saw active service with the British Army, as dispatch riders recruited in 1914 used their own machines. It was therefore possible for the Company to publish in 1915 a number of photographs showing Rudges in action, to help boost military sales. The rapid production of the Russian order was also emphasised by a notice to staff from W. G. Blatch, the Company Secretary,

A 1915 3½hp TT model Multi; Note the smaller diameter rear belt rim, dropped handlebars and lower mounting of the front Multi gear bracket, attached to the front down tube

"I am instructed to express the firm's cordial appreciation of the smart way in which the 400 Rudge Multis for the Russian Army were built and dispatched. The contract was signed on 2 October. The first lot left Coventry on 9 October and the last on 20 October. We have had news that all the machines have safely arrived at Archangel."

Although the Company already employed large numbers of women, there were plenty of men who joined the colours. Quite a number had become territorials in 1909, sufficient for the Coventry Works to have its own company of the 7th Warwicks. The racing team was also soon in uniform. Cyril Pullin joined the Royal Naval Air Service (which had Rudge Multis), Tommy Greene the motor transport section of the Army Service Corps, and Rowly Rowlandson was commissioned into the Ordnance Corps.

A majority of the management team were, of course, too old to serve with the colours but one exception was John Pugh's son Charles. He had been a keen motorcyclist before the war started and had ridden virtually all the models that the Company had produced. Unfortunately he died in the Battle of Ypres, a loss from which John Pugh never really recovered. When the latter died, his ashes were taken to the Continent and were scattered over his son's grave.

No. 25 Standard Full Roadster Imperial Service Model.

This machine has gradually been developed from our Standard Roadster as a model to stand up against the roughest usage. Long experience of special bicycles for the South African veldt; the rough country tracks of China; the jungle tracks and mountain roads of India; the backlands of Australia and for pioneering generally, has produced this Imperial Service Model which will withstand successfully the hardest usage to which a bicycle can be put. We recommend it for use at home by heavy, powerful riders who severely punish their machines. It is specially suited for Police and Military Service.

Frame. Flush-joint, 21-in., 23-in., 25-in. and 27-in. (see page 33). Extra heavy Tubes throughout.
Wheels. 28-in.
Rims. Nickel-plated Steel, lined black and red.
Tyres. 1½-in. "A" Roadster.
Handlebar. No. 76, Upturned, with Combination Celluloid-covering and Grips.
Brakes. Back and Front Rim, operated by Independent Rolling Levers, with Double Bell Crank Rear Transmission.
Free-Wheel. Silent Springless Ball-bearing.
Cranks. 6½ in. Cotterless.
Pedals. 4½ in. Rat-trap.
Gear. 67-in. (36–15).
Mudguards. Steel, V-section, with Beaded Edges.
Saddle. No. 115, mounted on 3-coil Enamelled Springs.
Finish. Frame, Forks and Mudguards, finest black enamel, lined red; patent black Celluloid-covering to Handlebar; other parts first quality Nickel-plate.
Equipment. 15-in. Celluloid Pump, Pump Clips, No. 739 Tool Bag, with Spanner and Oil-can.

Options without extra charge: 26-in. Wheels, with 21-in. Frame.
Nickel-plated instead of Celluloid-covered Handlebar.
Warwick instead of "A" Tyres.

No.	DESCRIPTION	PRICE £ s d	Payable by 12 Monthly Payments of s d	Cash Price (10% deducted) £ s d
25	As above Specification	8 - 8 - 0	14 - 0	7 - 11 - 3
2541	As No. 25, but with Coaster Hub Brake instead of Back Rim Brake	8 - 18 - 0	14 - 10	8 - 0 - 3
2542	As No. 25, but with Two Speed Gear (80 & 61)	9 - 4 - 6	15 - 5	8 - 6 - 3
2543	As No. 25, but with Three Speed Gear (94, 72 & 55)	9 - 18 - 0	16 - 6	8 - 18 - 3
2544	As No. 25, but with Three-Speed Coaster Hub Brake instead of Back Rim Brake	10 - 7 - 0	17 - 3	9 - 6 - 3

Production might have continued with replacements for Russia and Belgium but unfortunately the revolution in the former country and the fall of most of the latter to the German armies, ruled out further large sales. Early in 1915 a small order of a few hundred machines was received from Italy, but home orders were shrinking fast. Desperate efforts were made to find alternative markets and quite a number of machines were exported during April, to Copenhagen. A notable success was the sale of one to the Royal household, for the use of the King of Denmark, but this was one of the last Rudges to be sold for private use. During the same week of April 1915, a machine was presented to the Science Museum in London, where it may still be seen. By July, only military machines were being manufactured and production had dropped to just ten a day. This situation continued into early 1916 with only five a day being produced, production being split between Russia, Belgium and Italy with a few being exported to South Africa, Australia and New Zealand.

In 1916 the War Office considered producing a standard dispatch rider's machine made up of the best parts from British manufacturers. The Rudge Company contributed wheels to a number of the experimental machines and also provided two sets of frames and forks for experimental use. Thereafter production virtually ceased, except for one last order for the Belgium Army, which was completed during the end of 1916 and the

Rudge Multi

By Appointment Cycle Makers to H.M KING GEORGE

3½ h.p. (499 c.c.) Rudge T.T. Multi.

Brooklands Model.

THE winner of the International T.T. Race, the blue riband of the motor cycling world—the speedman's ideal—designed from the outset as a fast touring type of mount combining efficiency with reliability—its sloping top tube and tank (a design now being extensively copied) enabling the lowest possible riding position, and an extremely comfortable one at that—the most perfect steering of any machine on the road, due to correct weight distribution, angle of steering head and design of spring fork—nothing to watch but the road ahead! In short, a machine with a name and a reputation.

The Brooklands racing model shown in the inset is a similar machine in stripped form which has proved its ability to attain a speed approaching 80 m.p.h.

	Cash Price.	Credit or Exchange Price.
As specification opposite, with Multi-Speed Gear		
Brooklands Model, Fixed Engine		

Sturmey-Archer Three-Speed Gear can be supplied instead of Rudge Multi Gear without extra charge.

beginning of 1917.

On 3 November 1916 the Ministry of Munitions banned the production of motorcycles for civilian use. The Rudge factories swung into production of components and parts that had little to do with motorcycling. The ball bearing factory was working to capacity and was extended a number of times. Rudge wheels were also in great demand, mainly for Crossley ambulances and staff cars. The light, but strong, Rudge wheel was also used for aeroplane landing wheels. Probably the most unusual item produced by this division was for use on the Italian front. The Italian Army was fighting the Austrians in the mountains to the north of the country. This made the movement of troops very difficult and a series of aerial ropeways were designed. Four wheeled trolleys were

Rudge Multi

RUDGE WHITWORTH COVENTRY

By Appointment
Cycle Makers to
H.M. KING GEORGE

7/9 h.p. (1000 c.c.) Rudge Twin,

with 4-Speed Gear and Chain cum Belt Drive.

IN the model illustrated above, the 7/9 h.p. Rudge with four-speed countershaft gear and chain cum belt drive, we offer a luxuriously powerful sidecar motor bicycle. The Multwin is a double purpose mount, *i.e.*, suitable alike for solo or sidecar work, but the chain cum belt driven Rudge is designed throughout as a sidecar machine, and right well does it fill the bill. Its cool running engine, its braking power, its sturdy construction and up-to-date specification—all combine to place the latest Twin Rudge in the very forefront of passenger combinations.

The new introduction has received that careful attention to detail in the Drawing Office and subsequently in our workshops which characterises every Rudge production.

	Cash Price.	Credit or Exchange Price.
As specification opposite, with Free Engine Clutch, Kick Starter and 4-Speed Gear		

designed to run on these ropeways and the Rudge Company supplied these, each having 7ft wheels. The wheels were fitted with brakes controlled by a soldier who sat in a Rudge sidecar body, mounted in the centre. The whole effect was one of a gigantic pram!

The remainder of the Rudge factory was used for the manufacture of ammunition as the existing tools were easily adapted to the production of shells. A seventh floor was added to the main building at Spon Street, and the Sherbourne was decked over, to provide more storage space for the finished shells. By the time the war had ended in November 1918, the Company little resembled the Cycle and Motorcycle Company of four years previous.

Rudge Multi

By Appointment
Cycle Makers to
H.M. KING GEORGE

Rudge Sidecar.

THE RUDGE SIDECAR.

AS in the case of our 1915 model motor bicycles, the Rudge Sidecar has been improved where experience dictated, but mainly in the matter of additional comforts.

The upholstering is really luxurious. A compartment for spares, overalls and such like is provided under seat cushion, pockets with flap in door and opposite side and large pockets for maps and papers are placed on each side of seat.

A hood and screen can be supplied to order.

	Cash Price.	Credit or Exchange Price.
As specification opposite		
With Hood and Adjustable Screen		

The lamp set recommended for the Sidecar is Miller's Lightweight, per set.

Rudge Multi

RUDGE WHITWORTH COVENTRY

By Appointment Cycle Makers to H.M KING GEORGE

HINTS ON THE MANAGEMENT OF A RUDGE.

First see that the tanks are full—the oil tank with Price's Huile-de-Luxe or Vacuum T. T. lubricating oil, and the large tank with No. 1 or 2 petrol. If the machine is brand new, 3 or 4 charges of oil should be injected into the crank case before attempting to start, observing that the oil tap is open, *i.e.*, pointing downwards. Now turn on the petrol tap, flood the carburetter by depressing the button on the float chamber a few seconds, and with the machine jacked up on the stand, pedal the engine round. The valve lifter (left handlebar inverted lever) must be raised. The control levers should be placed as follows:

AIR (top lever right grip) closed.

THROTTLE (lower lever right grip) quarter open.

SPARK (controlled by tank lever) three-quarters advanced, *i.e.*, the arm on the contact breaker pulled up.

If when the valve lifter is released, the engine starts off at a fast rate, control its speed by gradually closing the throttle lever, and open the air lever to suit. The position of the air lever is soon found, as the engine will misfire if it is either too much opened or too far closed. In any case it should be the rider's object to use as much air as possible at all times—except when attempting to start, as the mixture is not strong enough to enable a start if the air lever be open at all. The maximum air supply conduces to a cool running engine and economy in petrol consumption.

Should the weather be cold and the engine stiff, an injection of a squib of petrol (oil gun in tank holster) will free the engine sufficiently to enable it to be turned freely. In wintry weather, a slightly thinner lubricating oil than is expedient in summer is desirable to obviate "gumming" up of the engine—Zero, Huile-de-Luxe, or Mobiloil A.

In the case of a brand new machine delivered by rail, it is wise to introduce a preliminary supply of oil to the gears and cams. First depress the inlet rocker, remove the vertical tappet rod, take the tappet out of the guide and inject an oil gun full of engine oil down the guide which is directly over the cam wheel. Then replace the parts. Once the engine is running the gears are automatically oiled by the splash feed in the crankcase.

It is always advisable to warm the engine by running it for half-a-minute or so on the stand before taking to the road. When the engine is warm, see that the lever of the Multi gear is the rearmost notch, release the clutch by the handlebar lever; a good test as to whether the engine is "free" is to put the back brake on, when the belt will stop, but the engine will continue to run—and with the left foot on the footrest, and also depressing the brake pedal, place the right heel against the stand and push off. Now let the clutch in very delicately—this is important to prevent straining the parts or stopping the engine—and gradually open the throttle, when the machine will glide away.

It is all very simple if one will only take the trouble to practise the control with the machine on the stand. Speed is increased by advancing the spark lever and pushing the Multi Gear lever forward gradually, so raising the gear ratio. The engine will stop firing altogether and allow the machine to float along if the valve lifter lever be raised; this is the simplest form of control, but in open country govern speed by the throttle lever.

POINTS TO REMEMBER.

Efficient lubrication is important to the life of a motor bicycle. Use only the best quality oils, and don't be too sparing. A charge every 6 to 8 miles is recommended for the single cylinders, and the Rudge Twin uses but little more.

Do not overlook the bicycle bearings and spring fork joints when wielding the oil can.

Carry spares all ready for use—it saves trouble and delay on the road.

In addition to the complete Rudge kit of tools, carry a spare sparking plug and washer, a belt fastener, a spare valve, spring and cotter complete. See that all are carefully and tightly packed to prevent damage by vibration in the tool bag.

Should blue smoke emerge from the silencer, it is a sign that you are over oiling, and should the engine stop firing altogether, take out the sparking plug and scrape away the charred oil from the points with a pocket knife. The points should be kept quite clean and separated by about $\frac{1}{32}$ of an inch. Reflex plugs are easy starters and never soot up.

RUDGE WRINKLES deals with the care and adjustment of a Rudge in detail, including tuning up for speed, and is illustrated by line and half tone blocks. Every Rudge owner should be in possession of a copy of this useful handbook, sent post free on application.

Multi Mechanism.

Extracts from The Times.

It is a singular fact, that although all vehicles which depend upon the petrol engine as a source of power would receive considerable theoretical advantages from the use of a gear giving infinitely variable ratios, it is only in the motor cycle that such a gear is found in actual practice. The reason why they exist only in motor cycles is that in this type of machine belt transmission still flourishes. The belt has contributed possibly more than anything else beside the magneto to the popularity of the motor cycle. It is a simple form of drive, by no means inefficient, and, what is of the greatest importance, tolerably elastic and operates extraordinarily well; it maintains its long established preponderance largely because it has itself been greatly improved in its composite canvas and rubber form.

From the "Motor Cycle." **Rudge Multi Acrobatics.**

The Gear that grips the gradient.

Chapter Eight
THE BRAVE NEW WORLD

AT the beginning of 1919 the armies of the world were being demobilised and factories were returning to peace time production. Automotive design had progressed rapidly during the war, although not for the motorcycle industry, which, like Rudge-Whitworth, had been engaged in other wartime activities. With the return of the young men to civilian life there was a demand for transport, particularly motorcycles. The Rudge-Whitworth Company was unable to take advantage of this demand as the factories had yet to be converted back from wartime production and many of the original workers had been killed in action.

Victor Holroyd, now General Manager, had been able to produce a few Multis for the Italian Army during 1918, although the total amounted to only twenty-five machines. Therefore when civilian production commenced at the end of January 1919, the production rate was only two or three a day. Unable to obtain an English magneto for these machines, Holroyd managed to import a number of Splitdorf magnetos from America, to get production underway.

The 1915 catalogue had listed ten models, plus a sidecar. These were the fixed engine design, the clutch model, TT, Multi and Ordinary Multi, in both 499cc and 750cc engine sizes, plus the 1000 twin with either a gearbox or a Multi gear. At the beginning of 1919 however, it was only possible to obtain the 499cc Multi in either Roadster or TT Roadster form. Although some sidecars had been manufactured for the Cable Cars mentioned earlier and also for the Belgium Army, they did not go back into production until April 1919. The situation gradually improved until in May the production rate had increased to five or six machines a day, of which one or two per week were of the 750cc type.

By July the production rate had been increased to twenty a day, almost up to the figures achieved in 1914. Supplies of the English CAV magneto were now becoming available and these gradually replaced the imported Splitdorf. Probably the most noticeable difference between the 1919 range and that offered in 1915 occurred in the frame of the TT Roadster. In all other years the difference between this and the standard

Multi Mechanism.

Engine.

3½ h.p. Engine.—Single cylinder, 85 m/m bore × 88 m/m stroke = capacity 499 cubic centimetres.

Engine Shop.

The compression ratio of the Rudge Engine is about four to one, that is to say, that when the piston is at the bottom of its travel the volume of gas is four times that of the space into which it will be compressed and exploded.

There are 11 finely cast cooling ribs on the cylinder which dissipate the heat engendered by the explosion. Below the ribs the plain cylinder barrel is not machined, as it is estimated that the finely matted surface left by the sand offers twice as much cooling surface to the air.

5/6 h.p.—The long-stroke single cylinder for sidecar has 85 m/m bore × 132 m/m stroke = 750 c.c.

7/9 h.p.—The Multwin 85 m/m bore × 88 m/m stroke × 2 cylinders = 998 c.c.

The charge is compressed to about 80 to 100 lbs. per square inch. The firing pressure is about three times this.

Multi Mechanism.

How pleasant it is not to be bound down to two or three arbitrarily chosen "step" gears.—**Extract from "THE MOTOR CYCLE."**

DRIVING AND ADJUSTMENT.—Do not attempt to change gear by forcing the lever while the machine is standing still, or some part will be broken. THE GEAR CAN ONLY BE CHANGED WHEN THE BELT IS RUNNING.

Belt Tensioning Device showing lever operating the movement of belt rim.

BELT TENSIONING DEVICE.—A neat lever screw has been added to the bell crank, which moves the rod controlling the opening and closing of the Multi belt rim. A turn of this screw will increase the effective diameter of the back belt rim, thus tightening the belt without the necessity of shortening. **This adjustment can be carried out by the sidecar passenger while the machine is in motion—IN FACT IT CANNOT BE DONE UNLESS THE BELT IS RUNNING, WITHOUT RISK OF BREAKING THE LEVER.**

Three types of Rudge F head engines at the start of the 1957 Vintage Rally during the Ise of Man TT Diamond Jubilee Week. *Left* - the 998cc 1922 Brooklands Twin, *Centre* - 1913 499cc Multi, *Right* - 1919 750cc Multi

Multi had been the lower handlebars and the higher gearing of the TT model. In 1919 however, the new Cyril Pullin low frame was used on the TT model, whereas the Multi and the 750 both retained the pre-war 'high' frame. It did not go unnoticed at the works that there was an ever-increasing demand for the TT model fitted with the lower frame. At the end of October 1919, the 1000cc vee twin was put back into production, only a month before the Olympia Show, where it was to make its first public appearance. There had been no motorcycle shows since it was first announced in 1915. The Show itself was a great success and the Company exhibited ten Multis, three vee twins, two 750s, three TT 500s and two standard 500 Multis. Sales resulting from the Show were quite satisfactory, particularly for the larger capacity models and the sidecars. The falling sales of the 500cc models were a little worrying, particularly as these models were now being out-performed by those of their competitors, whose machines were fitted with three-speed gearboxes and all chain drive.

Fortunately, Victor Holroyd was able to restart cycle production very quickly after the war and this became the mainstay of the Company. Special attention was paid to the lightweight racing cycle range and his efforts were well rewarded when all the winners of the British Amateur Championships of 1920 were mounted on Rudge-Whitworth cycles. In many ways 1920 was to be a vintage year.

By March 1920 between twenty and twenty-five motorcycles were leaving the factory each week, of which between five and ten were either 750 or 1000cc models. Export sales had been restored and machines were being sent to Italy, South Africa, Belgium, Japan, France, India and Greece. Others were dispatched to Denmark, New Zealand and Australia, but not in any great number.

The 7/9hp Vee twin machine of 1920. The magneto is an American Splitdorf, a type of magneto which was used for two years after the First World War when supplies of English magnetos were difficult to obtain

The magneto shortage of the previous year was now easing, as the factory was able to obtain large numbers of the new ML magneto. These were fitted to the 3½hp model. The CAV magneto was fitted to the 5/6hp models and the Splitdorf to the 7/9hp machines. By June 1920 the production rate had reached 30 a day, the highest rate ever reached for the production of Rudge motorcycles.

When the 1921 models were put into production on 1 July 1920, all had the new lower frame with the sloping top tube and were fitted with the ML magneto.

It has been said that the best engineers are those who have never received formal engineering training, but have developed a flair through interest. John Pugh certainly came within this category as he was committed to no particular engineering concepts, apart from the constant search for good quality. He was therefore able to switch from one approach to another, whenever the circumstances so demanded. For example, the problem of the belt-drive on the vee twin, which he encountered during 1915, was still unsolved by 1920. The power of the engine was too much for the transmission system. In 1915, the alternative of a gearbox failed through the shortcomings of the gearbox itself. There was only one answer – and that was to design one himself.

For the sake of simplicity, the first Rudge gearbox had three speeds and was most substantial in construction, the selector plates being ¼in thick for example. This gearbox was at first fitted to a 500cc machine, having a standard Multi type engine without the Multi gear ramps on the crankcase. As the final drive was now by chain, the spoking of the rear wheel was considerably simplified and the outer belt rim could be discarded. The brake flange was retained, however, with the normal, external shoe brake. This development gave John Pugh the opportunity to introduce a further improvement, interchangeable wheels. By adding to the front fork a similar brake to that fitted to the rear, in place of the less than satisfactory stirrup brake, he was able to use the same wheel design. The sidecar wheel had always been interchangeable with the motorcycle front wheel, so now it would be possible for all three wheels to be interchanged. Apart from these improvements and the use of a new clutch, the machine was very similar to the Multi, even to the retention of the pedal starter. The new clutch was mounted on the engine drive shaft, in the same way as a Multi, but in all other respects it was a completely new development. The Multi clutch consisted of approximately fifty plates, about the size of the old half-crown piece. The new clutch consisted of only two plates, and was of the same diameter as the flywheels. It was nowhere as smooth as the Multi clutch, but it was much slimmer and considerably reduced the overall width of the machine. It was also possible to mount the new clutch between the engine and the drive sprocket, whereas the Multi clutch had to be located outside the driving belt.

After extensive trials during the summer, a further 3-speed gearbox was produced and fitted to a 1000cc twin, on 27 October 1920. The transposition proved satisfactory and another 1000 twin with a 3-speed gearbox appeared on the Rudge stand at the Olympia Show, in November 1920. Eight machines, all with the Multi gear, were shown on the stand and comprised two each of the TT and 3½hp Multi, the standard 3½hp Multi, the 5/6hp Multi and the 7/9 Multi twin. One each of the last two models provided a further surprise as they were fitted with Lucas electric lighting, which was introduced as an optional extra in place of the standard acetylene lighting. Orders for 1921 were again satisfactory, although nothing outstanding when compared with the Company's major competitors. As Victor Holroyd kept production up to thirty machines a day, John Pugh pressed ahead with new designs, assisted by a young man who joined the Company in 1919, following demobilisation from the Army after service on the Russian front. He was a qualified metallurgist, who had joined the Research Department but was ultimately to make his name elsewhere. His name was George Hack.

At the time of George Hack's arrival, John Pugh was working on an engine which was unlike any Rudge that had been seen before. Although the drawings were commenced in 1919, it was July 1920 before they were completed. The specification was for a four cylinder in-line air cooled overhead camshaft engine. The block was a masterpiece of casting, with finned cylinder barrels and a car-type bolt-on sump. The camshaft was driven by a vertical shaft at the rear right-hand side of the engine and the bevel gear also drove the magneto, which was on the rear right-hand side. The camshaft operated two overhead valves on each cylinder, in-line down the centre of the cylinder head, with the sparking plugs off-set to the left-side of the engine. The inlet manifold was mounted on the right and the exhaust on the left-hand side of the head. Amongst other progressive features was a gear driven oil pump, shell-type main bearings and slipper pistons.

Many years later I discussed this engine with Graham Walker, who remembered it quite well. At the time it was fitted into cycle parts adapted from the vee twin. It had a very robust three-speed gearbox and all chain drive. When it was assembled in 1920, the Company's sales literature still referred back to 1913 and 1914 for successes and world records. This machine was capable of taking virtually any large capacity record of the day, including the world speed record. Unfortunately, it brought John Pugh into dispute with officialdom at the A-CU, the first of many occasions. In later years he was to write many letters to the motorcycling magazines, complaining of unnecessary restrictions on the freedom of designers. In the case of this particular engine, the bore was 85mm and whilst the exact stroke is not known it was approximately 75mm. This brought the

Multi Mechanism.

Details of Motor Bicycle Equipment.

Frame.—Made from weldless steel tube, with drop forged steel ball head and crankcase lug. The dropped frame, first used on the winning machine of 1914 T.T. Race, has caught on wonderfully, and has set the fashion to the Motor Cycling World. It will be found embodied on the Multwin as well as the single-cylinder Rudge.

Rudge Wheels. Strong steel rims, light car section, which have depressions for receiving the nipple heads; a similar practice to that which has been found so successful on Rudge-Whitworth detachable wire wheels for motor cars; with 10 gauge double-butted spokes and nipples and weather-proof ball-bearing hubs. The flanges set wide apart impart great strength to the wheel.

Front.—We realise the bad effect of wet roads on the front bearings—the water mixed with grit being thrown up by the tyres on to the mudguards, and dripping down the stays into the bearings. The amount of liquid mud coming down has been very much diminished on the Rudge Multi by putting the front brake forket and front stays entirely outside the mudguard, thus giving an unbroken smooth surface to the interior. In addition to this, a new type of hub flange has been designed which drains away all the water that comes down the stays from the entrance to the bearings; and, further, these are protected by dust caps, thus following very closely the practice which Rudge-Whitworth Ltd. found most effective in protecting the front bearings of motor cars. Front wheel bearing trouble has been non-existent for years.

The new design of flange also enables spokes to be used with only a very small bend under the head; another lesson that the Company has learned from its pioneer work in motor car wheels.

The Gear that grips the gradient.

Multi Mechanism.

The Rudge Sidecar.

Wheel.—Tyre, three-rib profile, 650 by 65 m/m. interchangeable with those on Rudge-Multi.

Mudguard detached.

Chassis.—The chassis is underslung, the main tubes being about 4in. below the wheel centre. In addition to the side tubes and two cross members, there is a diagonal tube connecting the left outside tube with the right inside tube, thus equalising the pull and increasing the strength of the chassis enormously.

Chassis, Springs and Carrier.

The Gear that grips the gradient.

Rudge Multi

By Appointment Cycle Makers to H.M KING GEORGE

Repairs and Spares.

TERMS OF BUSINESS.

THE spare parts listed on the following pages are of current pattern, but the descriptions and index numbers will serve for our earlier models, provided that customers when ordering always quote the number of the engine (stamped on back of crankcase), also the registered number of the Bicycle (stamped on seat lug of frame) in addition to the index number of the part required.

It is our invariable rule not to supply spare parts until after receipt of a remittance to cover their cost and carriage. When cash does not accompany the order an advance invoice, showing the cost of the parts required, will be sent to the customer and the order held in abeyance until cash is received.

Where it is anticipated that this invoice will cause delay and inconvenience we would recommend our customers to open a small credit account with us. A deposit of, say, £2 would allow of orders being dealt with by return and the delay of an advance invoice avoided. Goods will be invoiced out as supplied and a statement of account rendered periodically.

It is requested that customers taking advantage of this system should always reference their letters "Deposit Account" (Dept. F.M.). If on Tour mention Town of home address.

Complete Motor Bicycles or parts for repair must in all cases be consigned carriage paid, fully addressed to Rudge-Whitworth, Ltd. (Dept. M.C.), Coventry, and bear the name and address of the sender. A letter of advice giving full particulars of repairs required should also be posted at the same time.

Unadvised articles will lie here at Senders' Risk.

By the term "overhaul" we understand that the Motor Bicycle or Engine is to be completely dismantled, and all worn or broken parts renewed. Therefore estimates for this class of work cannot be submitted until the Bicycle or Engine has been taken down for examination. In the event of our estimate not being accepted, it is distinctly understood that the cost of taking down and re-assembling is payable by the customer. In most cases this cost will not exceed £2.

Crates and cases used in the packing of spare parts or repairs are not returnable.

capacity of the engine over the maximum permitted by the A-CU, so the machine could not be recognised for record attempts. A less forceful character would have redesigned the engine to come within the maximum limit, but not John Pugh. He abandoned the whole idea and the factory stayed away from racing and record attempts for two years.

There is, however, one amusing story concerning the running of this machine. It was taken out on the road to be tested and the rider opened it out on a straight stretch of road outside Coventry, early one morning. The power of the machine gave tremendous acceleration but placed unexpected stresses on the rear tyre. This separated the tread from the cover and the rider, who was crouching low over the tank and had no rear mudguard for protection, first knew of the trouble on receiving a number of hefty blows

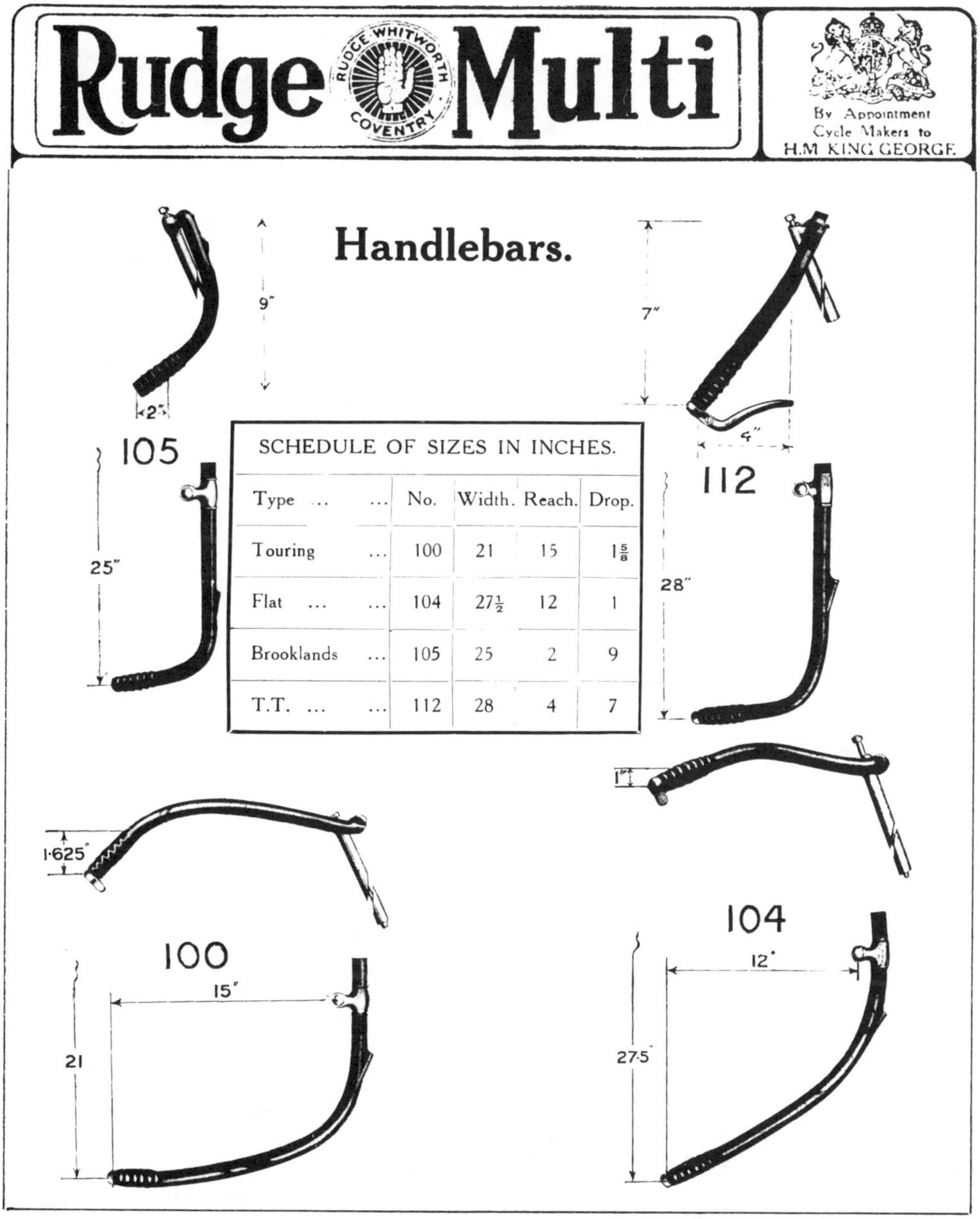

Rudge Multi

By Appointment Cycle Makers to H.M KING GEORGE

Handlebars.

SCHEDULE OF SIZES IN INCHES.				
Type	No.	Width.	Reach.	Drop.
Touring ...	100	21	15	$1\frac{5}{8}$
Flat	104	$27\frac{1}{2}$	12	1
Brooklands ...	105	25	2	9
T.T.	112	28	4	7

across his projecting posterior!

Graham Walker also remembered the end of this engine, which was also rather unusual. It had remained under a bench until after the Company had become bankrupt and the factory was about to close. Immediately before his last Christmas at the works, John Pugh was walking through the almost deserted Machine Shop when he saw the engine under the bench. Having partaken of quite a few whiskeys beforehand, he was in a melancholy mood and the memory of the time wasted on the engine did not please him. He called over two of the few remaining employees and had them carry the engine up to the balcony, which ran round the Machine Shop and throw it unceremoniously into the centre of the Machine Shop floor.

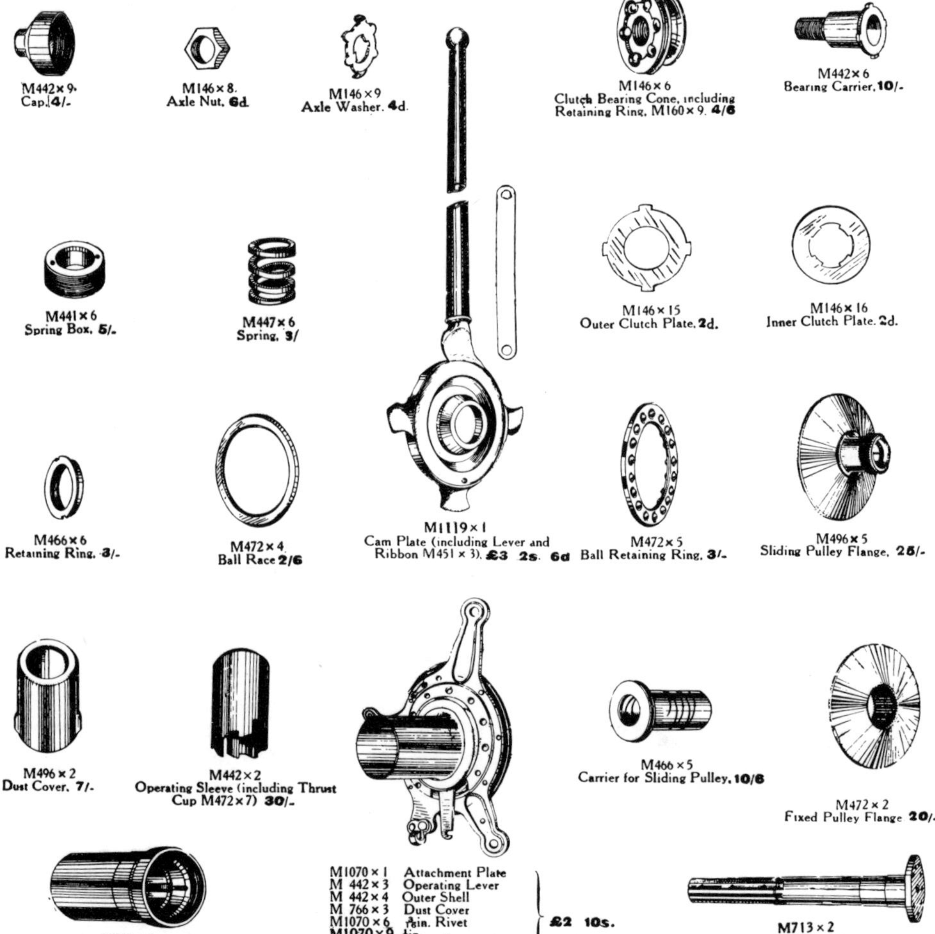

M442×9. Cap. **4/-**

M146×8. Axle Nut. **6d.**

M146×9 Axle Washer. **4d.**

M146×6 Clutch Bearing Cone, including Retaining Ring, M160×9. **4/6**

M442×6 Bearing Carrier. **10/-**

M441×6 Spring Box. **5/-**

M447×6 Spring. **3/**

M146×15 Outer Clutch Plate. **2d.**

M146×16 Inner Clutch Plate. **2d.**

M466×6 Retaining Ring. **3/-**

M472×4 Ball Race **2/6**

M1119×1 Cam Plate (including Lever and Ribbon M451×3). **£3 2s. 6d**

M472×5 Ball Retaining Ring. **3/-**

M496×5 Sliding Pulley Flange. **25/-**

M496×2 Dust Cover. **7/-**

M442×2 Operating Sleeve (including Thrust Cup M472×7) **30/-**

M466×5 Carrier for Sliding Pulley. **10/6**

M472×2 Fixed Pulley Flange **20/-**

M466×4 Flange Sleeve. **21/-**

M1070×1	Attachment Plate	**£2 10s.**
M 442×3	Operating Lever	
M 442×4	Outer Shell	
M 766×3	Dust Cover	
M1070×6	$\frac{3}{16}$in. Rivet	
M1070×9	$\frac{1}{8}$in. "	
M1070×7 & 8	Oil Hole Cover and Rivet	

M713×2 Axle. **32/6**

These prices are for the parts only, and do not include cost of fitting, which, if done, is charged extra.

All prices and conditions are subject to alteration without notice.

Orders are only accepted for execution at prices ruling at time of delivery.

Packing and Carriage extra, see page 2.

Chapter Nine
THE END OF AN ERA

DURING the first six months of 1921, the factory was still enjoying a boom period. Machines were being produced at the rate of thirty a day, the majority having the Multi gear. The vee twin with the 3-speed gearbox was also selling well, and one or two requests were received for the 500cc machine with this form of final drive. On 23 February 1921, it was decided that the prototype 500 should go into production and manufacture commenced at the end of March. Initially, as these models were made to order, the rate of production was only five a month. No form of shock absorber was fitted, so the early machines gave a much less comfortable ride than their belt-driven counterparts. When the 1922 models were put into production in July, a spring drive arrangement was built into the clutch and this gave some improvement. The pedal starter attached to the timing gears had been continued previously, but the introduction of kickstarters generally throughout the industry, necessitated the modification of the new gearbox. This was carried out in August 1921, when a solid shaft was mounted on two lugs behind the gearbox, upon which a kickstarter was pivoted, engaging with a gear on the end of the main shaft, on the outside of the gearbox end cover. Although this functioned quite satisfactorily, it introduced a weakness, causing the cast aluminium lugs on the gearbox to fracture with continued use.

It is claimed to be an economic fact, that the shortage of any commodity is usually followed by a glut. It appears to be human nature to rush into the production of items that are in short supply, to such a degree that there are then too many for the available market. This situation certainly occurred after the First World War, for the acute shortage of motorcycles in 1919 and 1920 was followed by over-production in 1921. The market reached saturation point in the middle of 1921 and many of the smaller manufacturers, who had rushed into the market, were forced to close down. The larger manufacturers also had their troubles, and were forced to cut back on the numbers of machines produced, leading to a price cutting war. By October 1921, Rudge production was down to fifteen a day, although the number of machines being sold with gearboxes

Rudge Multi

By Appointment
Cycle Makers to
H.M KING GEORGE

5/6 h.p. (750 c.c.) Rudge Multi.

A POWERFUL long stroke engine, ideal for sidecar work. No hill too long, no hill too steep. It embodies all the refinements common to other Rudge models. The engine is balanced in the most scientific manner, its heavy fly wheels ensure the greatest flexibility. The tube supporting the tank is looped to enable the cylinder to be readily removed.

If desired the 3½ h.p. engine can be fitted in this horizontal frame which gives ample room for tall riders.

For Prices, see page 8.

ADDITIONS TO SPECIFICATION ON PAGE 3.

Engine.—Powerful long stroke single cylinder, 85 m/m bore × 132 m/m stroke = capacity 750 cubic centimeters.

Silencer.—Extra large expansion chamber.

The Rudge 3 Speed Gear Box and All Chain Driven Motor Bicycle, (see page 5), can be supplied with this long stroke Engine.

Rudge Multi

By Appointment
Cycle Makers to
H.M KING GEORGE

7/9 h.p. (998 c.c.) Rudge 3 Speed Twin.

WE are the only British Firm producing a High-Powered Motor Bicycle, Engine and Gear Box complete, manufactured throughout in our own works. The Spring Drive on the Engine shaft absorbs all shocks, eases the strain on the chains and makes the Chain Drive smooth and silent as a belt. The Twin Cylinder Rudge Engine on the well tried lines of the $3\frac{1}{2}$-h.p. Single ensconced in the speedy dropped frame at once attracts attention. Its capacity is 85 bore × 88 stroke × 2 which equals 998 c.c.. Its power rating on test is 16-h.p. at 3,000 r.p.m. while its hill climbing with a Sidecar is remarkable.

The same engine as the Rudge Multwin.
For Prices see page 8.

ADDITIONS TO SPECIFICATION ON PAGE 3.

Aluminium.—Footboards and cover to front chain.
Clutch.—Dry plate with Ferodo inserts. Hand controlled.
Gear Box.—The Rudge Gear Box provides 3 Speeds and a neutral for the Kick Starter.
Transmission.—By Chain $\frac{3}{8}$" × $\frac{3}{4}$" pitch from Engine to Gear Box, and from Gear Box to back wheel. The standard gears are: 4, 7 and 10 to 1.
Wheels.—The Rudge Detachable and Interchangeable Wheels all have Brake Drums and are equally suitable for front, rear or Sidecar.

The same Engine as the Rudge Multwin.
The $3\frac{1}{2}$ h.p. or 5/6 h.p. engine can be fitted to the Rudge 3 Speed All Chain Drive Motor Bicycle as above Standard Gears 5, 9 and 13 to 1.

The effect of 30 years of neglect. A 1921 750cc Multi immediately after being discovered in a shed. The machine had been fitted with a sidecar, the brackets for which can be seen on the front down tube. This model was fitted with a particularly long and slim oil tank behind the saddle tube

had increased to twenty a month. A poignant sign for the future.

The front fork of the gearbox models had been redesigned in September 1921, so that the brake fulcrum was built into the leg of the right-hand fork. This gave much better leverage than the earlier bolted-on mounting.

The stand at the Olympia Show in November showed clearly the way things had gone since the previous year's show. In place of the array of Multis, there were now only two, one a 3½hp TT Multi and the other a standard 3½hp Multi. The remaining five machines were all fitted with the 3-speed gearbox, four of them being the newly introduced 3½hp model and the other the 7/9hp twin. The change proved to be sound strategy, for the sale of the 3-speed models increased to five a day, whilst the slump in sales of the Multis continued until they were selling at the rate of only five a day by the end of 1921. Early in 1922, John Pugh decided to reverse his no racing decision, in an attempt to boost sales through success in competitive events. The most obvious event was, of course, the TT in the Isle of Man, but this posed a problem. What sort of machine should be entered? Should it be the Multi geared machine which had won in 1914, or should the Company's colours be carried by one of the new 3-speed models? This simple question had a simple answer – enter five of each type to make doubly sure of success.

The machines had the Cyril Pullin designed frame which gave good road holding, but it was quite obvious that engine performance would have to be improved. A form of super-charging was achieved by reversing the cylinder head, so that the carburettor faced forward. The cylinder head was in fact an entirely new casting which was used only on this one occasion. The machines were also the first Rudges to have a mechanical oil pump. This was a Best & Lloyd drip feed type, mounted on the outside of the timing cover, although the machines still retained their auxiliary pump to augment the predetermined metered oil feed. The Multis in the team were also improved by the fitting of the front forks, wheel and brake from the 3-speed models. This provided considerable improvement over the stirrup type brake, still fitted to the production machines.

The mixture of the two types of machines, 3-speed and Multi, has to this day caused much confusion, as all the machines have been referred to as Multis. For example, in 1975, Volume 1 of the Keig Collection refers to O. M. Baldwin as riding a Rudge Multi, whereas he was riding one of the 3-speed models. To avoid confusion in the future, the machines used in the race are listed below.

Registration Number	**Model**
HP 3809	*3-Speed*
HP 3940	*3-Speed*
HP 3941	*Multi Gear, no clutch, 20 inch belt rim*
HP 3942	*Multi Gear, no clutch, 20 inch belt rim*
HP 3943	*3-Speed*
HP 3944	*Multi Gear, no clutch, 20 inch belt rim*
HP 3945	*3-Speed*
HP 3946	*3-Speed*
HP 3947	*Multi Gear, no clutch, 17 inch belt rim*
HP 3948	*3-Speed*

It will be seen that one of the five Multis had been replaced by a 3-speed model.

Interest at the factory in the race results was recognised by John Pugh, who arranged for a telegram to be sent at the end of each lap, showing the riders' position. This was to be followed in the evening with a celebration to mark the Company's success. After the race had started, interest reached fever pitch as the first telegram was expected. Time ticked on towards the end of the race and still nothing had been received. An hour after the race was expected to finish, the first telegram arrived and this announced that O. M. Baldwin had finished in 14th place, all the other machines having retired. A mood of great gloom settled over the factory. The 'F' head engine, which had proved so successful before the war was no longer competitive. It was still virtually in the same form in which it had won the TT in 1914 and had not kept pace with developments during the eight intervening years. One interesting coincidence was that H. Riddell, who retired on the sixth lap, was also a member of the ill-fated BSA team of 1921, where all five starters retired. After that disaster the BSA concern never returned to the TT with a factory team. The Rudge team disbanded after the race and another was not to be formed for some years.

Incidentally, O. M. Baldwin achieved two firsts as far as the Company was concerned. He was the first Rudge rider to complete the TT on a chain driven machine and the first to use the three-speed gearbox. In the latter respect his achievement was unique, as no other rider or Rudge machine ever completed the TT course using this gearbox. Unfortunately this sort of achievement does not help to sell motorcycles.

The 998cc three-speed Brooklands Twin. Note the engine shaft flywheel-sized clutch and the smaller shock absorber mounted on the gearbox mainshaft

The sales side of the organisation did not receive the boost that was expected and production dropped to about seven machines a day, of which five were Multis and two were 3-speed models. The Cyril Pullin type frame was now standardised for all machines, but this caused problems with the 750cc model, as the long stroke engine could not be accommodated. This model was therefore dropped, leaving two cubic capacities, 499cc and 998cc. In spite of failure in the Isle of Man, the majority of Multis made were to the TT model specification, although this comprised little more than lowered handlebars and a different gear lever.

Some consolation was obtained by successes at Brooklands, when R. E. Dicker won the 3 lap sidecar handicap race on 12 August. In October 1922 he was joined by J. H. Mathers, and together they broke six records from six hours and 500 miles upwards, on a 3-speed 1000cc twin.

The long distance records had shown that the machines had stamina, but a lack of competitiveness revealed a need for more speed. The 'F' type engine was very slow revving, having a maximum of about 3600 revs. The obvious answer was to produce a four-speed gearbox and this John Pugh put in hand immediately.

In the following month, at the Olympia Show, nine Rudge motorcycles were on display, three 3½hp Multis, two 3½hp 3-speed models fitted with ML magnetos, two more 3½hp 3-speed models fitted with BTH magnetos and two 7/9hp 3-speed twin machines.

There was another machine on the Rudge stand at Olympia. This was a miniature motorcycle and sidecar about 3in high which, after the Show, was presented to Queen Mary for her dolls house. One visitor to the stand who showed particular interest in the model was the Duke of York, who later became King George VI.

Before leaving 1922, it is interesting to read the tuning instructions for improving the performance of a standard machine. For example the enthusiast was recommended to drill the connecting rod to reduce reciprocating weight and to then file out the holes to make them square. A practice we now know leads to very expensive noises!

Chapter Ten
THE RUDGE FOUR

THE new Rudge 4-speed gearbox was not developed from the 3-speed design, but was entirely new. Unlike later practice, it was upside down, with the layshaft and kickstarter spindle beneath the mainshaft and the securing bolts at the top of the casting. The selector quadrant was to the rear of the box, like its successors, but unlike them the operating arm was mounted on the near side, behind the sprocket, and this was connected by a rod to the near side of the petrol tank. It was therefore necessary to have a cross-over shaft inside the petrol tank, to give the normal right-hand gearchange lever. With the new gearbox came a new clutch which, for the first time, was mounted on the gearbox and used a large central spring, similar to the Multi clutch, although the clutch plates were much larger. A new shock absorber was designed for the engine shaft which had two three-lobe cams working against each other, a device which was used in a number of modified forms until production eventually ceased. The engine and cycle parts were similar to those used on the 3-speed model, adapted where necessary.

With sales still falling, it was essential to take immediate action, as it was too long to wait until July for the introduction of the 1924 models. The prototype, with gearbox No. 1, was hastily assembled on 16 January 1923 and sent to the Glasgow Exhibition. On the return of the machine from the Exhibition, it was thoroughly tested and found to be fairly flexible, but with a modest performance when compared to contemporary sports machines. As a result gearbox No. 2 was fitted to a 7/9hp twin on 9 February 1923. This gearbox was very similar, except that the gearing was higher, giving a 3½ to 1 ratio in top, compared to 4 to 1 for the 500cc engine.

It is interesting to note that the third gearbox was fitted to a vee twin which was supplied the following day to the comedian Max Miller. It was noticeable at this time that the Company's advertising strategy had changed, as there were so few sporting victories to help sell their machines. The catalogues of this period are full of photographs of famous actors and actresses sitting on their Rudge motorcycles and/or sidecars, who listed 'Rudging' as one of their hobbies.

The 1923 7/9hp Rudge four-speed twin, the first model to be fitted with the Rudge four-speed gearbox. This machine is complete to the original specification apart from the tank top tool box which very few retained, and of course, the spark plugs. The pedal beside the footboard is the rear brake, while the pedal at the rear of the footboard is the oil pump operating pedal. This was also the first model with a clutch mounted on the gearbox, and an engine shaft shock absorber

Although the catalogue for 1923 gave the choice of Multi gear, 3-speed or 4-speed models, virtually no 3-speed versions were sold after February 1923, when the 4-speed version became generally available.

As far as the motorcycle industry was concerned, 1923 was a disastrous year. After the shortage of machines following the First World War, so many manufacturers had entered the market that there were far more machines than customers to buy them. Many makes disappeared, but those who survived found it necessary to cut prices to a very low level. The 3½hp 3-speed Rudge, for example, was priced at £94 in 1922, then dropped to £80 in 1923, whilst the 4-speed model was introduced at £85. The 7/9hp 3-speed twin dropped in price from £113 in 1922 to £97 10s in 1923 and the 4-speed version cost only £2 10s more, at exactly £100. Even so, sales were very slow and the year's production at the factory came down to a disastrous 1400 machines.

Having produced a workable 4-speed gearbox with a new clutch, John Pugh next turned to the engine. He was particularly concerned with the valve configuration and its effect upon engine performance. The 'F' head had been years ahead of its time in 1910, but it had now been overtaken by the overhead valve machines of other makers. One of these had a four valve ohv engine, designed by Sir Henry Riccardo. The engine had performed quite well but the steering of this model left something to be desired. The Rudge had a frame that gave good steering and needed only an engine with better performance to make it competitive. The four valve layout avoided a problem which John Pugh had met in his early experiments, the one of head distortion. A two valve head with valves large enough to serve his purposes would mean quite large diameter valves, which would tend to make distortion a probability. Retaining the same bore and stroke as the 3½hp 'F' head engine, the blueprints were prepared and the first experimental model was assembled on 27 July 1923.

The new engine had a bottom end which was fairly similar to that of the 'F' head engine. The magneto was mounted on the front of the crankcase and driven by a gear train, but the camshaft was now the first gear in that train and not the last. The Best & Lloyd pump, which had been used successfully in the TT, was substituted for the foot oil pump and also driven from the camshaft. This latter item consisted of a single lobe with a cam follower on each side. The valves themselves were parallel in a pent roof cylinder head and clearly showed John Pugh's concern about the damage that could be caused through valve breakage. Although the heads were only 1in diameter, the stems were 0.37in thick, a very sturdy stem indeed.

Under tests the engine produced over 15 brake horsepower, more than half as much again than the best that the 'F' head engine could produce. This was certainly a step in the right direction but it led to quite a number of unexpected problems. These boiled down to the fact that the cycle parts, which were quite satisfactory for the earlier machines, were now unsuitable for the additional performance that had become available. There were two answers, the first to redesign the cycle parts and the second to reduce the size of the engine. In typical belt and braces fashion, both were adopted and in September 1923 the engine was redesigned as a 350. The gearbox too had given rise to problems, with the selector on the left of the machine and its cross-over shaft inside the petrol tank. It was therefore redesigned, with the gearchange mechanism on the right-hand side, pivoting on the frame immediately below the saddle. The horizontal tube inside the petrol tank was retained however, and a spring mounted inside, to give the gearchange lever positive locations with the indentations of the gate on the side of the petrol tank. During October the cycle parts received attention, in the form of an entirely new frame. Although similar in external appearance to that used for the 'F' head 4-speed models, a pair of torque arms were added, running from the rear wheel to the bottom of the crankcase. A major improvement was introduced to the steering head, where the ball bearings were increased in size from 3/16 to ¼in diameter.

The steering cups, designed at this time, were used on all machines until production ceased in 1939. One of the last relics of cycle practice on the machine disappeared with the replacement of the handlebars which had, until then, been secured by a bolt which passed through their centre and into the steering stem. The handlebars were now brazed into the steering lug, which was secured to the top of the front spring and to the rear of the top shackle.

This was as far as the redesigning could be taken because the Olympia Show was fast approaching. The first two prototypes were assembled on 9 October 1923 and a third on 15 October. During the course of the month the front mudguard was redesigned to give it a width of 5in and the flattened 'U' shape, which was soon to become a Rudge feature. The rear mudguard was also redesigned to match, although initially it retained the flap at the rear which could be hinged up out of the way, during the removal of the rear wheel.

When the Olympia Show opened in November, the first two prototypes were put on display, the third being retained at the factory for testing. With all the work that had gone into the 350, there had not been time to redesign the 500, so the two 500cc four valve machines shown on the stand retained the earlier 4-speed gearbox with near side operating lever, and the earlier frame. To add to the mixture, the Company also displayed a standard 3½hp Multi, and two 4-speed 7/9hp vee twins, one of which was fitted out with electric lighting. As the last Multi to be made was assembled on 31 October 1923 and the last 4-speed vee twin on 2 November 1923, it is difficult to say why these machines were taken to the Show. I can only guess that it was done to achieve some continuity by introducing a fairly radical new machine alongside a tried and tested model, to give the buying public reassurance that new ideas were backed by a Company that really knew how to make motorcycles.

Prototype No. 1 went on to the Motorcycle Show in Brussels and No. 2 was sent to Velandini in Italy, for the Milan Show.

November and December 1923 were taken up with re-tooling and reorganising the factory, although one further prototype 350 was assembled on 26 December 1923, plus a further 500cc four valve model. This retained the old gearbox and cycle fittings. On 1 January 1924 production restarted at the rate of five machines a day, still the 500 'F' head engine with the old gearbox and cycle parts. Two of these were shown at the Scottish Exhibition in January but their days were numbered and production eventually ceased on 18 January 1924. Production then switched to the 350 four valve and the first three production machines were assembled on that day.

During the post-First World War period, when motorcycle production had first boomed and then slumped, the sidecar side of the Rudge factory had maintained a steady flow of completed units. Two or three appeared on the Company's stand at each Olympia Show and production throughout the period was maintained at about three or four a day. Although the touring sidecar achieved steady sales, the most popular was the lightweight version, which cost only £15, in 1923, having been reduced from £20 in the previous year. The touring sidecar was reintroduced in 1923 at a cost of £20. Sales went well after J. H. Mathers and R. E. Dicker attached a sidecar to the 7/9hp twin on which they had set up solo records in 1922, to take a further seven sidecar records in April 1923.

With the end of the 'F' head engine in January 1924, the rider lost an early thief-proof device advocated by the factory. In the handbook, it was recommended that the rider remove the inlet push-rod when parking his machine, to prevent unauthorised rides. With the relatively weak inlet valve spring and exposed rocker, this was a very simple practice, which was difficult to repeat on the new four valve engine, which had two valve springs to each valve and the rockers tucked away under the petrol tank.

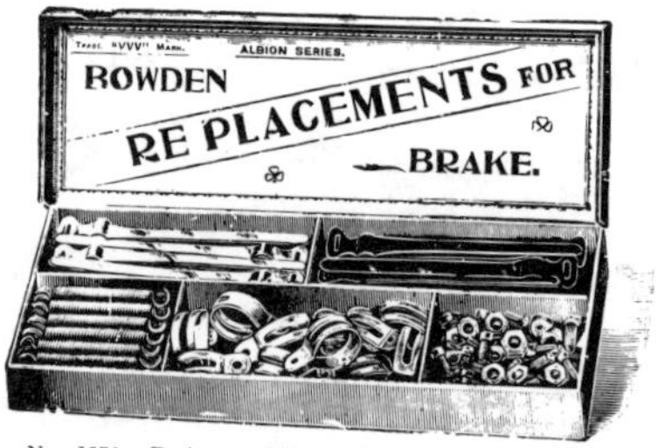

No. 1572.—Brake Sundries, assorted in boxes of one gross,' **2/3** per box.

Chapter Eleven
A SHAKY START

AT the start of 1924 the Rudge factory was producing a new and untried 350 which, in prototype form, had out-performed the previous year's 500 machines. The full development resources had been involved in producing this machine so it was all that the Company could market, once the 500 'F' head engine had been withdrawn in January. The obvious need was a new 500 to complement the 350, and be the power unit for the very successful range of sidecars, particularly the sports model, which was made in the ever popular bullet shape. February and March were therefore taken up with designing the new machine or, where possible, modifying parts of the new 350. By the end of April the new 500 was available and details were hurriedly released.

The new frame was very similar to that of the 350, complete with the torque arms from the rear wheel spindle to the bottom of the crankcase. Strangely enough, both frames incorporated a modification which had been brought about by the Multi gear, yet it was retained for a different reason. The Multi gearlever was mounted inside a gate on the left-hand side of the petrol tank. Continued use caused the tank to split as the tank brackets had no other support. The lower tank tube was therefore cranked to the left, so that it ran along the left-hand side of the tank, to give the needed support. On the TT Multi, the gearchange gate was mounted in a lower position on this tank rail, and the front down tube relieved the tank of any unnecessary stress. When the new frames were introduced in 1923 and 1924, the lower tank tube was still cranked to the left, to avoid the overhead valve gear. Whereas previously the offset was fairly angular, the new frame had a more pleasing gentle curve, from the steering head to the seat pillar.

Unlike the 350, the 500 retained the new gearbox with the left-hand side gear quadrant control. This involved fitting a cross-over shaft immediately behind the seat pillar, to keep the gearchange lever on the right-hand side of the tank. Strangely enough, this gearbox was later ignored when the Company reverted to left-hand gearchange ten years later, although access to the quadrant lever was somewhat restricted by the clutch. On both models the saddle was mounted cycle style, on a pillar inside the seat tube, the

The rear end of the 1924 350cc four valve machine showing the torsion bar which was fitted between the engine and the rear wheel. This was discarded in the following year when fears about the effect on the rear frame of the additional power proved to be groundless

The first electric lighting sets were 4½ volts and were controlled by a box mounted behind the headlight in a similar manner to the acetylene cylinder which it replaced

Timing side of the 1924 350cc four-valve machine showing the external Best and Lloyd oil pump which was in reality a total loss metering device

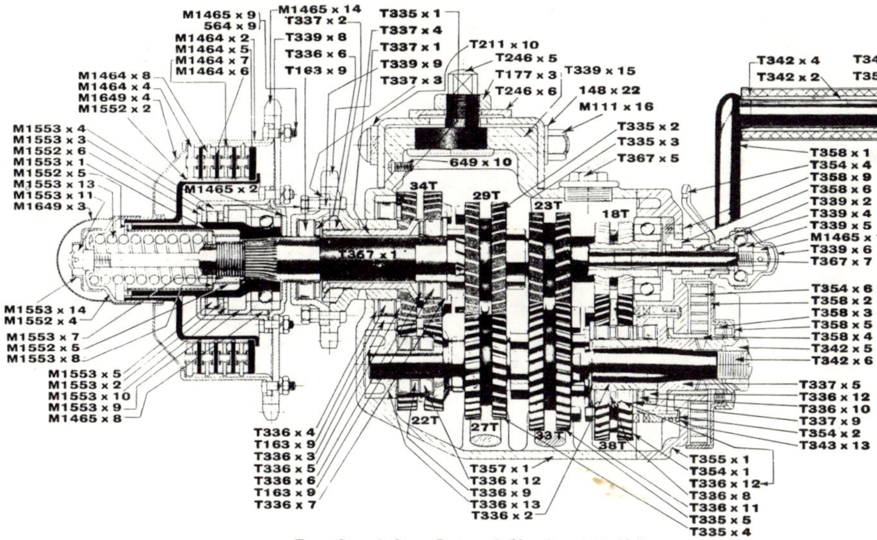

Four Speed Gear Box and Clutch. 4·99 H.P.

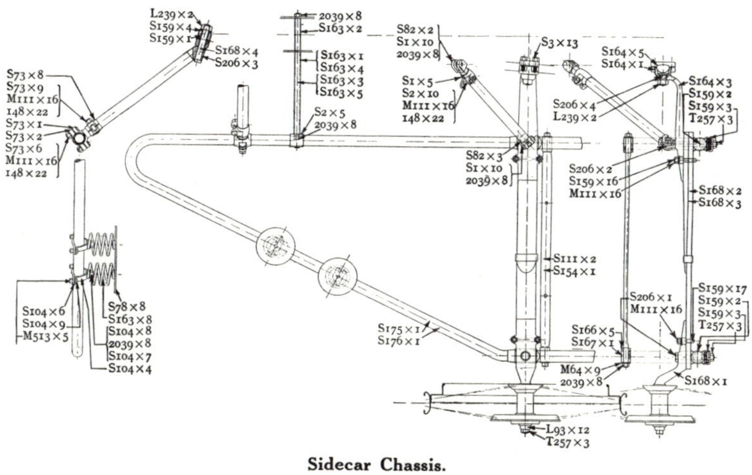

Sidecar Chassis.

last year that this method of fixing was used by the factory.

Although the 350cc and 500cc engines were fairly similar, the latter had a redesigned timing side and the camshaft was given two lobes, one for the inlet and the other for the exhaust, in place of the single lobe of the 350. This brought the push-rods into line with each other, in a vertical position, whereas on the 350 they were widely spaced at the bottom and close together at the top. The new 500 cost £64 6s, the 350 £58. Both were widely advertised as being fitted with electric lighting as standard, which cost an additional £5. Where lighting was specified, the ML magneto was replaced by the 4½ volt Maglita. On the drive side, one of the most noticeable points was the inverted gearbox, as this brought the clutch to a much higher level than the engine sprocket. The pressed steel chain cover was therefore tilted up towards the rear. The new clutch with the large central clutch spring projected through a hole in the chain case and was therefore given its own steel cover. It was necessary when riding, to remember not to move the left leg back too far, otherwise the back of the leg contacted the rotating clutch cover, which could prove quite painful!

Both machines handled well, although with a low compression ratio, performance was very modest. Quite a number were exported and in New Zealand, R. E. Canteloup, a 14 stone rider, rode a 350 up the side of Mount Eden, an extinct volcano near Auckland. Although footing was necessary, where the ground was soft, the engine did not stall on the 1200ft climb. The only adverse comment was that the rider had insufficient control over the throttle, using throttle levers and would have preferred a twistgrip. Unfortunately this plea went unheeded for several more years.

After such a major change in production within six months, from the 'F' head series to the new four valve arrangement, John Pugh might have been excused had he sat back and rested for a while. This was not to be however, for, starting in July, a whole series of improvements were incorporated before the next Olympia Show. First of all the gearbox was completely redesigned into the style that was to be used, with few modifications, for the next fifteen years. The kickstarter and layshaft were moved to the top of the box, giving a lower mainshaft and clutch position. Two parts of the Rudge slogan had already appeared and the third was to be added in October, when the front brake was coupled to the rear brake pedal so that both brakes could be applied by using the pedal alone. The factory could now proudly boast 'Four valves, four speeds, coupled brakes'. The rear carrier and mudguard were redesigned so that the whole unit behind the saddle would pivot forward to aid wheel removal, in place of just the mudguard flap. With both front and rear stands, the wheels were quickly detachable and of course, interchangeable. In place of footrests, the 500 was fitted with footboards, which were fashionable at the time, although footrests could be provided as a free optional extra. The literature proudly proclaimed that the 350 produced 10 brake horsepower, while the 500 reached 15bhp. Meanwhile the three sidecars had been joined by a fourth, known as the Boat Shape. This was not the sturdy little cruiser shape of later years, but a very long-nosed sidecar which was as long as the machine itself. Its shape was a clear indication of an extravagance yet to come.

Immediately before the Show, the factory took part in a sales promotion campaign, which upset some riders at the time, although the practice was not uncommon at the time. Riders were invited to complete a crossword and prizes for correct answers included complete motorcycles. One of the clues was 'a game played with a stick' in four letters. Another clue revealed that the last letter was O, so that virtually all entrants gave the answer as polo. They were then informed by their local Rudge dealer that the correct answer was pogo, but as they had been so close to the correct answer, they could have a 1924 Rudge at £5 discount. Two months later some were a little dismayed to see that the new models were reduced at prices below those which had been paid for the earlier model. The 350 was down to £42, the 500 £46, with electric lighting £4 extra.

When comparing the two years, there is no doubt that the 1925 model looked more sporting and purposeful that that of the previous year. One of the main reasons for this was the relocation of the lighting control box, from the handlebars to the frame tank top tube, and the mounting of the headlamp in front of the forks, instead of on top of them. During 1924 production reached almost 3000 machines, over double the number achieved the previous year.

The new 350 was soon in the record books when it was ridden at Brooklands and Montlhery by Col. Neil Stewart and his wife Gwenda. The records broken were all for long distances, confirming the durability of the machine and of Mrs. Stewart! She went on to greater things and is better remembered under the name Gwenda Hawkes as a record breaking Morgan three-wheeler driver.

Chapter Twelve
NEW IDEAS

ALTHOUGH the period of 1924 to 1926 is not remembered for innovations by the Rudge factory, nevertheless many new ideas were developed to become memorable features of the marque. Others were produced, only to be discarded before they reached the production stage. In the former category was the introduction of a linking cable between the rear brake pedal and the front brake, enabling the pedal to operate both brakes simultaneously. The prototype was designed during October 1924 and later introduced on the 1925 models. It was originally designed for a machine that did not go into production. Coupled brakes were, in fact, to remain a feature until production eventually ceased.

The machine for which the coupled brake was originally designed was a new four valve 350. This was also designed during October 1924, the top end and the method of valve operation being identical to that of the existing 1924 model. Although the crankcase separated vertically in normal motorcycle fashion, it extended to just below the main bearings. The lower part of the flywheels were enclosed by a car type sump, which contained the oil pump. This engine also incorporated another radical change, which was not to be introduced into the range for some years, positive oil feed to the big end rollers through the crankpin. Strangely enough, this engine had a bore of 71mm and a stroke of 88mm, whereas the next 350 prototype reverted to the more usual Rudge dimensions of a 70mm bore and a 90mm stroke. The second engine was identical to that of the standard production 350, although it was fitted with a two valve head. In addition to the use of a conventional two valve head, the rocker gear showed an interesting change in approach, when compared to the previous year. The 1924 production 350 had a spring mounted between the undersides of the two rockers, which held the rockers down against the valve stems. This assisted the rockers to depress the valves in operation, by working in opposition to the valve springs. Although the extra spring was intended to relieve pressure on the cam, it meant that any play in the system would appear at the top of the push-rod.

The not very effective front-brake fitted in the mid 1920s between the cycle type stirrup brake of the Multis and the very effective 8 inch brakes fitted in 1928. Note the second cable which linked the front brake to the rear brake pedal to give the first version of the Rudge coupled brakes

If this became excessive, or the machine was revved until valve bounce set in, the push-rod could quite easily fly out and immobilise the machine. On the prototype two valve engine, the spring was repositioned on top of the rocker, pulling each of these away from the valve and thus assisting the valve springs. Conversely however, this increased the wear on the cam and followers so the idea of the additional spring was dropped from all models at the end of 1924. The two valve engine did not perform as well as the four valve, as the valve heads were very little larger than those employed in the four valve engine. The two valve engine did not, therefore, progress beyond prototype stage. The third 350 engine of 1925 was little more than a 1924 engine with a redesigned crankpin and big end assembly.

Although the first 1925 models, which were produced towards the end of 1924, retained similar cycle parts to those used on the 1924 models, changes were introduced in April 1925. The torque stays had proved to be unnecessary and these were discarded, allowing the chainstays to be lowered to bolt to the engine plates, just behind the bottom of the gearbox. The engine plates themselves were of the cradle type and no longer surrounded the gearbox, which could now be removed more easily. The gear change pivot on the seat tube was also discarded and the tank lever was connected directly to a lever on the gearbox quadrant.

The front forks retained their existing style, although experiments were carried out in March 1925 with a bolt-up fork assembly. This comprised a series of tubes which were flattened at each point where the spindles were mounted. As no tube was permanently attached to another, but just retained by these spindles, in some places, on the fork shackles there were six flattened tubes held together by the spindle nuts. It did not take long for the testers to find out that riding a machine thus equipped was similar to cycling across an enormous jelly! The value of the Rudge rigid fork legs and fork shackles was confirmed.

On the sidecar front, another monstrosity appeared when the canoe sidecar was introduced. This was not to be confused with a canoe shaped sidecar, but was a 16ft single seater canoe mounted on a Rudge chassis. Just to prove it was no gimmick, G. E.

(Ernie) Nott, a works tester, took a Rudge and canoe sidecar through the Victory Trial and achieved a Bronze Medal. The canoe was not permanently fixed to the chassis, but had quick release clamps which enabled the nautical motorcyclist to remove it and take to the river should he be so inclined. Unfortunately, the records do not show how many of these sidecars were purchased but none is known to have survived. Although the Rudge advertising literature listed trials successes for this sidecar, it took a remarkable team effort to get the outfit to complete the course. Ernie Nott was an extremely tough rider, but Graham Walker later recalled that when the outfit took part in the trial it was necessary for the other two team members to complete their section and then go back to help Ernie Nott to manhandle his outfit round the more difficult parts of the course. Very few trials courses allow for a sidecar outfit that requires a 20ft turning circle!

The production of motorcycles in 1925 exceeded all expectations and reached a total of 7000 machines. It was clear, however, that the 350 engine needed redesigning as its performance did not compare with some of its contemporaries. When the 1926 models were introduced in July 1925, it was announced that the 350 model would be dropped from the range and that manufacture would be concentrated on the 500cc model. With only the 500 machine on the market, it was possible to develop the machine into two directions. The first was towards an all-weather motorcycle and leg shields were designed to go with the footboards, which were the standard fitting on these machines. It had not escaped John Pugh's notice, however, that the machines were performing well and in consequence they could now be obtained with footrests as a more sporting optional extra. The only other major change occurred within the gearbox.

When the Rudge 4-speed gearbox was first designed, the pinions were given helical teeth. This was to reduce wear and also to achieve an element of mechanical silence, as straight cut gears tend to be rather noisy. By 1925 improvements in gear cutting made it possible to fit straight tooth gears, which were easier to manufacture.

Despite the coupling of the brakes, the effect of the external brake shoes was far from impressive. In November 1925 a vee section brake rim was designed but as the rate of wear on the brake blocks became excessive, it did not go into production.

The 500cc model in both its guises appeared at the Olympia Show, together with a full range of sidecars. The sidecar chassis had been the subject of more of John Pugh's original thinking. It had been in use since the Company entered this market and it was constructed of very rigid steel tube. One of the main tasks of this chassis was to resist the bending stresses imposed by turning the outfit away from a straight line. What would happen if the rigid tubes were replaced by sprung steel, so that the chassis bent under stress, but returned to its original shape when the machine returned to the straight? On this occasion the idea worked and the Company was able to show on its stand the first spring steel sidecar chassis. It was a little unnerving for the sidecar passenger, however, first to have the nose of the sidecar pointed upwards, and then downwards, as the machine turned from lock to lock. Nevertheless, the design did improve road-holding.

With successes in trials and other similar motorcycle competitions, tentative steps were made towards re-entering the racing scene. This time the Company was not going to rush in like in 1922 and risk another publicity disaster. It was therefore decided to give works support to private entrants. In December 1925, racing handlebars were designed and also a forged Elektron racing piston, quite a change from the cast-iron component which had been used previously. Also produced at this time was a rather ingenious method of controlling the steering on a racing machine. The standard machine was not fitted with a steering damper and as a result steering could be very lively at high speed. There were a number of proprietary damper units on the market, which clamped between the top frame tube and the handlebars, but the Rudge design was quite different.

Rudge-Whitworth
Four Valve Four Speed

3·46 H.P.—10 B.H.P.

All Steel Frame -	With Drop forged ball head.
Brakes -	Front and rear acting on drum.
Carburettor -	Senspray, two lever control.
Chain Cover and Chain Guard -	Enamelled Black
Clutch -	Dry plate on gear box, hand controlled, spring drive and shock absorber on engine shaft.
Connecting Rod -	Drop forged steel, hardened and ground to receive roller bearing.
Electric Lighting -	From dynamo in same unit with magneto.
Engine -	70 m/m bore × 90 m/m stroke = 3·46 H.P.—10 B.H.P. Four overhead valves.
Gear Box -	Rudge-Whitworth Four Speed with double helical teeth always in mesh. Roller and Ball Bearings throughout, and enclosed Kick Starter.
Handlebar -	No. 110, covered with Black Celluloid with combination grips.
Lubrication -	Mechanical.
Magneto -	High tension, positive drive.
Mudguards -	With patent combined number plate, rear guard extension hinged for easy removal of wheel.
Petrol -	2 gallons tank, non-splash filler cap, 2in. diameter.
Piston -	Aluminium Rudge-Whitworth Racing Type.
Silencer -	Large expansion chamber with extension pipe to rear.
Spring Forks -	Perfect Steering. Complete insulation from road vibration at any speed.
Stands -	Back, spring operated, automatically resumes riding position. Folding front stand supports front mudguard.
Tool Bag -	Pannier, with necessary tools.
Transmission -	By Roller Chain, ½in. pitch × ·305in. wide from engine to gear box, and from gear box to back wheel. The standard gears are: 5 to 1, 7 to 1, 11 to 1, 17 to 1; or for sidecar work, 6 to 1, 8 to 1, 13 to 1, 19½ to 1.
Tyres -	Dunlop Cord 650 × 65, with two security bolts.
Valves -	Two overhead Celerity Inlet and two overhead Celerity Exhaust Valves, interchangeable in cylinder head.
Wheels -	Interchangeable, front, rear or sidecar. Specially strong steel rims. 10-gauge nipples and double-butted spokes. Weather-proof ball bearing hubs.

Code: "LITEFOR."

Without Electric Lighting Set - **£58** — **Extra for Electric Lighting Set** - - **£5**

Rudge-Whitworth
Four Valve Four Speed

4·99 H.P.—15 B.H.P.

All Steel Frame -	With Drop forged ball head.
Brakes -	Front and rear acting on drum.
Carburettor -	Senspray, two lever control.
Chain Cover and Chain Guard -	Enamelled Black
Clutch -	Dry plate on gear box, hand controlled, spring drive and shock absorber on engine shaft.
Connecting Rod -	Drop forged steel, hardened and ground to receive roller bearing
Electric Lighting -	From dynamo in same unit with magneto.
Engine -	85 m/m bore × 88 m/m stroke = 4·99 H.P.—15 B.H.P. Four overhead valves.
Gear Box -	Rudge-Whitworth Four Speed with double helical teeth always in mesh. Roller and Ball Bearings throughout, and enclosed Kick Starter.
Handlebar -	No. 110, covered with Black Celluloid with combination grips.
Lubrication -	Mechanical.
Magneto -	High tension, positive drive.
Mudguards -	With patent combined number plate, rear guard extension hinged for easy removal of wheel.
Petrol -	2½ gallons tank, non-splash filler cap, 2in. diameter.
Piston -	Aluminium Rudge-Whitworth Racing Type.
Silencer -	Large expansion chamber with extension pipe to rear.
Spring Forks -	Perfect Steering. Complete insulation from road vibration at any speed.
Stands -	Back, spring operated, automatically resumes riding position. Folding front stand supports front mudguard.
Tool Bag -	On carrier with necessary tools.
Transmission -	By Roller Chain, ⅝in. pitch × ⅜in. wide from engine to gear box, and from gear box to back wheel. The standard gears are: 4½ to 1. 6½ to 1, 10 to 1, and 14½ to 1; or for side-car work, 5½ to 1, 7½ to 1, 12 to 1, 17½ to 1.
Tyres -	Dunlop Cord 700 × 80, with two security bolts.
Valves -	Two overhead Celerity Inlet and two overhead Celerity Exhaust Valves, interchangeable in cylinder head.
Wheels -	Interchangeable, front, rear or sidecar. Specially strong steel rims. 10-gauge nipples and double-butted spokes. Weather-proof ball bearing hubs.

Code: "CHASIN."

Without Electric Lighting Set - **£64-6** — **Extra for Electric Lighting Set** - - **£5**

Victory Trial

1 Gold
2 Silver
1 Bronze

The Rudge-Whitworth Canoe,

14 feet in length, shown above passing through the watersplash at the bottom of Highoak Hill, demonstrated its suitability to be used as a sidecar, as it was piloted with ease by Mr. G. E. Nott on 4·99 H.P.—15 B.H.P. Rudge-Whitworth throughout the very difficult course of the Victory Trial, March 7th, and won a Bronze Medal.

The Canoe sidecar can be turned round in a circle of 20 feet diameter, which very few motor cars are capable of doing.

To river lovers it gives great mobility and makes it possible to become acquainted with half the rivers in the country.

3·46 H.P.—10 B.H.P.
£58
Or **£15 8s. 11d.** Deposit and 12 Monthly Instalments of **£4 1s. 2d.** Full Insurance against Accident, Fire, Theft, and Third Party Risk included.

4·99 H.P.—15 B.H.P.
£64:6s.
Or **£17 12s. 8d.** Deposit and 12 Monthly Instalments of **£4 12s. 5d.** Full insurance against Accident, Fire, Theft, and Third Party Risk included.

British Throughout.

Electric Lighting Set on either Model £5 extra.

Rudge-Whitworth, Ltd.,

and All the best Agents. **COVENTRY**

A metal band was inserted inside the steering head between the two steering cups. The inner surface was covered with a friction material and through this ran the fork stem. A bolt was attached to the end of the band and this passed through a hole in the side of the steering head to the right-hand side of the machine, where it was secured by a winged nut. As the wing nut was screwed down, the band tightened round the fork stem, giving a very effective damping effect. With the wedge shaped tank in use at the time it could be reached easily for adjustment and it was retained on the racing machines until the bulbous saddle tank came into use during 1928.

In September 1926, the crankcase and timing cover were redesigned to dispense with the external Best & Lloyd oil pump and it was replaced with an integral Rudge pump. Like the Best & Lloyd pump, the Rudge component was really a metering device, which allowed oil to flow from the oil tank at a pre-determined (and adjustable) rate, in a total loss system. The oil pump was mounted vertically in the timing cover and was driven by a worm gear on the end of the intermediate gear pinion. In addition, an oil tell-tale plunger was mounted on the timing cover, a feature which was continued on all subsequent models.

A more substantial clutch was designed, of larger diameter but much slimmer than its predecessor, thus allowing the metal primary chain cover to be reduced in depth. The clutch incorporated four friction discs, two rivetted to the chain wheel and two to a secondary plate which had tongues slotted into the chain wheel. This clutch proved to be very smooth in operation and remained in use for several years, until the power of the 500cc engines increased to such a degree that a stronger unit became necessary. Even then it was not discarded as, in a slightly modified form it was used on the 250 models from 1931 to 1939.

When the 1927 models were introduced in July 1926, they had large diameter clutches with four friction discs, but on these the secondary clutch plate was rivetted to the chain wheel. Very few of these clutches were fitted before the new clutch, described above, was used, in time for the Olympia Show in November 1926.

Also produced in time for the Show was a new version of the gearbox. Although very similar in many ways to the gearbox which it replaced, this was the version which was to continue in production until 1939, although a number of modifications were introduced as shortcomings became apparent. One major fault within the new gearbox was the design of the second and third speed gears. On these, the selectors ran in grooves which had teeth on either side. As these grooves were not in the centre, the teeth on one side were particularly short. Experience was to show that these teeth would not stand up to misuse as this would cause one to break off, with dire results within the gearbox! This fault was soon corrected and the gearbox became another easily recognised feature of the Rudge motorcycle. Anyone who has taken one of these to pieces and explored the delights of over one hundred needle roller bearings will know exactly what I mean. Although the gearbox is often much maligned because of the needle rollers, these helped to produce a gearbox which was very smooth and positive in operation. This, as much as the engine, contributed to the successes which were yet to come.

The cylinder head also received attention and was redesigned with longer valves having much slimmer stems of three-eighths inch diameter. The exhaust ports still emerged directly forward from the head, a feature that had not previously caused any problems.

The redesigned machine was now really fast and this in turn threw up an old problem. The brakes still consisted of two external shoes bearing on the outside of a dummy belt-rim. Even though the brakes were now linked so that the foot pedal would operate them both at once, the retarding power was far from satisfactory. In the event of

Timing side of the 1927 Standard model. Note the external Best and Lloyd total loss oil pump

Drive side view of the 1927 500cc Standard model. The ML Maglita, mounted at the front of the engine, runs at engine speed so starting can sometimes be a little hazardous if the engine kicks back! A recommended optional extra for this model is a cap which can be put over the carburettor to put out the resulting fire

The Andre shock absorber fitted to the Special and Sports Special models. Note also the steering damper, controlled by the wing nut just below the upper steering cup

The 1927 500cc Special model. Notice the difference between this and the standard model also illustrated in this chapter. The most obvious feature is the cast aluminium expansion box on the Special model and the broad sweep of the exhaust pipes. The Special model was also fitted with a fork damper on the off-side

wet weather, the rider had to be going up hill against a headwind to have any chance of slowing down in a hurry. With John Pugh thinking again of re-entering the racing field, it was necessary to come up with something more efficient. In April 1927 the first drum brake was produced. The brake drum was 8in in diameter and the brake shoes were 1½in across. These dimensions alone were quite outstanding for 1927 but even more remarkable was the fact that inside each drum were six shoes. Each shoe covered 60° of the drum and was retained at each end by a spring. Behind the shoes, running round the hub centre, was a cam plate which was attached to the brake operating lever. As the lever was raised, the cam plate rotated and forced the brake shoes against the drum. An ingenious, but rather complicated idea, when compared to the normal two shoe internal expanding brake. The brake drum had been made 8in in diameter in order to accommodate the cam plate. When the brake was redesigned with only two shoes, the drum was retained 'because it was there' and its size soon gave an excellent name for good braking to the machines to which it was fitted. The experimental brake also gave rise to another feature which was to make the Rudge unique. Although the six shoe brake was complicated, it was also very efficient and some concern was felt about the effect on steering of such a powerful brake, mounted on one side of the wheel. The wheel was therefore designed so that the back plate of the brake came directly in-line with the centre of the wheel rim. To achieve this, it was necessary to offset the spokes to one side, and this feature was also retained until production ceased in 1939.

Another modification tried at the same time, but discarded, was a pulley to achieve chain adjustment, without need to move the rear wheel.

Although the foundations were being laid for the successes that were soon to follow with the four valve machines, the Company suffered a serious blow on the management side. This occurred with the death of Bernard Pugh, who was responsible for the Company's finance. When I discussed this event with the late Jim Sheldon, he expressed the opinion that the death of Bernard Vernon Pugh was responsible for the subsequent bankruptcy and eventual liquidation of the Rudge organisation. Up to the time of Bernard's death, the Company had expanded from a simple cycle business into a conglomerate which produced parts for the cycle, motorcycle and car industries. From this profitable position it took less than six years for the official receiver to be appointed.

Another reason that I have heard advanced for the subsequent failure of the Company was the payment the Company received for war work during the First World War. It has been suggested that if the Company had accepted payment instead of the ball bearing factory, it would have had sufficient funds to have survived. Yet another reason put forward was the massive redesigning and retooling of the motorcycle range in 1927 and 1928.

Personally, I think that the failure was due more to an unhappy series of events, rather than any one particular cause. Had the Company accepted payment for war work in place of a factory, this money would surely have been ploughed into the business long before the Company ran into financial difficulties. The death of Bernard Pugh deprived the Company of a financial expert and his guidance was sadly missing when the world slump hit the business. The redesigning programme of 1927 and 1928, although expensive, led to unforeseen successes for the marque, which might have saved the Company, but for the depression.

In 1926, however, the Company was still a thriving concern and 7000 motorcycles were produced during the year. The continuing process of development of the four valve machines was taken a step further. With all the development work which had taken place in making the machines go faster and improving their performance, the 1927 TT offered a good opportunity for the factory to return to racing. In 1926 two private owners, with factory help, competed with reasonable success, S. Ollerhead finishing in thirteenth place and Frank Whitworth in fifteenth place. George Hack became the Racing Manager and was to supervise things in the Isle of Man. In view of the length of the race, a large petrol tank became necessary but the frame tubes restricted the size of the design. The wedge tank was therefore replaced by a saddle tank which had similar square lines, so it did not look too unlike the roadgoing machines. The new internal expanding brakes were tried but not the Rudge oil pump. The external Best & Lloyd pump was retained, additional oil being fed to the rear of the cylinder. This sprayed oil directly onto the rear of the piston, as piston seizure had been a real problem following the change to aluminium from cast-iron.

The cylinder head had also caused problems. At high speeds, the head had cracked between the two ports and, although the crack did not extend as far as the valve seats, it meant that a new head had to be designed. On the new head the exhaust ports came straight out of the head at an angle, while the compression ratio was raised to 6½ to 1. The exhaust pipes curved out of the head to each side and in one continuous bend swept back to a point beyond the rear spindle. The Company had yet to learn the effect of resonance, for all they had produced was an exhaust system which was pleasing to the eye and which was to become another identification point. The Senspray carburettor had already revealed severe limitations at high speeds, so it was replaced by a flange fitting Amac carburettor.

To ride the machines the Company engaged Frank Longman and C. T. Ashby, while the third member of the team was one of their employees, Ernie Nott. Unlike the previous year, when the Rudge entries in the TT had stamina but were short of power, the 1927 entries had the power but not the stamina, and all three retired. Fortunately George Hack did not give up but took the machines on the Continental Circus. No races were won but Ernie Nott achieved second place in the Belgium Grand Prix, Frank Longman was second in the Ulster Grand Prix and C. T. Ashby finished third in the

Grand Prix d'Europe, run at the Nurburgring. The machines were now capable of 100mph and produced twenty-eight bhp, so all looked well for the 1928 season.

Back on the home front a new approach was being made to marketing, which had progressed from clever tricks. The Company produced a book called *The Rudge Book of the Road* which provided 124 pages of excellent reading in the form of a handsomely bound volume, a considerable number of which have survived to this day. Mixed with information about architecture, the weather, hills and ferries were chapters about the many aspects of owing a Rudge, written in a humorous manner. It was explained, for example, that "it took five minutes to remove the rear wheel if you were ham-handed, but two minutes if you were not". The new clutch was also featured as being heat-proof, oil-proof, slip-proof and young brother-proof. Who could resist this subtle salesmanship?

To head the new marketing drive it was decided to appoint a new Sales Manager, a man who was well respected in motorcycling. At the end of 1927, John Pugh persuaded the Sunbeam Competition Manager to come over and head his Sales Department. The new man was Graham Walker. Graham later described to me the shock he received once he had taken up his new appointment. At Sunbeam, the management was extremely paternal and everybody was on the best of terms so that nothing ever got done. At the Rudge factory, however, everybody was united against the 'gaffer', John Pugh, and as a result, everything that had to be done was done. Meanwhile, as George Hack sought more racing successes and Graham Walker accustomed himself to his new surroundings, John Pugh was working on the 1928 models.

Another new item in 1927 was the first publication of the Pitman *Book of the Rudge* which ran to four editions and eight reprints over the next 25 years.

With George Hack in charge of design, development and racing, and Graham Walker the 'Sales Gaffer', John Pugh set about a facelift of the road going machines. In 1927, the range comprised a 500cc single in three guises, Standard, Special and Sports. These were basically the same machine, with the Special a de luxe version of the standard model and the Sports being the top of the range model. The price of the Standard model, with electric lighting, was £50, that of the Special £55 and the Sports £60. Like modern car production, the differences were mainly cosmetic, the Standard model having an expansion box in front of the crankcase, with a black tail pipe, whereas the Special and the Sports models had nickel plated exhaust pipes sweeping back to aluminium silencers fitted with nickel plated tailpipes. The Special had an adjustable Andre damper on the front forks and the Sports model boasted a tuned engine. In its tuned form, it was claimed that the engine produced 28 brake horsepower at 5200 revs, nearly three times the power produced by the Multi engine only four years earlier. This additional power was certainly needed, for one additional item which appeared in the 1927 catalogue. This was the Rudge caravan, which could be purchased complete with motorcycle and semi-sports sidecar for 130 guineas. The caravan was 7ft 3in long, 4ft 7in high and 4ft 10in wide and was fitted out with two bed settees, a table, and lockers for food, clothing etc. No provision was made for a wash basin and cooking stove; these you had to provide for yourself, and it was recommended that they be used outside the caravan, particularly the stove, as the whole caravan was made of wood! When parking, it was recommended that the tow-bar be lashed to the nearest hedge and the rear corners fitted with ropes and pegged down. The caravan was also available in commercial versions, together with a box sidecar, and in this latter form it proved to be quite popular. There are reports that the Coventry Co-op were still using the commercial caravans for delivery of milk and bread as late as 1944.

Although Ashby and Longman had retired in the TT, they, together with Ernie Nott, had some success on the continent and in Ireland. The improvements that had been introduced on the works machines were therefore incorporated in the production models as quickly as possible. The very large internal expanding brakes were now a standing feature of the 1928 models and wired rims were introduced at the same time, to replace the beaded edge type.

The works machines for 1927 had saddle tanks, although these had retained the square shape of the general production models. For the 1928 season, a new rounded saddle tank was introduced, of soldered up construction. In April, however, a change was made to a welded petrol tank and purchasers of the soldered tank were offered one of the new type in exchange. As a result, very few of the soldered tanks survived.

The mudguards too were redesigned and came out in a rather flat section, described as 'car section'. They were now 6in wide.

Early in 1928 the Rudge competition riders consisted of C. T. Ashby, Jack Amott, Frank Longman, Ernie Nott and Graham Walker. They were soon to be joined by a young Irishman who had finished thirteenth in the 1927 TT on a Triumph – H. G. Tyrell Smith.

The problem with redesigning at short notice usually results in a large number of obsolete parts left over at the factory. This was avoided in 1928 by retaining the standard model with its square tank and rim brakes, and selling it at an increased price of £51 5s 0d, as the Roadster model. The cost of retooling was apparent with the other two machines, as the Special had increased to £60 5s 0d, and the Sports model to £65 5s 0d. In each case the price was reduced by £5 5s 0d if the machine was delivered without electric lighting.

The change which was to take place on all three machines was the use of the Amac carburettor. The Senspray had been used by the Company on its machines for fifteen years, which was not surprising as the carburettor was manufactured within the Rudge-Whitworth group. During 1927 it became apparent that the carburettor was not up to the speeds and performance now being obtained from the engine. Another link with the Multi had been severed.

To complement the new range the Company retained the three sidecars already in production, the divan touring sidecar costing £18, the streamline sporting sidecar £20 and the divan semi-sports sidecar at 18 guineas. The caravan was also continued, although it now offered a table, washing basin and cooking stove as part of the full specification!

The caravan, or rather a trailer version, caused Tyrell Smith some embarrassment soon after he joined the Company. It was the works practice to send the machines and the riders to the Isle of Man by rail. Two of the riders were required to take over the spares and a hack bike. The spares were loaded into a box sidecar and a trailer so that the whole outfit weighed approximately a ½ ton. Although the sidecar wheels had brakes operated by cable from the motorcycle foot pedal, they were of the external rim type. The machine was also a Roadster model. Ernie Nott was riding the hack machine and together they were cruising at about 40mph when a constable stepped out from the side of the road to halt them. Tyrell hit the brakes hard but there was no chance of stopping the outfit in a hurry and it sailed on past the policeman and eventually stopped 100 yards further down the road. Seeing the problem, Ernie Nott pulled up beside the policeman to show that he interpreted the signal to apply to him. The policeman was not so readily convinced and he set off down the road, after the outfit, to accuse the rider of having no brakes. When he tried the time honoured method of testing the brakes, by pushing the outfit with the brakes applied, he couldn't move it an inch, which is not surprising considering the weight it was carrying. He therefore let the riders go with a warning about being a bit more observant in the future. It was a good thing that he knew nothing of the effect of inertia!

The 1928 Speedway Rudge. This is one of the first speedway models fitted with the triangulated strengthening struts. These were later found to be more of a hindrance than a help, and were discarded

The special timing gear used on racing machines to reduce the magneto revolutions from engine speed to half engine speed

Chapter Thirteen
SUCCESS AT LAST

ASK the motorcycle enthusiast who knows something about the Rudge story which year the Company really came to prominence and he will probably say 1928. One of the reasons for this is likely to be the employment of Graham Walker as Sales Manager who, in addition to fulfilling this role more than adequately, was an excellent Public Relations Officer long before this latter function gained recognition. Another reason will probably be the Company's racing successes, even though these occurred late in the racing season.

Initially, 1928 did not start too well, as the TT results were rather disappointing. C. T. Ashby failed to start while Graham Walker and Ernie Nott both retired during the Senior Race. H. G. Tyrell Smith came home in fourth place, while Jack Amott finished eleventh. As TT results affected sales of road going machines, Graham Walker had been very keen to win this race. At the start of the last lap he had been leading by three minutes but was forced to retire with big end failure, at the 28th milestone. This failure might well have been avoided had two recommendations he made to George Hack been taken up. The first was that the machine be fitted with a foot oiler, similar to those used on the earlier Multi range. This would enable the rider to provide additional oil to the metering device used on the total loss system. It was, however, the Company's policy to race machines which were similar to those available to the general public and the return to a device that had been dropped four years earlier was not viewed with favour. During practice, Graham's machine had been smoking, so the metering device was reset by George Hack, to cut down the oil flow. Unfortunately the reduced supply proved insufficient during the race. The second request, which was also rejected, was for a signalling station near Ramsey. At the beginning of the last lap, the pits informed Graham erroneously that he was leading by only three seconds and as a result he pressed on over the Mountain until the big end failed. Had there been a signalling station at Ramsey, the error could have been corrected, enabling him to nurse the sick engine to the finish, giving him his first TT victory. Ironically, the race was won by Charlie Dodson on a Sunbeam, the marque which Graham had recently left.

By the time the Ulster Grand Prix was due, Graham had his foot oiler and was ready to take on the Sunbeams. In theory, the Rudge had the advantage, but this did not take into account the differences between the two riders. Charlie Dodson had a very small physique which gave him a great advantage over Graham who, not only was more substantially built, but had been quite severely injured during the First World War for which he was in receipt of a disability pension. This not only restricted the use of his left foot, but also caused mental disorientation, which meant that he had to take the early part of a race somewhat carefully. In the event, the two fought a race-long battle, which Graham eventually won by 200 yards at a speed of 80.078mph. This was the first time a road race had been won at over 80mph and helped to establish the Ulster as the fastest road race in the world. Graham was not slow to see the publicity that this could bring and when the 1929 models were introduced a month later, the Sports machine was renamed 'The Ulster'. This machine remained in production for ten years and established a firm reputation as a fast, sporting, road-going motorcycle.

The second event which enhanced the Company's name was the brain-child of Ernie Nott, who had progressed through trials into road racing. In 1927 he had suggested to George Hack that the machines were fast enough to take the 100 miles in one hour title, as this had never before been achieved on a motorcycle. The Company had been the first to achieve 50 miles in an hour and here was a second milestone, ready for the taking. Unfortunately, the idea was rejected as Ernie Nott did not have the necessary track riding technique and so the record went elsewhere. After the 1928 TT, when George Hack had designed a more substantial crankpin, Ernie Nott suggested that this be thoroughly tested by an attempt at the 200 miles in 2 hours record, at Brooklands. This time George Hack agreed and the record attempt was on.

During his practice for the event, Ernie Nott revealed his inexperience in track-craft, causing many raised eyebrows amongst the track fraternity. When the day for the event came, the centre of the track was crowded with riders who had come to see the fun. If they were expecting a monumental failure, they were to be disappointed, as Ernie completed the 2 hours at an average speed of 100.23mph, including refuelling stops. Just to show that he had learnt something about the Weybridge concrete saucer, Ernie Nott competed in the 200 mile race and finished in third place.

The only other major racing success of the year came in the Dutch TT, which Graham Walker won at a speed of 75.96mph. Although Graham provided the only two wins, the others were still riding to good effect and H. G. Tyrell Smith followed him home in third place in the Ulster Grand Prix. In the German Grand Prix, Graham Walker came second and Ernie Nott third. At the Grand Prix d'Europe, the order was reversed, with Ernie Nott second and Graham Walker third, and Ernie Nott followed this by taking second place in the sidecar event.

A third memorable contribution to the good name of the four valve machines came from an entirely different source. Stan Glanfield, a motorcycle dealer and Flt. Lt. Sparks, who was serving in the RAF, decided to do something a little different and motorcycle round the world. In these days, when most countries have some form of road system, it is difficult to imagine a journey of this magnitude, which required a fair amount of skill in navigation as well as physical endurance. They set out during July 1927 but later disagreed over the route. Stan Glanfield chose the longer journey through Turkey, Arabia, India, Malaya, Australia and North America. The journey is worthy of a book in its own right, with its many trials and tribulations. Two anecdotes later related by Stan may give some idea of the unexpected problems which he met. When crossing the desert near Basra, after making reasonably good progress, he found it necessary to manhandle the outfit through thick black mud for over twenty miles. Little did he know at the time that the mud was a mixture of sand and oil and that he was crossing an undiscovered oil field!

While crossing Australia at speed over a track covered with fine sand, the sidecar wheel hit a hidden tree stump and sheared off at the spindle, causing the whole outfit to turn over two or three times. One of the handlebar levers penetrated his leg and it was necessary to apply some rudimentary first aid to stop the bleeding. The next problem was to find the sidecar wheel, which had continued on its way after the crash. This was eventually found more than a quarter of a mile away, after an hour long search. Fortunately, Stan was carrying a spare spindle and he was able to refit the wheel and head towards the nearest town for medical attention. The journey was completed during April 1928, when he met his original companion in London.

Rudges were providing customers with speed, endurance and reliability. The Company could now proudly proclaim in its catalogue that the Sports model, and its replacement, the Ulster, could achieve 85mph, the result of a 20bhp power output.

In 1928, a new motorcycle sport was becoming popular in England, dirt track racing. Initially, any sports bike was used, but it did not take manufacturers long to realise that here was a new sales area. First into the field were the Douglas machines, which had considerable success. This development was not lost on the Rudge management and by June 1928 the first Rudge dirt track model was assembled. Many existing parts were used in its manufacture, the engine being the 1927 works type. The frame parts were standard components, while the brakeless hubs were of the 1927 type, fitted into 1928 rims. There was, however, one error in the design in that it was decided that the fairly springy Rudge frame should be stiffened to aid performance. Additional struts were therefore added from the steering head to the front of the engine and to the rear spindle. This caused a tragedy at the works when the prototype was wheeled out into the yard, during a lunch break. One of the assemblers was allowed to ride it down the yard, to try its performance. Acceleration was excellent, but when he came to lay it over to turn round, the rigid frame held the machine upright and he was thrown off against the wall, receiving injuries from which he subsequently died. Nevertheless, the machine performed reasonably well on the cinders and was put into production during June 1928. In these days of 'Women's Lib', it is interesting to note that the seventh machine, produced early in July 1928, was sold to Fay Taylour, who had established quite a name for herself in motorcycle sport.

Once the dirt track machines were in production, attention was turned to the standard production range being offered by the Company. There was, of course, a choice of three models, but all were of 500cc capacity. In June one of these had been enlarged to 595cc, for the 600cc sidecar class, but this development was taken no further. Quite obviously the easiest solution would be to reintroduce the 350, using most of the existing 500cc parts. In July 1928 a new 350 engine was designed, which was little more than a scaled down 500. It was apparent though that the Company would still miss out on the growing lightweight market, even with a new 350. But with design work concentrated on the improvement of the 500 and the reintroduction of the 350, there was little time left to deal with anything else. The only answer was to produce a machine using a number of proprietary parts. The first of these was fitted with a Villiers 250 two stroke engine and a Burman gearbox. Unfortunately (or fortunately?) this did not provide the sought-after performance and was soon discarded. On 15 October 1928, two further prototype 250s were assembled, the first with a side-valve JAP engine, and the other with an overhead valve engine of the same make. These proved more satisfactory and when the Company exhibited at the 1928 Olympia Show they were able to display seven 499cc Specials, three 499cc Sports models, renamed Ulsters, two 350s and one each of the new 250s.

The underside of the 1929 Ulster cylinder head. On this particular example the side spark plug mounting has been blanked off and a centre sparking plug substituted. Note the parallel valves and the four bolt fixing

Top view of the 1929 Ulster cylinder head with the rockers pulled clear of the valves so that the feet can be seen. This is again the cylinder head with a centre spark plug substituted for the standard side position. The large nuts on the rockers contain needle roller bearings

Whereas most of these machines followed current practice by being displayed with black paintwork and nickel plating, one of the Specials had a chrome plated finish.

By 1929 Rudge Motorcycles had become a force to be reckoned with, both in sport and on the road. Although the steering was not perfect, it was good by the standards of the day and the large diameter brakes established an excellent reputation. Sadly, the Company's success was already too late as the stock market crash and the world-wide slump that was to follow were imminent. Even so, the successes in sport boosted sales and 7000 machines were produced during the year, the same as 1928.

Early in the year further successes were gained in trials events and a very large number of cups was added to the Company's 'sideboard.' These successes reached a peak in the summer when J. H. Amott, a member of the road racing team, put up the best solo performance in the Scottish Six Days Trial and G. R. Butcher put up the best sidecar performance. Altogether, Rudge riders took five Silver Cups and two Gold Medals. Following these excellent performances, G. R. Butcher was selected to join the ISDT Trophy team. He completed the event with a Gold Medal and no loss of marks, and the team gained the International Trophy. No other team competing for the Trophy finished without loss of at least one rider.

The Rudge-Whitworth No. 2 Team won the 500cc class for the Manufacturer's Team Prize, the team consisting of J. Williams, G. F. Povey and Pycroft. The marque also claimed the Manufacturer's Team Prize in the 600cc sidecar class, the team being G. R. Butcher, C. Edge and R. Neisse.

It is interesting to note that although a majority of the machines used in the ISDT by Rudge riders were 1929 models, three 1930 models were entered and all three riders won Gold Medals.

Before looking at the changes which were introduced in the summer of 1929, it is necessary to go back to the performance of the machines in the TT. Like 1928, this was another race which might have been. This time the Manx pixies struck at Tyrell Smith, who had every chance of winning when he started his last lap. Unfortunately, he crashed at Glen Helen and eventually finished third. Although this position still stands in the records, there might have been grounds for an appeal against him on the subject of outside assistance. Following his crash, which deposited him and his machine in a heap in the road, he was escorted into the pub and revived with a large glass of alcoholic beverage. When he returned from the bar, the machine was restarted with the aid of the spectators, which was very necessary for it was later discovered that in the crash he had broken several ribs. As the course at that time was particularly bumpy and the machines had rigid suspension, it says much for his physical endurance that he finished the race at all. Ernie Nott followed him home in fifth position, while the third member of the team, Jack Amott, retired having been injured in a fall at Greeba Bridge.

Ernie Nott, having been bitten by the Brooklands bug the previous year, took his Brooklands machine back to the track on 27 July 1929 for the 200 mile race. On this occasion he was successful and won at a record speed of 100.07mph, the only time that the Brooklands 200 mile race was won at over 100mph. Later in the year, on 24 November, he and Tyrell Smith took the machine to Montlhery and put up another world record by completing 200 miles in under 2 hours, at a speed of 102.9mph. Five days earlier he had raised the hour record to 106.49mph and the 100 miles record to 106.45mph.

Back on the road everything was at last beginning to go the Company's way. On 10 August, Graham Walker won the Leinster 100 for the second year running, at a record speed of 79.9mph and with a record lap of 80.4mph, whilst team-mate Tyrell Smith took second place. The factory also took the Andy Doyle team prize. In the Dutch TT, Ernie

RUDGE-WHITWORTH
Features of Interest

THE FOUR VALVE ENGINE. Racing, that most searching of all tests, has once more vindicated the Rudge-Whitworth principle of using four valves per cylinder in the case of engines with a large or medium bore. The 500 c.c. Rudge-Whitworth has proved itself fully as fast and more reliable than its rivals, this freedom from trouble being particularly noticeable under the exacting conditions of the Dirt Track.

The advantage of having four valves is that a very large port area can be obtained with valves which, while no heavier, are immensely stronger than an equivalent two valve design.

Valve breakage under normal conditions is consequently unheard of.

The "Ulster" Engine

PURSUING our policy of making our Sports engine almost an exact replica of the power units used in the previous year's racing, the 1929 Rudge-Whitworth "Ulster" engine has the deeply ribbed crankcase with both ball and roller bearings on the drive side and a single roller bearing on the timing side which was used on our 1928 T.T. machines.

With the exception that still further improvements have been effected in the cylinder head, and by enclosing the valve gear, the rest of the engine, flywheels, big end, connecting rod, pistons, cylinder and lubricating system, with an oil feed to the back of the cylinder is identical with the racing engines which have gained so many laurels during 1928.

350 c.c. Engine

ALTHOUGH the manufacture of this type was discontinued in 1925 there are hundreds of 350 c.c. Rudge-Whitworths on the road to-day whose owners are unanimous in their praise of the reliability and sweet running of these delightful little machines.

The remarkable run of successes gained by F. T. Sibley with a 350 c.c. Rudge-Whitworth combination is still talked of, while as early as 1925 J. H. Mathers obtained a speed of 90 m.p.h. with a similar machine.

The design closely follows that of its big brother, the 500 c.c. engine, and it has been brought right up to date with the latest pattern radial port head and embodies many other improvements suggested by recent research in four-valve engine design.

The Lightweights

WHILE the principle of using four valves in a large bore cylinder has amply proved its efficiency, the need for this design becomes less acute as the cylinder size decreases so that for the new 250 c.c. lightweights we feel justified in adopting the simplification of two valves per cylinder without a serious loss of power and the prospective owner need have no fear that the performance of the 250 c.c. Rudge-Whitworth will suffer as compared with that of other machines of its size.

For those who favour a side valve engine the new Rudge-Whitworth will be found a delightfully tractable little mount which will attain 50 m.p.h. and will maintain 40 m.p.h. indefinitely.

For those who prefer rather more power, speed and liveliness, we have introduced an overhead valve edition of the same machine.

RUDGE-WHITWORTH—THE MACHINE WHICH WON

Lubrication

MECHANICAL Pumps are standard on all models with tell-tales or sight drip feeds and easily adjustable delivery. Except on the Sports and Dirt Track models, which have an external oil feed to the back of the cylinder, there is only one external oil pipe.

The Rudge-Whitworth pump is driven by a worm on an extension of the intermediate timing wheel shaft.

By means of a face cam bearing against an adjustable stop, the plunger is caused to rise and fall, a flat cut in the bottom of the plunger acting as a valve.

Rotation of the adjustable stop alters the timing of the pump and so varies the supply of oil.

The Four-Speed Gear Box

THE joy of using an efficient four-speed gear box, which provides just the right ratio for any condition, and on which gear changing can be effected with ease and certainty, must be experienced to be realised. One may fly up long grades on third, instead of labouring on top, or crawling on second ; while the close ratios make for easy changes at all speeds and yet permit of an emergency bottom gear low enough to cope with even a freak hill.

For 1929 in order to keep pace with the increased power output of the Rudge-Whitworth engine the gear box has been still further strengthened and improved.

All gears are in constant mesh, so teeth cannot be damaged when changing gear.

Clutch

THE clutch as shown in the illustration, is of the dry plate type, asbestos fabric lined. It is light to control and so well up in its work that clutch trouble is unheard of.

Rudge-Whitworth Wire Wheels

PIONEERS of Wire Wheel construction since the earliest days of motoring, the quickly detachable and interchangeable wheels fitted throughout our range embody the latest principles of wire wheel construction. Whether for heavy touring or racing, wheel trouble on a Rudge-Whitworth is unknown.

For 1929 the chain sprocket is mounted directly on the brake drum, thus eliminating any back lash in the drive and permitting of the use of improved wheel bearings which may be adjusted while the wheel is still in the machine.

This construction, however, does not prevent the interchangeability of front, back and sidecar wheels, in fact the rear wheel can be changed even quicker than before. Knock-out spindles are used on the 500 c.c. models.

Provision is now made on all sidecars for the carrying of a spare wheel.

Proportional Coupled Brakes

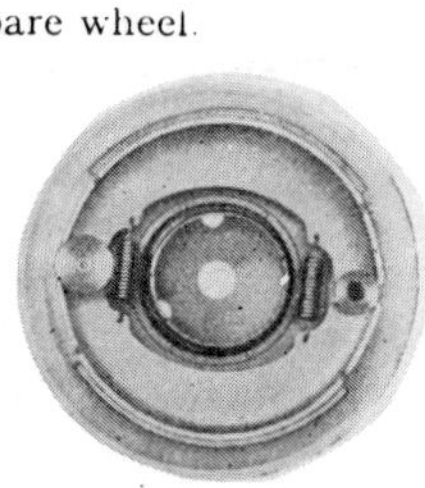

THE secret of Rudge-Whitworth braking lies in the Proportional Coupled Brakes. When braking gently in the usual way, the braking is best divided equally between the front and back wheels. When braking harder, weight is taken off the back wheel and thrown on to the front wheel, and equal braking will then skid the back wheel long before the front is fully braked.

The Rudge-Whitworth Proportional Coupled Brakes, when put on gently, brake the back and front wheels equally, but when put on harder, they brake the front wheel harder in proportion, while still braking the back wheel gently, thus getting the maximum retardation on each wheel without skidding either.

The O.H.V. "250" MODEL

SPECIFICATION.

ENGINE. 62.5 mm. bore × 80 mm. stroke, 245 c.c. J.A.P. engine, roller and plain bearing main shaft, roller bearing big end, aluminium alloy piston and fully floating gudgeon pin. Two overhead valves operated by push rods, detachable head.

LUBRICATION. Best and Lloyd mechanical duplex pump with sight feed and one external pipe only.

CARBURETTER. Amal, two lever or twist grip control optional.

ELECTRIC LIGHTING. 6 volt M.L. Maglita set, dynamo in same unit with magneto. Battery carried on seat tube.

FRAME. All steel straight tube frame with drop-forged steering head.

FORKS. Parallel ruler type with enclosed central spring.

BRAKES. Rudge-Whitworth Proportional Coupled Internal Expanding 6¾ in. × 1 in., actuated together by a single pedal. Front brake can be applied alone, by inverted handlebar lever. (See page 5).

FOOTRESTS. Thick rubber pads.

MUDGUARDS. ⌒ Car section 5 in. wide.

TANK. Streamline saddle tank, finished in black and gold. Capacity 2½ gallons of petrol, 3 pints of oil. (Use Castrol XXL oil). (See page 6).

EXHAUST SYSTEM. One 1¾ in. pipe to a large plated sheet metal silencer thence by an extension pipe with a 6 in. fish tail end. Capacity 16 times that of the cylinder.

TRANSMISSION. By roller chain (½ in. pitch by .205 in. wide) from engine to gear box and from gear box to back wheel.

CLUTCH. Asbestos fabric lined dryplate clutch.

GEAR BOX. Rudge-Whitworth improved four-speed gear box. Enclosed kick starter. Gate control on tank. Gear Ratios: 6.0 to 1, 8.3 to 1, 10.9 to 1, 20 to 1.

WHEELS. Interchangeable on machine only with readily adjustable bearings. Fitted with Dunlop Cord 25 in. × 2.75 in. tyres.

STAND. Central spring-up girder stand.

CARRIER. Optional, fitted without extra charge.

SADDLE. Soft top Lycett.

KNEE GRIPS. Adjustable pneumatic type.

TOOL KIT. In special lined metal case attached to seat pillar tube.

GREASE GUN SYSTEM. Tecalemit.

WEIGHT. 211 lbs.

FINISH. The highest possible throughout. Black and gold.

PRICES.

Without Electric Lighting Set **£43 0 0**

or by £**10 15 0** deposit, and 12 monthly payments of £**3 7 1** which includes full insurance cover. **Code: "Oles."**

With 6 volt Electric Lighting Set (Front and Rear Lamps) **£48 0 0**

or by £**12 0 0** deposit and 12 monthly payments of £**3 13 10** which includes full insurance cover. **Code: "Olit."**

Nott beat Graham Walker into second place, completing the course at a record speed of 75.75mph. On 7 September, Graham Walker returned to the Ulster Grand Prix, which he won at another record speed, this time 80.6mph, with a record lap of 82.36mph. H. G. Tyrell Smith won the German Grand Prix at a record speed of 63.38mph and also the Czechoslovakian Grand Prix.

Success was not only the province of the works team as local riders soon added their names to the list of winners. In South Africa, for example, J. Sarkis won the South African Grand Prix at an average speed of 62.94mph, with a record lap of 73.69mph. Other Rudge riders came home first in the Spanish Championships, the Austrian TT, the Italian TT and the German Eifelrace. It was quite obvious that the 1930 prototypes, which the works riders were riding, were proving faster and more reliable than their 1929 counterparts. What were the essential differences?

First of all, a new frame had been designed which provided a longer wheel base. The works machines were also fitted with a left-hand rocking pedal foot-change, but the main improvements lay in the engine. Up until 1929, the engine had been lubricated by various forms of metered, total loss oiling systems. In 1929 however, the vertical pump was redesigned and transformed into a reciprocating, double acting pump. This converted the engine to dry sump lubrication. The opportunity was also taken to redesign the crankcase mouth at the same time, which, until then, had a square flange, with a stud in each corner. With the increase in compression ratios, it was necessary to provide the cylinder barrel with a round base, which permitted the use of six studs. The compression ratio could then be increased to 7.25 to 1. In 1929, a third bearing had been added to the crankcase on the drive side and this was reinforced with six webs. For machines intended for racing however, two additional webs were added beneath the bearing.

There was no such thing as a 'replica' at this time, although a number of promising private entrants were supplied with racing machinery. For the sporting rider on the road, the Ulster was available in one of three guises. First of all it could be purchased without electric lighting for £69 and was guaranteed to do 85mph. The same machine with electric lighting cost £74 5s 0d. The pride of the range was available for an extra £10, for which a tuned engine was provided, accompanied by a certificate stating that the machine could achieve 100mph.

Many years later Graham Walker recalled that this offer cost the works team many hours of additional riding. Owners with machines which had been issued with this certificate would return to the factory with the comment that his machine could not achieve the guaranteed speed. Graham's first check would be to look at the underside of the footrest rubbers and if these were in mint condition it usually meant that the lack of performance was the rider's fault. The rider and machine were then taken out to a regular course around the public roads, where the owner was invited to demonstrate the lack of performance over a timed lap. One of the works riders would then take the machine round the same lap and never failed to prove the machine's speed, returning with a red hot engine and very little rubber under the footrests! Later on, it was discovered that less scrupulous owners were bringing their machines back for the test and then selling them 'as previously ridden by Graham Walker, Tyrell Smith' etc. This accounted for the apparently large number of works machines that appeared to exist at one time. In practice, very few of the works machines were sold to private owners. Although a number were sent overseas to help with export sales, the majority were broken up at the factory. George Hack had been trained as a metallurgist and was well aware of the problems of metal fatigue. Many a famous frame finished its days under a hacksaw. The engines, however, were retained for testing purposes and this is why many more original engines survive than cycle parts.

Whilst on the subject of testing, the name of an unsung hero of the Rudge saga comes to mind. Other manufacturers are remembered for having their own wizard of tuning, who became part of the company's history. In the case of Rudge-Whitworth the hand on the test bench was that of Jim Dalton. He and Ernie Nott toiled for countless hours tuning and modifying engines under George Hack's direction, to achieve incredibly high brake horsepower figures.

When the Motorcycle Show opened in December 1929, the Company displayed a full range from the JAP engined 250s to the 100mph Ulster. Mechanically, the two 250 models were unchanged, but they had been improved cosmetically by chrome panels on the petrol tank. All the Rudge-engined machines had the circular cylinder base flange, and the dry sump lubrication system was now standard on all but the dirt-track machine. The dirt-track engine had been redesigned, however, and with the new front forks which had been designed for it, it proved a very successful mount for many riders such as Jim Kempster. Greater efforts had been made to keep the road-going machines quiet and all now sported Brooklands style silencers, which contained two large baffle tubes. Another link with the past was broken with the introduction of a sturdy centre stand, in place of the rear stand which had been used in various forms since motorcycle production commenced.

The gearbox had also been redesigned to move the selector plates to the side of each sliding pinion, thus giving each pinion longer and stronger teeth. The kickstarter return stop was moved inside the box, thus removing a design fault which eventually led to the end cover fracturing.

To assist roadholding, a more substantial front fork spring was fitted and, to mention one further modification, the oil was contained in a separate compartment within the petrol tank in all but the Ulster models. This latter machine was now available in three states of tune, at £70 for the standard version, £75 for one with a guaranteed top speed of 90mph and £85 for one having a guaranteed 100mph. Electric lighting was available for an additional £5 10s 0d in each case, although this was recommended only for the standard model.

A full range of sidecars were also available, mounted on the sprung steel chassis. The divan touring sidecar cost £18 and the divan semi-sports sidecar was more select at 18 guineas! For the faster rider, the light touring sidecar cost only thirteen guineas, whilst for the sporting man, the streamline sporting sidecar could be purchased for £20. The milk-truck sidecar and the delivery box were also listed, but the caravan was no longer available. The sidecar wheel was still interchangeable with both of those on the motorcycle, so it was necessary to specify which machine was to be attached to the sidecar, to make sure that the correct type of wheel was fitted.

Orders from the Show looked promising despite the depressed state of the economy, but George Hack was already thinking of redesigning the cylinder heads. The rocker gear had already been made more rigid on the Ulster by having cast-in rocker pillars in place of the bolted-on plates. The shape of the combustion chamber had been improved by making it as hemispherical as possible, but this was limited by the fact that each of the pairs of valves had to be parallel to react equally to the movement of the rockers.

Before leaving 1929, it is worth looking at some ideas which were tried but did not progress much further than the experimental shop. The first was a unique arrangement for varying the valve timing on an engine, without removing the timing cover. The cam followers in the crankcase were mounted on an eccentric pivot pin. As the pin was rotated, the followers moved across the top of the cam, thus advancing or retarding valve operation in relation to the stroke. Spark variation was controlled by the usual handlebar lever, which was a limiting factor in the range that could be used. Although this was a useful device when experimenting with new engines, no use could be found for it on road-going or racing machines.

Before finally dropping the idea, a further development followed whereby the valve timing could be varied independently. With this application the inlet valve cam follower was mounted on a sleeve and the exhaust valve follower on a spindle, which passed through the centre of the sleeve. Each was eccentric, although there was sufficient clearance between the spindle and the sleeve for each to be rotated independently of each other.

In November 1929, after a year of successful road racing, a 5-speed gearbox was produced. The 4-speed gearbox was extended and an extra pair of pinions were added, but the extra width itself created considerable problems. This project was not therefore continued.

Another interesting experiment carried out in November was the constant clearance brake shoe. Although the Rudge single leading shoe brakes were probably the best available for racing machines of the day, this did not prevent George Hack from looking for an even more efficient arrangement. The arrangement was not dissimilar to the earlier device, with eight eccentric arms, except that the new version controlled two shoes. Each arm was at a trailing angle to the drum and when the brake lever was applied, the levers turned at right angles to the drum, each one moving in a slot in the brake shoe. This forced the brake shoe outwards and the shoe contacted the drum equally around its circumference. This arrangement provided a slightly more effective brake, but this advantage was offset by the additional unsprung weight.

Another attempt at improving the existing brake was tried during the same month, when the brake operating cam was replaced by a ratchet. At the end of the brake shoe the operating cam was extended and serrations were cut on the side facing the brake shoe. The ratchet was inserted between the two serrations, to provide a more positive brake operation. This too did not show any great improvement over the much simpler cam and spring system, and was therefore dropped.

No. 1530. — "Miraculum," Cycle size Tubes, **2/6** each retail; **21/-** per doz

A 1930 Special which was exported to Sweden. This model has a combined petrol and oil tank, the oil pipes can be clearly seen between the tank and the vertical oil pump immediately in the front of the push rod tube

One of the six models that were made for the Company following the 1, 2, 3 victory in the 1930 Junior TT. This particular model was presented to George Hack and is now the annual trophy awarded to the best Bristol apprentice. Five of these models are still known to exist

Chapter Fourteen
THE RADICAL, RADIAL RUDGE

THE years 1929 and 1930 are considered by many to be the Golden Years of the Rudge motorcycle. Certainly 1929 had proved very successful, with sales of motorcycles matching sporting successes. Although the successes continued in 1930, the seeds of the Company's destruction were being sown in the outside world. The slump was really beginning to bite and by the end of 1930, the Company only just managed to maintain the sales of machines at 7000. This was not the sort of reward the Company had anticipated from their outstanding sporting successes and it did very little to contribute towards the costs of racing and developing new machines. Seen in the light of the general motorcycling market, however, it was a success story, as UK motorcycle registrations fell from 731000 in 1929 to 724000 in 1930. At the beginning of 1930, all looked well for a glowing future. Rudge riders continued to gain successes in trials, following the excellent performances which had been put up in the ISDT. The first major success of the year was gained in South Africa by Joe Sarkis who, for the second year, won the South African TT at a record race speed of 75mph, with a record lap of 78.6mph. With the road racing season yet to start in the United Kingdom, the racing team took time off at the beginning of February to take part in the Brighton run for old machines, where Graham Walker (1911 free engine 2½hp), Ernie Nott (similar model) and Tyrell Smith (1912 3½hp Multi), all won pioneer plaques.

The next event occurred during the first week in April, when Ernie Nott took his racing machine to Brooklands for a match race against Jack Dunfee's Ballot racing car, at the *Motor Cycle* sponsored open meeting. This was one of a number of similar match race events against cars, race horses etc., to further Graham Walker's publicity drive. Over three laps, from a rolling start, Ernie Nott won by approximately 30 yards, at a speed of 99.61mph. The machine was, in fact, his 1929 racer as the 1930 500's were not yet available.

At the end of April, the team took their machines to Ireland, for the North-West 200. The race was won by Ernie Nott, quite easily after the retirement of Graham Walker, who had contested first place for fifteen laps. Tyrell Smith also retired, but only after setting the fastest lap of 74.1mph. Second place went to Patrick Walls, a local Rudge-mounted rider.

The 1930 racing 500s appeared to be little different from those of 1929. Externally, the most obvious feature was the left-hand rocking pedal gearchange and the use of a carburettor spacer. The engine had, in fact, been redesigned with a more substantial cylinder head, having more fins to aid high-speed cooling. Larger tyres were fitted but even so, the machine in racing trim weighed less than 300lb. With the successes that had been achieved in the previous year, it was decided not to make major alterations to a winning design. Nevertheless, it was true that although the Company marketed smaller machines, only the 500cc class was being contested in sporting events. What could be better then than to try out radical ideas in an entirely different class, where an established reputation would not be jeopardised by failure. Fresh thinking on valve layout was applied to a new 350cc engine. The designs were completed in April 1930 and the machines assembled by the end of the month. Even so, it was necessary to provide an alibi against failure, and the motorcycle carried stories to the effect that the machines were experimental, that they would only just be ready for the race and would be entered purely to obtain data. The secret of the development work on the radial was well kept and as late as 5 June *Motor Cycle* was able to say only that the valve gear was unorthodox.

Four radial valves in a cylinder head was not a new engineering development, as the arrangement had been tried on aero engines some time earlier. It was, however, the first time that it had been tried on a racing motorcycle. The sparking plug was located in the centre of the head, with the four valves disposed radially around it. Each push-rod operated a single rocker, which opened a valve on the timing side. In addition, it operated the first of two rockers which were mounted across the head and simultaneously opened the second valve. The ends of each rocker were ground in such a way that the contact was one which gave a rolling motion, rather than a rubbing and wearing contact.

On 16 June 1930, the three 'experimental machines entered to obtain data', swept the board and became the first Junior machines to complete the seven lap course at an average speed of over 70mph. First was Tyrell Smith, at 71.08mph, second was Ernie Nott at 70.89mph, and third was Graham Walker at 70.77mph. Ernie Nott made the fastest lap at a speed of 72.2mph. Three Rudge motorcycles were entered for the race — and their finishing order was one, two, three — what a moment to savour.

It was reported at the time that, following the race, John Pugh, full of confidence, tried to back his team to finish first, second, third and fourth in the Senior. The bookie, however, could not stand the odds which were reckoned to be 423 to 1, and so the money was returned, fortunately for John Pugh as it turned out. The 500cc entries still retained the parallel valve heads. The fourth rider on this occasion was Walter Handley and his inclusion revealed the unselfishness of the existing Rudge team. Walter was due to ride a Belgium FN but this did not materialise and it was suggested he be given a spare Rudge as the Company had five machines in the Island. John Pugh considered refusing him a mount on the grounds that it would be unfair to his three regular riders but they not only persuaded him to change his mind, but gave Walter the fastest machine which otherwise would have been ridden by Tyrell Smith. It is interesting to note that this machine had a compression ratio of 7 to 1, whereas the remaining team machines had a ratio of 7.25 to 1.

As expected, Walter Handley won the race at a record speed of 74.24mph, with a record lap of 76.28mph. Graham Walker followed him home into second place, but the two other team members were slowed by mechanical trouble. Tyrell finished in sixth place and Ernie in seventh. The remaining machine, ridden by Pete Coleman, retired. Nevertheless the result was good enough to give the Company the second Manufacturers Team Prize of the week.

With so much success in the larger classes, very little attention is ever paid to another first which was created by the Company in the 1930 TT series. The Company did not produce a 250cc engine, but it did produce 250cc motorcycles fitted with JAP engines. One of these was entered in the lightweight race by G. Himing, who finished in a creditable eleventh place. As the delighted Rudge camp left the Island for the Continental Circus, they could hardly suspect that the races were the last Senior and Junior Tourist Trophies to be won by the factory and also the last by a push-rod engine.

In the designing and racing of a brand new engine, John Pugh and George Hack had approached the limit of current technology. Although they had won the Junior TT, the new 350 had not been all plain sailing. During practice all the pistons had cracked along the skirt, under the gudgeon pin. As no alternative pistons were available, the cracked pistons were put back in for the race and fortunately they did not crack any further. This was very similar to the earlier cylinder head problems, where the head cracked but became no worse. The outcome was a number of piston experiments made during the following year. These involved running in a piston then trying it flat out at 5600 revs for as long as possible. In these tests the full skirt pistons seized after 5 to 10 minutes running, while the Invarstrut type lasted 18 minutes. When the skirt was relieved above and below the gudgeon pin bosses, the piston lasted longer but the cracks returned. This led to the production of a slipper piston which was run for one hour flat out, without problems. The slipper piston was therefore adopted as standard for the racing and fast road-going machines.

Having had such an outstanding success in the Isle of Man, great things might have been expected in the following European Grand Prix. One must remember, however, that in many of these events the capacity classes were all run together, so the riders had to choose the one class in which they expected to succeed. With the 350 radial not yet in production for the private owner, as only five had been produced by the end of June 1930, preference had to be given to the 500cc class, where the machines were well proven and any successes would help boost sales. Although the 350 had been race proven over approximately 250 miles in the Isle of Man, the cracked pistons gave cause for concern and the valve gear was still far from perfect. The fact that the TT was intended to do little more than test the machines was confirmed by the fact that the riders were not given any signals, and were left to ride as they thought fit. Graham Walker, for example, with his own physical difficulties, completed a very slow first lap but was faster than the other two Rudge riders over the succeeding six laps. Graham Walker and Tyrell Smith therefore concentrated on the 500cc class, and Ernie Nott raced a 350.

At the beginning of July this arrangement was used at the European Grand Prix, held at Spa, in Belgium. It proved very successful. Ernie Nott headed the 350s home at a speed of 70.66mph, finishing over eight minutes ahead of Arthur Simcock, in second place. In the 500cc event, Tyrell Smith came home first, at a race speed of 74.26mph and with a record lap of 76.00mph; Graham Walker followed him home, in second place. This reversed the position of the German Grand Prix, held earlier on 29 June, which was won by Graham Walker, with Tyrell Smith in third place, behind Stanley Woods.

The same team arrangement was tried at the Ulster Grand Prix, which was run in pouring rain, but the marque could only gain second place in the 350cc class and third in the 500. By the end of the racing season, however, the 500cc racing models had taken first place in the Dutch, Italian and Austrian Grands Prix, as well as the Royal Grand Prix of Rome. To round off the most successful year in the Company's history, E. R. Merrille

THE

"ULSTER GRAND PRIX" MO

Winner for the second year in succession of
the World's Fastest Motor Cycle Road Race

RUDGE-WHITWORTH COVENTRY

Without Electric Lighting Set **£70 0 0**
or by **£17 10 0** deposit, and 12 monthly payments of **£5 5 8** which includes full insurance cover. **Code : " Ulles."**

Smith Front Wheel Internal Drive

Guaranteed 90 m.p.h. £75
For particulars of

A 1930 cylinder head showing the cast in rocker pillars used for parallel valve heads from 1930 to 1936. The rockers are allowed free movement by needle rollers retained in the pillars by steel side plates

SPECIFICATION

ENGINE. Similar to the 1929 Rudge-Whitworth T.T. engine. 85 mm. bore × 88 mm. stroke, 499 c.c. Four overhead valves with fully enclosed roller bearing rocker gear carried by pillars cast on the radial port detachable cylinder head. Two-ring dome-topped Aluminium piston with fully floating gudgeon pin. H section connecting rod with roller bearing big end. Ribbed crankcase with ball and roller bearings on the drive side, roller bearings on the timing side.

LUBRICATION SYSTEM. Dry sump circulating system with tell tale, oil being fed under pressure by a duplex pump enclosed in the timing gear to the big end, main bearings and rear of the cylinder. Surplus oil is collected in a sump cast on the crankcase whence it is returned by the pump to the oil tank. Cool filtered oil is continually being circulated within the engine.

MUDGUARDS. ∩ section 6in. wide. Detachable flap on rear guard permits of easy wheel removal.

PETROL TANK. 3 gallons capacity. Large quickly operated non-splash filler caps, 2½in. diameter.

OIL TANK. On seat tube, 3 pints capacity. Castrol XXL Oil recommended.

SILENCER. Two 7¾ in. wide angle radial exhaust pipes from the cylinder head to two large plated sheet metal silencers, thence by extension pipes with 6 in. fish tail ends. Capacity 16 times that of cylinder. (See page 6).

TRANSMISSION. By roller chains ½ in. pitch by .305 in. wide from engine to gear box and from gear box to back wheel. The front chain runs in a cast aluminium sound proof case.

CLUTCH. Asbestos fabric lined, dry plate clutch.

CARBURETTER. Sports Amal. Two lever or twist grip control optional.

ELECTRIC LIGHTING. 6 volts 30 watt M.L. Maglita set, dynamo in same unit with magneto.

FRAME. All steel straight tube frame with drop-forged steering head.

FORKS. Parallel ruler type with enclosed central spring. Redesigned with increased travel and incorporated shock absorbers.

BRAKES. Rudge-Whitworth Proportional Coupled Internal Expanding, 8 in. × 1¼ in., actuated together by a single pedal. Front brake can also be operated independently by inverted handlebar lever.

FOOTRESTS. Adjustable with thick rubber pads.

HANDLEBAR. Adjustable Sports type, covered with black celluloid. built-in steering damper.

GEAR BOX. Rudge-Whitworth four-speed gear box, with improved and strengthened teeth. (See page 5). Control lever in gate on tank. Enclosed kick starter. Gear ratios: Solo Gears 4.4 to 1, 5.4 to 1, 6.9 to 1, 11.0 to 1. Sidecar Gears 5.2 to 1, 6.4 to 1, 8.2 to 1, 13.1 to 1.

WHEELS. Quickly detachable and interchangeable—front, rear or sidecar, with easily adjustable bearings. Fitted with Dunlop Heavy Cord 27 in. by 2.75 in. wired-on tyres.

STANDS. Girder stands to front and back wheels; the latter of the central spring-up type.

CARRIER. Instantly detachable. Optional.

KNEE GRIPS. Adjustable pneumatic type.

TOOL BAG. On Mudguard stay.

GREASE GUN SYSTEM. Tecalemit.

WEIGHT. 288 lbs.

FINISH. The highest possible throughout. Black and gold. Crank case sandblasted Polished chain case. For optional finishes see page 6.

With 6 Volt Electric Lighting Set **£75 10 0**
or by **£18 17 6** deposit, and 12 monthly payments of **£5 13 2**
which includes full insurance cover. **Code: "Ullit."**

:—Non-Trip £2 5 0 Trip £2 10 0

Guaranteed 100 m.p.h. £85

see separate List.

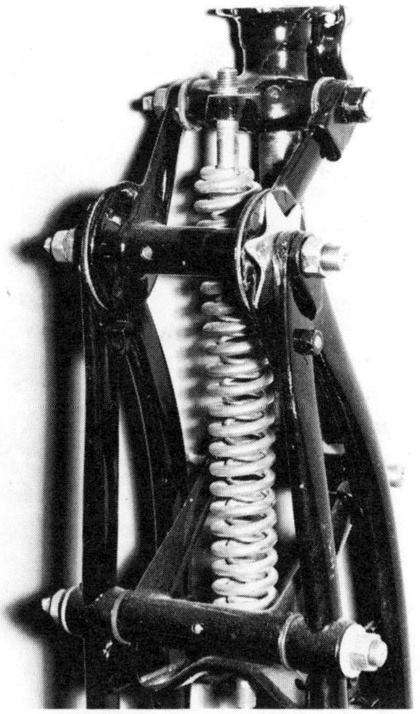

The 1930 'D' section bolt-up front forks with the front fork spring covers removed. Visible are the two-coil springs which provide the front suspension. The one-piece fork shackles contributed to the good steering of these machines won the Senior Manx Grand Prix, followed home by G. W. Wood, who was also riding a Rudge. Unfortunately this latter victory was followed by some bad feeling, as accusations were made that the two riders were mounted on works machines and not on those which were available to the general public. John Pugh went to great lengths in the motorcycle press to point out that the works machines were elsewhere at the time, in the hands of the factory racing team. The machines in question did, however, have a number of modifications not found on the 100mph Ulster model listed in the catalogue. This again brought to light the fact that the Company's manufacturing year started mid-year and that by September, the following season's modifications were already being included. This dispute revealed that it was unwise to have the road-going sports machine and the private owners' racing machine both listed under the name Ulster. From then onwards, a new name came into the Rudge catalogue, the Replica.

To complete his year's riding, Ernie Nott took his machine to Brooklands at the end of September, for the postponed 200 mile race. This year the machine was plagued by a misfire which was only cured by changing the sparking plug. While motoring to good effect in second place, Ernie suffered a repeat of the Rudge misfortune of ten years earlier. A large section of the rear tread broke away from the cover, which gave him a blow reported to have reminded him of his school days! Jack Levene brought his Rudge home into second place, but suffered similar tyre trouble after crossing the finishing line in his slowing down lap, and had an exhausting push back to the pits. It is interesting to note that Ernie Nott's speed for the first 100 miles was 102.16mph, not far short of the world record for the distance which he then held, which had been set up on a deserted track.

Although the 350cc radials had won the TT straight from the drawing board, the design team were far from complacent. New ideas were tried out to improve valve operation, without any loss of performance. The first new design, in August 1930, took the form of a three valve head, with one inlet and two exhaust valves. This successfully reduced the reciprocating weight on the inlet side, but the performance was not as good as that of the four valve layout so the project was discontinued.

Another modification was tried in October when a Mr. Watkinson wrote to the Company suggesting improvements. His suggestion was that the valves could be operated by only four rockers, in place of the train of six currently being used. It was proposed that the right-hand rockers should run at an angle of 45° from the push-rods, across the top of the valves. The second rocker would then be at right-angles to the first, running across the top of the left-hand valve. He suggested that where the rockers met, the circumference should be gear cut so that the two meshed. This idea was later modified in the drawing office so that the remote rocker was operated by the normal Rudge leverage method. The disadvantage of this design was that it would have required eight pillars in the head, on which to mount the rockers, and so this idea was also discarded.

Another item to be discarded was one associated with motorcycle production from the very early days. The instruction book issued with every new motorcycle was now called just that and no longer rejoiced under the name of *Rudge Wrinkles.* This latter name might seem a little odd so its origin is worth recording. At the time when Rudge motorcycles were first being produced there was a very useful volume on the market called *The Wrinkle Book.* This was a compendium of hints and tips for the modern man and went from such extremes as 'how to build a rabbit hutch' to 'how to beat your neighbour at chess'. As the word wrinkle then implied a good hint or tip, what better than to call the handbook *Rudge Wrinkles.*

While on the subject of wrinkles, the motorcycle magazines of the day were already publishing ideas on overcoming a shortcoming in the Rudge design that was to remain for another six years. The tops of the push-rods mushroomed outwards to give a larger surface where they located into the rocker arm. The tops were flat, but the cup inside the rocker arm was concave, to give a rolling rather than a rubbing motion. Once this convex surface had worn down, the push-rod soon wore its way through the arm and came out through the top. A number of methods were advocated for repairing the rocker, such as cutting a thread in the hole and inserting a high tensile screw. Many such dodges are still being used today by the owners of pre-1937 open valve Rudges.

Although much has been made of the road racing successes of the machines, successes in other areas of sport were becoming too numerous to mention. G. R. Butcher in particular was having many successes in the trials field, and Rudge entrants again took three Gold Medals in the International Six Days Trial. In speedway racing, the dirt-track Rudge was more than holding its own in the hands of riders like Jack Parker. Graham Walker was never one to miss an opportunity for publicity and in August he took Ernie Nott along to Brandon Speedway to present Jack Parker with the Golden Helmet which he had won. One of these speedway attendances was almost Graham's undoing, as he hurt his 'gammy' leg again during a guest appearance, which made it even more difficult for him to start in subsequent road races. In the heady atmosphere of success, John Pugh continued to follow a very independent line when considering fresh fields to attack. In spite of the time wasted ten years earlier on the in-line four, he again proposed building a four cylinder engine to put in a motorcycle for record attempts. After attacking the FICM limit of 1000cc, a vee four engine was designed and assembled, although nothing is known of its subsequent history. At the time John Pugh approached Captain Irving, of Sunbeam and Humber fame, to assist with the streamlining of the motorcycle in which the engine was to be fitted, but unfortunately he was too busy and the whole project was shelved.

At the Motorcycle Show in November, the radial 350s took pride of place and the Company claimed eleven first places in eleven classic events for its racing machines. 350 and 500cc Replicas were now available in place of the tuned Ulster, and the JAP-engined 250s had been dropped. This did not mean that the factory had lost interest in this class, for the design staff were hard at work on a new project which would shortly make its mark and for many years to come.

A 1930 racing timing pinion, showing the camshaft, oil pump drive and magneto drive sprockets

Drive side view of the 1930 works engine showing the massive casting that supports the outrigger bearing

Chapter Fifteen
THE GATHERING STORM

AFTER the successes of 1930, the Company could have expected bumper sales in 1931 but the world economic slump hit hard, so that by the end of the year only 2500 machines had left the factory. This was less than half the figure produced in the previous year, which meant that the high costs of racing and developing new models could not be recouped.

At the end of 1930, the complete redesign of the range was in hand, commencing with the 350. The 1931 Replica, as its title implied, was an exact copy of the 1930 racing machines, but the road-going machine bore no resemblance to the previous year's model. The valves were now fully radial and the opportunity had been taken to redesign the crankcase, so that the magneto was mounted behind the cylinder. In its place, at the front of the engine, was a separate dynamo, driven by chain from the engine mainshaft. This chain, and the primary drive, were covered by a one-piece metal pressing, which had no inner section and therefore contained no oil. The oil tank was a new, separate unit, mounted on the right-hand side of the frame, immediately beneath the saddle.

The Special had also been redesigned in the same manner, except that it had retained parallel valves. The same improvements had also been made to the Ulster, except that the primary chain cover was cast in aluminium alloy, again not of the oil bath type.

On all three models the most notable change was the new oil pump. This had been given a greatly enlarged capacity and was now mounted horizontally at the base of the timing chest. The dirt-track machine was very little changed, retaining the parallel valves with bolt-on rockers. In advertisements the Company proudly proclaimed that in 1930, most of the successful speedway riders rode Rudge machines.

By the end of March 1931 the Australian TT had been won again by a Rudge, whilst Rudge riders had won the Victory Cup and the White Trophy in the Cotswold Trial. The pattern of 1930 appeared to be repeating itself, even to the problem of the design team having too little time to look at far too many problems. With the success of the fully radial 350, there was an obvious possibility of the 500 racing machines being redesigned with a similar head. But the current racing team had shown that the existing machines were very fast and might well continue to win for another season, with very little development. One expensive item, as far as the factory was concerned, was the 250, as it was necessary to buy the engines from J. A. Prestwich Limited. It also meant that the machine was similar to many others produced by manufacturers who also used the same engine.

The first racing machine for the 1931 season was assembled in March 1931, and this was a 250, entirely of Rudge design. The cylinder head was virtually a scaled-down 350 full radial, but the bottom end was completely different. Having redesigned the road-going machines with rear mounted magnetos, the new 250 also followed this trend, having this item driven by chain from the end of the camshaft.

It had been the Company's practice to race a new design and then introduce the road-going version immediately after the TT, calling it the following year's model. With time running out on the financial side however, the new 250 road-going machine was introduced immediately, before its racing counterpart had gained any measure of success. On this occasion it was however, necessary, to modify the ordinary 250, to reduce the weight to compete with the very light Villiers-engined machines that were available from competitors. The magneto was therefore discarded in favour of a Miller coil ignition set, the contact breaker being set into the timing cover. The machine was lightened in many other ways, including discarding the front fork spring covers and fitting a single coil barrel shaped spring, something which had been fitted previously only to the dirt-track machine. The experimental 250 racing machine was followed by five more, so that six were available at the beginning of the racing season. Attention was then turned to the 350s, which were also redesigned to provide a rear mounted magneto, driven by chain from the camshaft. Six of these were also assembled and then, at the beginning of April, work started on the 500s. Here some time was saved by making the 350 bottom half common to both capacities but the cylinder head came out in an entirely new guise.

In January 1931, experiments had been carried out with a new cylinder head, which had radial exhaust valves and parallel inlet valves. This modification reduced the number of moving parts in the rocker gear and showed an interesting increase in power over the parallel valve heads. As the performance was very similar to that provided by the radial valve head, the new valve arrangement was used on the 500cc racing machines, of which seven were produced.

At the end of April the new machines made their first appearance in the North West 200, in which the three classes are run together. Tyrell Smith rode a 250, Graham Walker a 350, and Ernie Nott a 500. On the new 250, Tyrell Smith broke the lap record on his first and second laps and was leading comfortably when he was forced to retire with lubrication trouble on the twelfth lap. The oil pipes had been connected up back to front, a problem that was to cause concern on a number of later occasions. Graham Walker pressed on and won the 350cc class at an average speed of 67.39mph, being followed home, on another Rudge, by H. Taggart. Ernie Nott set up the fastest time for the third year running, winning the race at a new average speed of 72.97mph.

Two other interesting developments took place at this time, which were to prove of considerable assistance to the riders. First of all a redesigned timing cover incorporated a rev counter gearbox, the instrument itself being mounted on the side of the petrol tank, immediately above the rider's right knee. Secondly, a number of experiments had been carried out to investigate the effect of resonance on the exhaust system. It was found that if the exhaust pipe was 'tailored', to the exact point of resonance of the engine, the output of the engine was improved. On the Rudge racing machines, this required an open pipe 54in long, which brought the end of the exhaust pipe level with the rear wheel spindle. These experiments were later taken further and resulted in the introduction of a megaphone system to the racing machines. Finally, it is worth noting that the two new cylinder heads used on the 250 and the 500 were fitted with 14mm sparking plugs, in place of the 18mm type which had been used previously.

Before moving onto the TT itself however, it is necessary to look at another project which John Pugh was investigating at this time. In the previous year he had had dreams of going for the motorcycle land speed record with a 2000cc uncharged engine, which had been thwarted by the FICM limit on engine capacity. Supercharging was, however, permitted so in April 1931 he produced a supercharged 250 vee twin engine. Both the 125cc cylinders had radial valve heads, with a centrally placed 14mm sparking plug. The engine generally followed normal Rudge practice, except that the magneto was mounted parallel to the engine on the timing cover, being driven by a skew-gear coupled to the front camshaft. The rear cylinder head was mounted back to front so that the inlet stubs faced each other. Unfortunately, the engine produced only approximately 85% of the brake horsepower of the unsupercharged 250 single, so the project was dropped. It is a pity that this engine was not developed further as an unsupercharged unit, since it might have had useful potential. As it was, it was only produced because there was no data on supercharging a single cylinder engine, whereas data was available for a twin. John Pugh therefore reverted to his ideas on streamlining, but more of that anon.

Before the TT the factory claimed another prize when the team of A. D. Stewart, Jack Williams and R. MacGregor won the manufacturers team prize for over 350cc machines in the Scottish Six Days Trial. The Ulster, which now weighed 310lb, was still relatively light and suitable for this type of event. Noticeable, however, was the development of the separate trials team. In earlier years, the works riders tackled events in all classes of motorcycle sport but competition was bringing with it specialisation and a separate racing team concentrated on road and track events. This did not mean that the riders did not try other events as works supported 'privateers'. For example, Jack Williams was a brilliant all-rounder and in 1935 gained fifth place in the lightweight TT, on a Rudge.

Initially, practicing for the 1931 TT was held in rainy conditions and Rudges appeared on the leaderboard in all three capacities, although the speeds were relatively low. When the roads dried out, Tyrell Smith took the lightweight machine round the course at speeds very close to the existing lap record. Also, as the roads dried, Graham Walker and Ernie Nott took out the Senior machines and Graham subsequently described to me the result of that practice session. "We went out with high hopes and handfuls of throttle and came back with white faces and full trousers". The machines, which had all the power the riders could use, would not steer at high speeds. Later, when it became apparent to most observers that the riders were having great difficulty in staying on the road, the message was put about that the wrong chainstays had been fitted at the factory. The story suggested that longer chainstays had been fitted, thus lengthening the wheel base, causing the difficulties. Anyone who has ever tried to fit the wrong chainstays will know that, as a result of the two bolt fitting behind the gearbox, it is not possible to line up the bolt holes at the rear wheel without considerable modification. Graham thought that the real reason for the difficulty was the whip in the chainstays which allowed the rear wheel to flex. From subsequent discussions with George Hack, I think the answer lay in the weight distribution. The 250 was a new machine designed entirely from scratch, with the magneto behind the engine, and this gave no problems. The 350 and 500, however, had been redesigned with the magneto behind the engine. This had shifted the weight forward, thus altering the centre of gravity. The subsequent change back to a

GENERAL SPECIFICATION of 1931 MOTOR CYCLES

LUBRICATION SYSTEM. Dry sump circulating system with tell-tale, oil being forced by duplex pump, integral with crankcase, to the big end, main bearings and rear of the cylinder. Surplus oil is collected in a sump cast in the crankcase, whence it is returned by the pump to the oil tank. Cool filtered oil is continually being circulated within the engine.

CARBURETTER. Amal. Twist-grip control or two lever, optional.

ELECTRIC LIGHTING. 6-volt Miller dynamo and lamps with battery fitted on seat pillar.

MAGNETO. M.L. chain driven and running at half engine speed.

FRAME. All-steel straight tube frame, with drop-forged steering head.

FORKS. Parallel ruler type with enclosed central spring. Adjustable shackles and incorporated shock absorber.

BRAKES. Internal expanding, working on the Rudge-Whitworth Proportional Coupled system. Front brake can be applied independently by hand lever.

HANDLEBAR. Adjustable Semi-Sports type with steering damper.

PETROL TANK. Streamline saddle tank, capacity approximately 3 gallons.

OIL TANK. A separate oil tank is supplied on all models and is fitted on the seat pillar. Capacity approximately 3 pints.

EXHAUST SYSTEM. Large radial pipes to two large plated silencers with 6" fish tail ends.

TRANSMISSION. By ½" pitch roller primary chain and ⅝" pitch roller rear chain. Adjustment of rear chain on 500 c.c. models effected by eccentric keyed to spindle, thus maintaining wheel alignment and rendering wheel removal the simplest of operations.

CLUTCH. Asbestos fabric lined dryplate clutch.

GEAR BOX. Rudge-Whitworth four speed gear box with continuous large teeth. Folding kick-starter, with enclosed mechanism. Gate control on tank.

WHEELS. Interchangeable, having easily adjustable bearings with locknuts.

TYRES. Avon Heavy cord wired-on.

MUDGUARDS. Deep section guards with hinged flap to facilitate removal of rear wheel. Strengthened mudguard stays with additional support for the hinged flap.

CARRIER. Instantly detachable, fitted without extra charge.

STANDS Efficient central spring-up stand, with girder stand for front wheel.

SADDLE. Soft top Lycett.

KNEE GRIPS. Adjustable and pneumatic type.

TOOL KIT. In specially lined metal case attached to rear chain stays.

GREASE GUN SYSTEM. Tecalemit.

FINISH. Black with gold lining and lettering on tanks. All bright parts chromium plated.
Optional finish as above, but with chromium plated tank with black or maroon panels and black with maroon guards and tank panel.
Smith front wheel internal drive Speedometer, Non Trip, £2 5 0.
Trip, £2 10 0.
Smith eight-day Clock fitted into steering damper anchor plate, 30/-.

General Specification for all Sidecars.

CHASSIS. Flat laminated spring steel axle and cross members built into triangular shape.

WHEEL. The Rudge-Whitworth Detachable and Interchangeable Wheels used on 500 c.c. machines are equally suitable for front, rear or sidecar. The spare detachable wheel is carried on the back of the sidecar. On the 350 c.c. machines the wheels are not interchangeable with that of the sidecar. When ordering it will be necessary to state whether for attaching to "Ulster," "Special" or "350" model, to ensure the correct wheel being fitted.

Extra for Electric Lamp and length of cable, 10/-.

FOR PARTICULARS OF GUARANTEE SEE FULL CATALOGUE.

IMPORTANT. Hire-Purchase Prices shown DO NOT INCLUDE Insurance. All Hire-Purchase transactions must carry a comprehensive Insurance Policy which Rudge-Whitworth can arrange at current rates.

"350" Model

ENGINE. 70 mm. bore × 90.5 mm. stroke .. 349 c.c. Four overhead valves radially disposed in spherical combustion chamber operated by roller bearing rockers carried in sheet metal side plates. Detachable cylinder head. Two ring aluminium alloy piston. Crankcase assembly similar to 500 c.c. engine.
BRAKES. 6¾" × 1".
GEAR RATIOS. Solo 5.3, 7.2, 9.5, 17.2. Sidecar 6.0, 8.2, 10.7, 19.5.
WHEELS. Interchangeable. 27 × 3 Avon tyres, alternative size 26 × 3.25 or 28 × 3.5 at extra cost.

Price £54 10 0

or by deposit £13 12 6 and 12 monthly instalments £3 13 7. Plus Insurance.
With Electric Lighting, £60 0 0
or by deposit £15 0 0 and 12 monthly instalments £4 1 0. Plus Insurance.

T.T. Replica Model. Price £82

or by deposit £20 10 0 and 12 monthly instalments £5 10 9. Plus Insurance.

"Ulster" Model

ENGINE. 85 mm. bore × 88 mm. stroke .. 499 c.c. Four overhead valves with fully enclosed roller bearing rocker gear carried by pillars cast on the radial port detachable cylinder head. Two ring dome topped aluminium piston with fully floating gudgeon pin. "H" section connecting rod with roller bearing big end. Stiffened crankcase with ball and roller bearings on the drive side and roller bearings on the timing side. Central sparking plug.
BRAKES. 8" × 1¼".
TRANSMISSION. Front chain enclosed in polished aluminium case.
GEAR RATIOS. Solo 4.3, 5.4, 7.0, 11.1. Sidecar 5.3, 6.6, 8.6, 13.7.
WHEELS. Quickly detachable and interchangeable, 27 × 3.25 Avon tyres. Alternative size 26 × 3.25 or 28 × 3.5 at extra cost.

Price £70

or by deposit £17 10 0 and 12 monthly instalments £4 14 6. Plus Insurance.
With Electric Lighting £75 10 0
or by deposit £18 17 6 and 12 monthly instalments £5 1 11. Plus Insurance.

T.T. Replica Model. Price £85

or by deposit £21 5 0 and 12 monthly instalments £5 14 9. Plus Insurance.

Special Model

ENGINE. 85 mm. bore × 88 mm. stroke .. 499 c.c. Four overhead valves with fully enclosed roller bearing rocker gear carried by pillars cast on the radial port detachable cylinder head. Two ring dome topped aluminium piston with fully floating gudgeon pin. "H" section connecting rod with roller bearing big end. Stiffened crankcase with ball and roller bearings on the drive side and roller bearing on the timing side.
A touring engine based on the Ulster Model, with enclosed rocker gear. Fitted with de-compressor to ensure easy starting.
BRAKES. 8" × 1¼".
GEAR RATIOS. Solo 4.5, 6.2, 8.0, 14.6. Sidecar 5.3, 7.2, 9.5, 17.2.
WHEELS. Quickly detachable and interchangeable, 26 × 3.25" Avon tyres. Alternative size 28 × 3.5" at extra cost.

Price £59

or by deposit £14 15 0 and 12 monthly instalments £3 19 8. Plus Insurance.
With Electric Lighting £64 10 0
or by deposit £16 2 6 and 12 monthly instalments £4 7 1. Plus Insurance.

Dirt Track Machine

Price £79

(Not illustrated).

Streamline Sports Sidecar

BODY. Coach built on airship lines, feather-weight, streamlined, with door at top. Re-designed with more roomy seating accommodation. Finished in polished aluminium and upholstered in black. Black apron screen and long floor cushion.
LOCKER. Behind seat squab. Wide mudguard attached to and sprung with body.

Price £22

forward magneto, to eliminate the handling difficulty, seems to confirm this theory. The situation was confirmed in the races themselves, when the lightweight Rudges romped home, Graham Walker winning at the record speed of 68.98mph, followed home by Tyrell Smith in second place and Ernie Nott, who was fourth. The race could have been another Rudge one-two-three, as Ernie Nott was leading on the last lap, having set a lap record at 71.73mph. A tappet locknut loosened so, having no spanner, he held it in place with his hand to finish the race. In the Junior, Ernie Nott achieved third place, with Graham Walker fifth, while in the Senior it was Ernie Nott fourth and Graham Walker fifth. The Rudges were no match for the camshaft Nortons, which had no steering problems. Rudge riders also took eleventh, twelfth and thirteenth places in the Senior and seventeenth place in the Junior, but results overall were a disappointment. The engines were certainly not lacking in power, as was proved when they were tested after the race. Ernie Nott's 500 was turning out 33bhp at 5800 to 6000 revs, at the standard compression ratio of 7¼ to 1 with a 53 carburettor jet. Tyrell Smith's 350 recorded 24.5bhp at 6200 to 6400 revs, on a compression ratio of 8 to 1. The figures for the 250 were 19.5bhp at 6600 to 6800 revs on a 10.6 to 1 compression ratio.

Another successful season on the Continent was expected after Ernie Nott won the 350cc race in the FICM Grand Prix and Graham Walker won the 250cc race. In the Dutch TT the Isle of Man story was repeated, when Tyrell Smith won the 250 race at a speed of 72mph, while Ernie Nott finished second in the 350 class and Graham Walker third in the 500. The only other success on the Continent, however, was the German Grand Prix, where Tyrell Smith claimed first place in the 350 race, but the marque could only manage third place in both the 250 and the 500, while in the Belgium Grand Prix the only place was second, in the 350 race. 1931 was not to be a repeat of the successes of the previous year.

Back home in September, the Ulster provided a better performance when E. M. Mitchell won the 250 race, followed home by C. W. Johnston and C. H. Manders, also on Rudges. In the larger classes, the Nortons continued to dominate, although Ernie Nott was second in the 500 and T. Wallace third in the 350 race. Rudge riders also claimed the 250, 350 and sealed handicap prizes. In the Senior race, Walter Handley finished fourth on a Rudge and Graham Walker seventh, the latter having been delayed by a most unusual trouble. During the race his front mudguard had broken away from the front fork bridge and four times it had spun round the wheel to the ground, locking the wheel! On one occasion this threw him up the bank into the spectators; not the best treatment for someone who was physically handicapped. Yet he continued to finish the race.

At Brooklands, where good cornering ability was not quite so essential, the marque was still a force to be reckoned with. In July L. R. Courtney won the 500cc event, completing one of the laps at over 100mph, thus winning his Gold Star. This was the first Gold Star to be won by a non-works rider. In August, the Handicap Race was won by W. C. Marshall, followed home by T. L. Reynolds who was also on a Rudge. The main event of the day was the 600cc scratch race and this was won by J. H. Pringle, who had won the Australian TT in January on a Rudge. Unfortunately, on this occasion, he rode another make. The second man W. C. Marshall was, however, Rudge mounted. In the trade-supported handicap L. R. Courtney was third.

Before leaving the racing scene in 1931, it is worth recalling the contribution made by riders of other nationalities. The Company had made great efforts to export machines during its existence and there were Rudge dealers all over the world. As the Replicas became available they were also distributed widely and were used extensively by local riders. In addition to the successes already recorded, the Company could claim first place in the 500cc class of the Royal Grand Prix of Rome, the 500cc class in the Italian

TT and the 250 class in the Swedish Grand Prix.

It is very difficult, where a Company is successful, not to resort to lists of the achievements of the period. Although these successes are part of the Company's history, they make very boring reading. Even so there were two further events where success confirmed the versatility of the machines. First of all, in the Scottish Six Days Trial, the 500cc Rudge team of J. Williams, R. MacGregor and A. D. Stewart won the Team Prize and Rudge riders claimed three Silver Cups and one Gold Medal. This was followed by the International Six Days Trial, where the six Rudge entries achieved six Gold Medals. The Rudge team included a lady rider, Miss Betty Lermitte, and she, together with Jack Williams and Bob MacGregor, won the 500cc manufacturer's team prize. They lost no marks, as did the two members in the Dutch team, who were riding Rudge Ulsters. It was this latter team that won the International Vase. Success brought its problems, however, and one unusual occurrence took place at the Company's depot in Coventry, where the Travers Trophy was on display. The trophy was stolen in a smash and grab raid, which must have been one of the few occasions when such a raid took place on a cycle and motorcycle shop!

With the drop in sales now apparent, it was necessary to take immediate action if the Company was to remain solvent. The Company therefore started to offer engines and gearboxes to other manufacturers as proprietary parts. In proprietary form the components were renamed *Python* and the engines were available in all capacities and types, i.e. Ulster, Special, 350, 250 and three Replicas. One of the first manufacturers to use these components was Grindlay-Peerless, to be followed shortly by Cotton and HRD in this country, Eynsink in Holland, Imperia and Zundapp in Germany and Durandal in France. Although not sold in as many numbers as the JAP engines, the Python was used by quite a number of English and Continental manufacturers during the following four years, among the better known British makes not already mentioned being AJW, Dunelt, Newmount and Rex Acme; 1931 was also a year of experimenting with new materials. Elektron had been used for the crankcases and the gearbox castings of the works machines, but other ideas were also tried. Although the engines were performing well, there was a problem of heat dissipation as the finning on the engine was still fairly modest. The high temperatures were transmitted to the valve gear and melted the grease, thus increasing the wear in the bearing surfaces. The first idea was to produce a cast-iron cylinder which was little more than a liner and cast round it copper fins. This did produce better results than cast-iron fins but it was a rather expensive process. The next possibility was to change the material of the cylinder head itself. Copper was too soft, so the new cylinder head was cast in bronze. Although this was heavier than its cast-iron equivalent, the improved heat transfer of this material was such that it was subsequently used for the Ulster, Replica and racing machines.

During August 1931, experiments with the 500cc three valve head were resumed. The maximum brake horsepower was 33, which was no better than the existing engine and the larger inlet valve caused a number of problems. The worst of these was that valve bounce set in at much lower revs than on the four valve head. The four valve head was therefore redesigned with smaller inlet valve stems, which allowed slimmer guides to be fitted. The inlet port was machined to an oval shape to compensate for the volume occupied by the end of the valve guide and the valve stem in the port. This engine showed an immediate improvement and produced 36bhp at 6000 revs. These developments were then incorporated into the 1932 racing machines. In September this experimental engine was tested on a compression ratio of 10 to 1, using RD1 fuel, and the power output increased to 40bhp at 5800 revs. Another idea, previously used only on the lightweight racing engine, was a duralumin conrod working directly onto the crankpin. This worked successfully on the 250, and on the experimental engine it was able to cope with high compression ratio and power outputs, so it was incorporated into the 350 racing machines as well. Also in September 1931, George Hack ran a number of experiments with different fuels, in conjunction with ICI. The highest readings came from methanol, where the 500cc engine produced 42.5bhp at 6000 revs on a 10 to 1 compression ratio.

Earlier, John Pugh had returned to his pet project, the world motor cycle speed record. In place of the supercharged 250 vee twin, he designed a 500cc supercharged flat twin. The crankcases were split vertically into front and rear sections and incorporated a very large finned sump. The magneto was mounted on top of the engine and was driven by a chain from the front mainshaft. The cylinder heads were standard 250s. Although this engine was built, financial difficulties prevented the attempt on the record taking place and as far as is known the engine was not fitted into a frame.

When the Motorcycle Show opened in November 1931, the 1932 models revealed a number of important changes. On the road-going machines, the primary chain cover had been replaced by an aluminium oil bath chaincase. This involved the use of a longer gearbox mainshaft and engine driveshaft to allow for the thickness of the inner chaincase. The opportunity was therefore taken to redesign the clutch on the 350 and 500 models, to cope with the ever-increasing power. This unit was not much more substantial, with two Ferodo inserted plates and two friction rings, the latter being rivetted to a much more substantial chain wheel. A centre stand operating lever was also incorporated for the first time and it is worth recording the way in which it came about. John Pugh had always been conscious of the weight of motorcycles and had always endeavoured to make them as light as mechanically possible. During a discussion with his design team about the new models, it was pointed out that the new clutch and chaincase increased the weight. This meant that the rider had to put more effort into lifting his machine onto the centre stand. John Pugh went away to sleep on the problem and, in the morning, returned with the rough drawings of the stand lever. Using the lever, it is possible to put a Rudge onto its centre stand, using only one finger.

The Special had acquired deep valances on the front mudguard and, as in the previous year with all models, it was possible to have a chrome and black finished petrol tank in place of the plain black finish or, alternatively, to have maroon on the tank and the mudguards. Another optional extra introduced for the first time was an upswept exhaust pipe for competition work, although this was not fitted to any model as a standard item.

The Ulster and the 500cc Replica both incorporated a modification which I have never been able to explain satisfactorily. Both had fully radial cylinder heads even though the racing machines the previous year were semi-radial. The Ulster retained the magneto behind the cylinder, whereas the Replica had reverted to a forward magneto, on both the 350 and the 500 models. A 250 Replica was introduced for the first time and this was very similar to the previous year's racing machine, with the magneto behind the cylinder. The road going 250 was now available with three alternative specifications, with coil ignition, or with a magneto or a Maglita.

The sidecars continued unchanged from the previous year, as did the delivery box and side carrier, but the trailer was reintroduced, this time with a fabric covered body and having rated capacity of 8cwt. With this range the Company looked forward to 1932.

Although John Pugh continued to be involved in the design of Rudge motorcycles, the job of Chief Designer was now held by F. Anstey, who helped put into effect the Managing Director's ideas as well as many of his own.

A very potent 'Python' - a 250cc four-valve Chris Tattersall Special, now fully restored

Chapter Sixteen
THE BEGINNING OF THE END

IN spite of a reasonably successful year's racing, the sales figures for 1931 had been a disaster and 1932 was to be no better, with only approximately 2500 motorcycles sold during the year. Quite obviously economies had to be made and these were first felt on the racing side. The 1932 racing machines were greatly reduced in number and there were only three 250s, three 350s and four 500s. The new 250 engine produced 19bhp at 6600 to 6800rpm with a 9 to 1 compression ratio and proved very reliable on test. The 350 provided 25.5bhp at 6200 to 6400 revs on an 8 to 1 compression ratio, while the 500 produced 39bhp between 5800 to 6000rpm, with a 10 to 1 compression ratio. This latter figure was increased to 41.5bhp when methanol fuel was used.

Particular attention was paid to the carburation and quite a number of experiments were carried out using air filters. These had a fairly adverse effect upon the engine output, so they were replaced by a carburettor bell mouth.

Generally speaking, the 350 and 500 engines were basically the 1930 design with a front mounted magneto. It was hoped that by reverting to this layout, the handling problems would be solved. This change involved a return to the vertical oil pump, which was given an enlarged capacity to provide an additional oil feed to the cams. Following Graham Walker's experience in the previous Ulster, rubber buffers were attached to the lugs on the front fork to prevent the mudguard breaking free when the forks bottomed. It is interesting to note that the 500cc racing machines retained semi-radial valves whereas the road going Ulster and Replica both had fully radial heads.

This was the only year that the 500cc engine was fitted with the fully radial head and the explanation has so far eluded me. I can only assume that it was intended later to fit a fully radial head to the racing engine, but such a change never took place. Another peculiarity was the oil pump on the racing machines which was identical in dimensions to the 1930 type. The synosidal groove was reversed, however, so that the pump ran in the opposite direction to its predecessor. This proved very confusing to the mechanics who had worked on the earlier engine and in one race Tyrell Smith had to retire when his little end seized because the oil pipes had been connected in the 1930 style, thus starving the engine of oil.

In road racing, the year started as well as its predecessors, with first place in the 500cc class of the Australian Grand Prix and victories in the North West 200, in both the 350 and 500cc classes. The new 250 was also making itself felt in reliability trials and the list of victories included the Kickham Memorial Trophy and the 250 classes in the Bemrose, Wye Valley and Cambrian trials.

A full team was entered for the TT that included Walter Handley, who had signed up to ride in each race. The Rudge engines for the race were certainly a match for the Nortons but the steering problems had still not been solved. The machines would hold a straight line perfectly and would corner well at low speeds, but at high speed corners required great respect. On the 1931 racers, the tendency for the machine to sit up on corners and thus take off at a tangent was quite marked, even at moderate speeds. For 1932 the change of engine and frame design raised the speed at which this problem occurred. In the Lightweight TT, bad luck struck again when Ernie Nott blew up his engine when leading on the last lap. Walter Handley was also dogged by sparking plug trouble and changed three during the course of the race, yet still managed to finish in third place, two minutes behind the winner. Graham Walker, riding his usual reliable race after a slow start, finished second. Walter Handley set a record lap at a speed of 74.08mph, which was to stand until 1935. In the Senior and Junior races however, there was no way that the Rudges could match the road holding of the Nortons, although the Junior with its lower average speeds provided the best opportunity. Walter Handley finished second, with Tyrell Smith third and Graham Walker fifth. In the Senior race Ernie Nott was fourth, Graham Walker sixth and Tyrell Smith eighth.

On the Continent, where circuits tended to be faster, the team did not achieve one win, recording two second places in the 250 and 500cc classes of the Belgium TT, and two third places in the 350 and 500cc classes of the Dutch TT. The Ulster Grand Prix provided an encouraging end to the season, with first and second places in the 350 and a third place in the 500cc races.

The Continental picture was not entirely gloomy, however, as large numbers of Replicas and works machines had been sold to Rudge distributors for the use of local riders. The Company was therefore able to claim successes in a number of local races, including first places in the Austrian 500cc TT, the 250 and 500cc classes of the Spanish TT and the 250 and 500cc classes of the Leinster 200. At Brooklands, the marque won both the 350 and 500cc Grand Prix races, but a greater success was to be recorded in another field of sport. The British 'A' team in the International Six Days Trial comprised Graham Walker, Jack Williams and Bob McGregor, all mounted on Rudges. The team also won the Manufacturers Team Prize and two other Rudge riders won Gold Medals. This followed a similar success when the Rudge team won the Manufacturers Team Prize in the Scottish Six Days Trial, taking the Premier Solo Award plus three Silver Cups.

All round, the performance during the year was quite remarkable when considering the low volume of production. But this unhappy situation was to become worse in 1933. The main effect was the cancellation of projects which might have brought great benefit to the Company in succeeding years. One of these was a new speedway machine, which was very necessary as the existing model was now being well beaten by JAP-engined competitors. The new machine had very similar cycle parts to the existing design but the engine was totally new. The cylinder head retained the four semi-radial valves but the bottom end had been completely redesigned. A very much lighter cylinder barrel was fitted, with fairly small fins. This was retained by six through-bolts, which screwed directly from the head into the crankcase. The flywheels had been reduced to 7in in diameter, and the engine had a compression ratio of 10 to 1, producing 40bhp at 6000 revs. Approximately twelve of these machines were made and they proved to be very competitive indeed. Sadly, there was no money available for their further development.

Another interesting development was produced by Johnnie Leete, who was the Chief Engineer at West Ham Stadium. He was an excellent Rudge tuner and in 1928 had modified Rudge speedway machines to his own specification. He had been one of the first to discard the strengthening stays and a number of his ideas were incorporated in the 1929 dirt-track model, which started the long list of Rudge successes. In 1932 he produced a speedway machine with right-hand drive, as many of the problems of maintenance were caused by having the chain and final drive on the left. This he achieved quite simply by reversing the engine, leaving the cylinder head in its normal position. The only modification was to reverse the push-rods in order to reverse the direction of rotation of the engine, as the cam profiles were similar.

A new development which was never marketed under the name of Rudge was the four valve 175cc engine. This was to take advantage of the lower road tax in some continental countries for under 200cc engines. The 175 had many parts in common with the 250, including the crankcase and flywheels. The cylinder barrel and head were, of course, smaller and the reduced power allowed a number of lighter cycle parts to be used. The machine never went into production however, although the engine was produced in some quantity. The 175 class was very popular on the Continent however, and the engine was marketed under the Python name and used by French, German and Italian manufacturers. The fact that this was not generally known in this country caused problems when a number of the barrels were sold off when the Coventry factory subsequently closed. As the flange and head fittings were identical to the 250, the barrels were sold as replacements for the 250 by the dealers who had purchased them. To make them fit, it was necessary to bore the barrel out and this resulted in a very thin cylinder wall. In a number of cases the barrel fractured below the fins, and this became known as a 250 failing.

When the Motorcycle Show opened in November, the machines on display showed very little change when compared to those of 1932. The 250 was now only available with a magneto, coil ignition having been discontinued. The 350 was still available and both models had fully radial heads. The 500cc Special looked very similar to that of the previous year but now it was proudly described as the Silver Vase model, to capitalise on the ISDT success. The 250 Replica was also very similar to the previous year, with the magneto behind the cylinder. The two larger Replicas and the Ulster, however, followed the works racing practice and had the magneto returned to the front of the cylinder. The 350 Replica remained fully radial while the 500 Replica and the Ulster reverted to semi-radial valve gear. The dirt-track machine had been dropped, leaving the field clear for the JAP-engined machines to sweep the board in succeeding years. The Divan Touring sidecar was retained, while the Divan Semi-Sports was replaced by the Sunshine Saloon, and the Streamline Sports sidecar by the Launch, which followed the fashion of disguising a sidecar as a small boat. The delivery box and trailer were also continued in 1933. Thus the Company looked forward to 1933 with race proven machinery, but with steadily shrinking sales.

A race ready 1933 350cc Replica. Note the fully radial rocker gear, twin fillers on the oil-tank and left-hand brake pedal operating the right-hand brake

Timing side of the 1933 350cc Replica showing a rocking pedal gear change and TT type carburettor

Chapter Seventeen
THE STORM BREAKS

THE lack of sales over the last few years had already taken its toll on the Company's finances. Failure to gain numerous orders from the Motorcycle Show confirmed that the situation would not improve in the immediate future. Drastic action was therefore required and on 15 January 1933 the Company issued the following official statement.

> "Rudge-Whitworth have definitely decided not to participate officially in track racing, road racing or competitions or trials of any character in 1933. They still believe that road racing is the best means of improving the breed but instead of racing officially they intend to put their racing organisation onto development work, pure and simple, and they believe that by this step they will definitely raise the general level of their product and will also produce machines which in competent hands will win races.
>
> "In adopting this policy, Rudge-Whitworth is following that of many eminent car firms who don't race officially, but their cars behave not without distinction in racing."

The members of the Rudge team were aware of this situation before the announcement was made and they met with Graham Walker in an informal bar-room conference to discuss the future. The Company still had its racing machines and the tools available to make more, without becoming involved with additional development costs. With the members of the team employed at the factory, it would be quite easy for machinery to be borrowed and raced without involving the Company in any direct expenditure. Graham Walker proposed to form a Syndicate, which would make the racing machines available to the riders, who would thus appear as a group of private entrants. Even so, at this time, quite a few works machines lay around the factory unused and sorely tempted a number of employees unofficially to follow Graham Walker's example, and use one as a private entrant. During the First World War the river, which flooded the

A rare model, this 1933 Ulster with a forward mounted BTH mag-generator. This particular machine was exported to South Africa where it has been discovered and restored

The timing side of the 1933 Ulster showing the linking cable on the front wheel which connects the front brake to the rear brake pedal. The rocker cover and push rod tube are missing from this machine

Two works engines, the first 1930 and the second 1933. These clearly show the enormous development work that had been done on the cylinder head, while the bottom end has remained quite similar. The oil pump has however been reverse between the two years

factory in 1900, was decked over with a platform to provide additional storage space. As employees could be searched leaving the gate, the method of lifting the parts from the factory was more down the river rather than over the wall. Parts were attached to packing cases which were floated down the river under the bridge and the empty handed employee only had to walk through the gate and then further down the river to collect his prized part. In this way quite a number of interesting racing parts came into private ownership.

The no racing announcement was shortly followed by another, which was even more surprising. John Pugh, who had led the Company throughout the period of motorcycle production, resigned as Managing Director, and was replaced by Frank G. Woollard. He continued as Chairman for the time being, however.

The Syndicate continued to use the 1932 250 and 350 racing machines whenever they needed them during the racing season. Graham Walker somehow managed to persuade the Company to produce four new 500cc racing machines for the Syndicate, in May 1933, but there had been no development work in the racing department since October 1932, the machines were very similar to the previous year's models. They were very carefully assembled Replicas although two had aluminium bronze cylinder heads and each had a separate oil feed to the camshaft. In an attempt at solving some of the handling problems, the petrol tank was extended rearwards so that it fitted round the peak of the saddle, maintaining a similar capacity to that of the previous year. The front hub and the forks were lightened to reduce weight, and a heavier two-plate clutch was introduced. Even with the additional weight of the tank and clutch, the whole machine weighed only just over 300lb.

The Syndicate started well, winning the 500cc class in the North West 200, but this was to prove the only major win during the year. In the TT the 500cc machines were outclassed, with Ernie Nott finishing in fifth place, Graham Walker sixth and Tyrell Smith ninth.

The Syndicate went on in the 500cc class to claim second place in the Belgium TT, third in the Dutch and also in the Ulster. In the 250 TT, the Syndicate was not allowed to enter but C. H. Manders came home in third place on his own machine. Rudges also came home in eighth, thirteenth and fourteenth places, in the hands of L. G. Martin, L. P. Hill and W. Kitchen respectively. In the Junior, F. Aranda, a promising Spanish rider, brought his Rudge home in twelfth place.

At Brooklands, a number of Rudge riders continued to keep the marque to the forefront, including Ernie Nott, although he did not have the success of previous years. Particularly fast Rudge riders were D. W. Ronan, J. H. Lafone and a rider who was to make his name with BMW and later Associated Motorcycles – J. M. 'Jock' West, who won a Gold Star for a 100mph lap during 1933.

The lack of sales and the chronic shortage of finance had taken their toll, however, and H. H. Graham was called in to act as Receiver and Manager on the 27th March 1933. Before the full effect of the slump had been felt, the Company had shown a steady level of profit. For example, in 1928 the surplus was £11,690 while in 1929 it still amounted to £9,178 after charging for racing development. In the subsequent years the drop in sales had been so dramatic that the loss for 1931 was £33,503 – for a range of motorcycles evolved from the Senior and Junior TT winners!

The factory did however remain in production but the range of machines was drastically reduced. When the Motor Cycle Show opened in November only four models were available. The 350 capacity had been dropped completely and the 250 and 500 racing Replicas were no longer available.

Looking first at the work-horse of the range, the Special, there were a number of

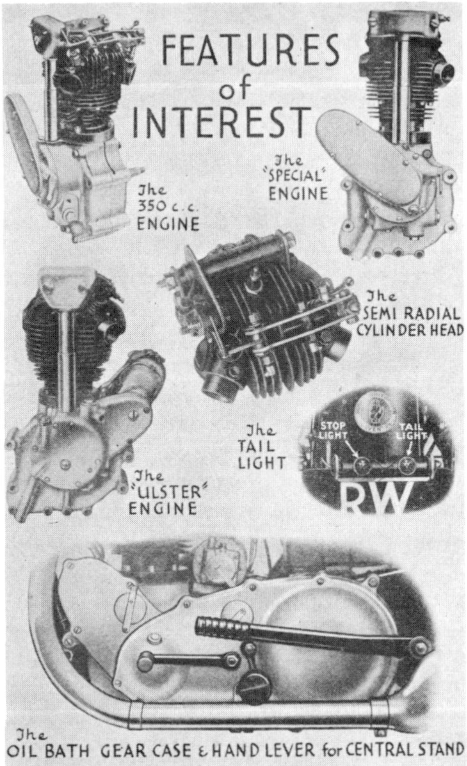

detailed improvements, most important of which was the new big end. The Rudge manufactured unit had been replaced by a Ransome & Marles assembly which used two rows of ¼in by 5/16in rollers in place of the less substantial 0.1814in needle rollers used previously. The other major modifications were cosmetic, the hand-change pivot being concealed beneath the right-hand knee grip, a metal shield added to the right-hand side to cover the end of the gearbox and attention to the gearchange mechanism. The oil tank was reshaped, from a fairly round design to a square shape, which matched the battery mounted on the opposite side of the seat frame tube. The battery was now enclosed in a battery cover, which gave a symmetrical appearance.

The Ulster had also acquired a new R & M big end assembly, but this contained three rows of ¼in by ¼in rollers. Apart from this, the bottom end was identical to that of the Special, with a forward mounted dynamo and a rear mounted magneto. It can be said that the only difference between the two, apart from the big end and heavier duty main bearings, was the prefix 'S' on the Special crankcase and the 'U' on the Ulster crankcase! The Ulster also acquired the new oil tank and battery cover, plus the gearbox shield. One interesting development was the introduction for the first time of upswept exhaust pipes and barrel type silencers, in place of the Brookland style silencers used previously.

On the standard 250, which had also acquired an R & M big end, the bearing consisted of two rows of ¼in by ¼in rollers, but the most interesting development was the transfer of the oil tank to a position immediately in front of the crankcase and the front down tube. The machine also acquired the battery cover, but not the gearbox shield.

The final model in the range was the 250 Sports, which was externally very similar to the standard model, except that it was also fitted with upswept pipes and barrel type silencers. The engine was however fitted with a slipper type piston, a hotter cam and heavier valve springs.

A less obvious modification on all models was the new rear mudguard. Previously, the rear section of the mudguard had hinged upwards to assist in the quick removal of the rear wheel. The new rear mudguard consisted of two pieces, the short fixed section mounted immediately behind the gearbox and the main part of the mudguard which was held in place by two nuts securing the stays and two bolts which passed through brackets on the seat stays into the valances on each side of the mudguard. Although for many years the road-going range had been offered with electric lighting, it was always possible to buy a machine without the lighting set fitted, at a lower cost. From 1934 onwards, electric lighting ceased to be an optional extra and only one price was quoted. The prices for 1934 were higher than those of the previous year, which did not help sales at a time when more and more manufacturers were turning to cheap proprietary parts to cut costs. The Special now cost £63 10s 0d compared to £56 10s 0d the year before, the Ulster cost £73 10s 0d compared to £65 10s 0d and the standard 250 £52 10s 0d compared to £46 10s 0d. The new 250 Sports model cost £55 10s 0d.

The Company continued into the 1934 season with the four model range, under the guidance of a Receiver and under the chairmanship of Sir Edward DeStein, the merchant banker.

Although the Company had embarked on a non-racing policy, it did not completely abandon the need to add improvements. Graham Walker could be extremely persuasive where the Syndicate was concerned! In February 1934, a new cylinder head was produced for the racing 500, using the existing pattern. The variation was the use of a bronze cylinder head skull, surrounded by aluminium fins. This would have achieved a considerable saving in weight, with the advantage of good heat dissipation, but the biggest problem was the difference in expansion rates of the two materials. These problems proved too difficult to solve with the limited resources available, and the project did not proceed any further at that time. It is interesting to note that when A. L. Bailey attempted to improve the Rudge cylinder head in the early 1950s, he also tried this approach, but with similar lack of success.

One experiment using two different materials which was a success was the finned brake drum, designed in March 1934. A thin aluminium ring was cast and then shrunk onto the standard brake drum. This greatly improved the cooling of the drum but added to the unsprung weight. This was partially offset by the use of a lighter, high tensile steel wheel rim. This brake drum was used on both the 250 and 500cc racing machines during 1934.

As the 250s had done so well in the hands of private owners who were using the previous year's Replicas, during 1933, three new racing machines were assembled in March 1934. These were very similar to the previous year's Replicas, except that they had the new R & M big ends. In addition, two 500cc racing machines were produced, again similar to the previous Replicas, with the new big end assembly and also dural push-rods, even though the solid steel push-rods were retained for the 250. The carburettor was given a 10° downdraft, with a 1in extension to allow the circular inlet to blend into the oval shaped port. The front fork links were also changed, in an attempt to achieve better steering, and an extra rubber buffer was fitted to prevent the telescopic spring cover from fouling the upper fork link. Graham Walker rode one of these machines in the Senior TT and finished in sixth position, while another was ridden by L. G. Martin, who failed to finish. Without the backing of a development department, the machines were now becoming out-classed.

The 1934 250cc Sports machine. The most noticeable feature is the oil tank mounted in front of the crankcase, the only year that this arrangement was tried

In the Lightweight TT, the Rudge riders consisted of Graham Walker, Ernie Nott and L. T. Hill, who finished thirteenth in the previous year's race. Graham Walker recruited for the Syndicate Jimmy Simpson, a rider who had previously competed in twenty-three Tourist Trophy Races, without ever having won. I spoke to Jimmy Simpson several years ago about this and he admitted he had been a victim of his own philosophy. His attitude had been that, if a machine was worthy to win the race in the Isle of Man it had to be able to stand being ridden as hard as possible. As a result Jimmy Simpson frequently set up the fastest lap, but more frequently retired when the machine failed to last the race. For the 1934 Lightweight however, the day was wet and foggy and he had already decided to retire, at the end of race week. As a result, his feeling for survival overcame his normal hard riding approach. On the first lap the machine did, in fact, partially seize but the pit manager refused to allow Jimmy to retire so he went on to win the race. In second place was Ernie Nott and third was Graham Walker, giving the Rudge concern another clean sweep. L. P. Hill, the other Rudge rider, failed to complete the race. H. G. Tyrell Smith followed the success by taking a 250 to the Continent. He won the Belgium and German Grand Prix and finished third in the Swiss Grand Prix.

In spite of these successes, the Company turned to the 1935 models without any sign of improvement in sales. In fact, by the end of 1934, they had achieved sales of only approximately 2000 machines – almost the same number as had been sold in 1933. Another sad blow to the Company during the year was the regrettably worsening health of John Pugh, who was forced to retire completely from the Company. Against this background and with negligible finances, George Hack set about producing the 1935 models.

SPECIAL FEATURES

ENGINES

All engines are fitted with four overhead valves operated by roller bearing rockers which ensure long life and dispense with the necessity for adjustment. It will be observed that the disposition of the valves differs in the case of the various models. There is sound reason behind such differences. Years of research on the bench and on the road have proved that the full radial lay-out is most suitable for an engine of 250 c.c. capacity. For an engine of 500 c.c. capacity, such as the Special designed for constant hard work, the parallel valve layout gives perfect reliability and maintained tune. In the Ulster Model, which is designed for maximum speed and competition work, the semi radial valve layout gives the necessary increase in performance, coupled with high speed reliability which has been proved throughout the world. Pistons throughout the range are of special heat treated aluminium alloy, combining minimum weight with maximum strength, and adequate cooling. Lubricant is supplied under pressure direct to the big end bearing and to the rear of the cylinder. The dry sump system (with tell-tale), in conjunction with the large capacity separate oil tank, ensures a continuous supply of well cooled oil which is kept clean by passing through a large Tecalemit filter which is removable from the oil tank for cleaning purposes. All bearings by Ransome and Marles Ltd. Whilst the performance of the engines is exceptionally high the design is so robust that the margin of safety ensures trouble-free service over very long periods.

GEAR BOX SHIELD

Standardized on the 500 c.c. models, this feature adds considerably to the "clean to ride—easy to clean" Rudge layout. Full accessibility to clutch cable adjustment and gear box filler cap is provided, and the whole shield is easily detached by removal of two finger screws and the footrest hanger.

BRAKES

All models are fitted with the Rudge-Whitworth patented Coupled Braking System. An improvement in the 1934 range consists of the standardization of the aluminium shoes which have proved so successful in racing work during recent years. The largest braking area with the maximum heat dissipation is provided, and the benefits of the Coupled System (now so widely imitated) are such that this layout gives the highest braking efficiency known to road transport. The front brake can be applied separately by means of an inverted lever on the handlebar.

HAND LIFT STAND

This ingenious patented fitment, standardized on the 500 c.c. models, overcomes all the usual difficulties associated with placing a comparatively heavy machine on its stand. The method is simplicity itself. Without dismounting from the machine the rider, by a gentle upward movement of the hand lever, places the machine on the stand feet. An equally gentle downward movement places the stand up, leaving the machine ready to ride away.

FORKS

Of girder construction with central compression spring. The design is such that maximum lightness is obtained giving the perfect steering for which these machines are noted. Shackles are individually adjustable. Hand operated steering damper and shock absorbers are incorporated. On 500 c.c. models rebound buffers are built-in.

BATTERY COVER

On every model the battery is enclosed in a neat quickly detachable metal case which makes inspection and topping-up a matter of moments. Not only does this case protect the battery from climatic conditions, but it matches the oil tank, giving that symmetrical appearance so necessary to machine beauty.

DETACHABLE REAR MUDGUARD

In order to facilitate the quick removal of the Rudge-Whitworth Detachable wheel, the rear mudguard complete with carrier or pillion pad, is quickly detachable from the saddle stays. It is only necessary to remove two screws and slacken two nuts to achieve this object. Provision has been made, by means of detachable plugs, to disconnect rear and stop light cables when carrying out this operation.

EQUIPMENT

Electric lighting is standardized on all models. Head lamps are fitted with special two-filament bulbs giving main beam and dip light operated by handlebar switch. An automatic brake operated stop light is incorporated in the rear lamp. Lucas high frequency electric horn, Smith chronometric trip speedometer, and best quality licence holder, save the Rudge owner from any further expense. The 500 c.c. models are supplied with a matched 8-day clock by S. Smith & Sons, which, together with the speedometer, is incorporated in a neat and inconspicuous handlebar panel.

SADDLES AND PILLION PADS

All machines are fitted with soft top saddles by Lycett. 250 c.c. Speed and 500 c.c. Ulster Models have rear pillion pad as standard. 250 c.c. Standard and 500 c.c. Special Models are fitted with carrier. Where pads are fitted carriers may be had as optional equipment if specified at the time of ordering.

OIL BATH CHAIN CASE

Primary chain cases on all models are of cast aluminium. Both primary and dynamo chains thus run in a constant oil bath ensuring maximum life for the transmission. Accessible filler caps to ensure correct level of oil, and inspection caps are provided for both chains. A further advantage of the cast aluminium type of case consists of the sound-absorbing qualities inherent to the design, giving perfect silence to the transmission. Rear chains are lubricated by crankcase oil impregnated vapour, and have effectively valanced guards giving protection from all weather conditions but at the same time providing perfect accessibility to the rear wheel.

RECOMMENDED OILS

Vacuum Mobiloil "D," Wakefield's Castrol XXL, Aero-Shell. These lubricants are suitable for both engine and gear box.

ADDITIONAL ITEMS TO STANDARD SPECIFICATION

S. Smith & Sons' 8-day clock in steering damper arm on 250 c.c. Model	£1	10	0
Leg Shields, all Models		15	0
Rudge-Whitworth Pillion Footrests		6	6
Rudge-Whitworth quickly detachable and interchangeable wheel on Watsonian or Swallow sidecars	£1	15	0

SIDECARS

We recommend Swallow and Watsonian Sidecars for Rudge Motor Cycles. Full particulars and prices of these are obtainable direct from Swallow Coachbuilding Co., Ltd., Foleshill, Coventry, and Watsonian Sidecars, Ltd., Albion Road, Greet, Birmingham.

See what these Famous Riders say of Rudge

J. H. SIMPSON.

I chose a Rudge for the 1934 Lightweight T.T. because I wanted a machine which would stand up to my alleged "flogging," whilst at the same time possessing enough speed to win. I had carefully watched the progress of the Rudge 250 c.c. since it startled the Motor Cycle World by winning the 1931 Lightweight T.T., which race marked its first appearance in Competitions.

Since then it had always been "placed," and had proved amazingly trouble free.

The opinions I had formed were confirmed by Wal Handley who told me, after the 1932 T.T., that the Rudge was the most comfortable and perfect steering machine he had ever ridden.

Owing to various reasons I never did a practice lap on my own mount, and we thus started the Race more or less unknown to each other. The weather was appalling, and riding conditions had never been worse.

It seemed doubly cruel to thrash a brand new machine under these circumstances, but it had to be done. It speaks volumes for the Rudge that in spite of a very slow first lap, due to a stop at the Pits to change my saturated goggles, I had no difficulty in gaining the lead in the third lap. Steadily increasing my average speed throughout the race, my last lap proved to be the fastest one of the day, so it requires no assurance from me to prove that the splendid tune of the Rudge had been maintained.

The 1934 Lightweight Race marked my 21st attempt to win a T.T., and was the first occasion on which I had ridden a Rudge in the Island.

The Rudge stood up to all I could give it, and in return gave me the ambition of my riding career. Can I say more?

J. H. Simpson.

G. E. NOTT.

As the chap responsible for the final testing of the Rudge Models sold to the Public, I know how little my own Racing Machines differ from the standard product. This is because the Racing jobs are developed from the standard designs in the first place; then anything which we discover to be of advantage in the Races is built into the next series of standard models. I don't mean by this that the "Ulsters," the "Specials" and the 250 c.c. jobs are Racing Machines, because they are not; they are machines designed for day-in day-out hard work on the road, combining wonderful steering and braking with 100% reliability. Successful Racing experience has, however, given them something else in addition, and that thing is performance: maximum speed, acceleration, flexibility, and above all that feeling of safety when making fast averages which only a race bred machine can give.

G. E. Nott.

H. G. TYRELL-SMITH.

The fact that Rudge Machines finished 1st, 2nd, and 3rd in the 1934 Lightweight T.T. is proof of the outstanding reliability of the breed. I think, however, that the detailed history of *one* of the Team Machines makes even more convincing testimony—Ridden by G. E. Nott it finished 2nd in the "Leinster 200." With the same rider "up" it was 2nd in the Lightweight T.T. I then took it on the Continent where it finished 6th in the Dutch T.T., 3rd in the Swiss Grand Prix, 5th in the Circuit de Lario, 1st in the German Grand Prix, and 1st in the Belgium Grand Prix. Finally Nott rode it in the Ulster Grand Prix winning the 250 class at the amazing speed of 77.08 m.p.h. with a record lap of 78.84 m.p.h. It is still going strong, having maintained a 100% history of finishing in every race in which it has been entered.

H. G. Tyrell-Smith

5

● LIGHTWEIGHT T.T. SIMPSON WINS (Photo by Courtesy of "Motor Cycling.")
● Dr. GALLOWAY and his RUDGE ULSTER IN THE INTERNATIONAL SIX DAYS' TRIAL. Winner of Gold Medal and NO MARKS LOST (Photo by Courtesy of "Motor Cycle").
● LIGHTWEIGHT T.T. SIMPSON AT RAMSEY HAIRPIN (Photo by Courtesy of "Motor Cycling").
● LIGHTWEIGHT T.T. THE VICTORIOUS TRIO (Photo by Courtesy of "Motor Cycle").

Chapter Eighteen
BANKRUPTCY

WITH the Company facing bankruptcy one would not have expected any change in the range of machines offered for 1935. Certainly the Special model continued into 1935 without change, and was offered under the slogan 'Designed – Developed – And Now Perfected'. The Ulster too looked very similar but it now sported the petrol tank shape of the previous year's racing machines, which extended back either side of the saddle nose. The cylinder head, which appeared similar to the previous year was, in fact, completely redesigned to take more substantial rockers. It should not be assumed however, that no development work took place at all as, in July 1934, George Hack had experimented with a water cooled version but this experiment never looked like reaching the production line.

Most of the development work during 1934 had taken place on the 250 range. The new Sports model was continued in 1935 in its fully radial four valve form, the only major change being the transfer of the oil tank from the front of the crankcase to the more usual position on the right-hand side of the machine, immediately under the saddle. Again the cylinder head had been redesigned to take more substantial rocker gear. Although fairly similar, the crankcases were also new, as these were the same as those that were being used for the new model of the range, the 250 Tourist. This was a fairly radical development for the Rudge Company as the machine was fitted with a two valve head. The exposed rocker gear on the four valve models required frequent adjustment as it was exposed to the elements and prone to wear when working with a lubricant mix of grease and road grit. The new two valve model provided very similar performance to its four valve predecessor but reduced the amount of maintenance necessary to keep it in tune. At the experimental stage in November 1934 a Lucas Magdyno was tried, but in its final form the model remained faithful to the Maglita.

A year had passed since the Company had withdrawn from racing, yet it was possible to look back on the previous twelve months as a period when many successes had been recorded, both by Graham Walker's Syndicate and by private owners. In addition to what has already been mentioned, local riders had won the Targa Florio 500cc class, the

The 1935 Ulster, clearly showing the rocker gear on the exhaust side and the left-hand exhaust valve. The rocker adjustment is on the pillar immediately above the exhaust pipe

Esthonian TT 250 and 500cc classes with, in addition, second place in the latter race and the first, second, third and fourth places in the 500cc class of the Greek TT. In the ISDT, the marque had claimed two Gold Medals, one of these being achieved by Dr. Galloway, a member of the British team that won the Silver Vase.

Graham Walker had retired from racing at the end of the 1934 season, so the Syndicate was disbanded. This was virtually the end of a factory supported team, although H. G. Tyrell Smith did have a 250 to take round the Continental Circus in the 1935 season. This was one of the 1934 models and with it he finished second in the Lightweight TT, second in the Swiss and third in the German and Belgium Grands Prix. Ernie Nott and Jack Williamson joined him in the TT, to take third and fifth places respectively, to claim the Manufacturers Team Prize for the second year running. Not a bad record for a company that had ceased to support racing eighteen months earlier! L. P. Hill, also riding a Rudge, finished in ninth place.

Although no new racing 250s were produced in 1935, a number of 500 racing machines were assembled. These were constructed to the 1934 specification and ten were produced. Five of these were immediately exported to Germany and the remaining five were sold to private owners in the United Kingdom. One of these, fitted with engine number 804, was probably the most powerful ever to leave the works as it developed 42 to 43bhp at 6000rpm. Another engine, in a higher state of tune, reached 48bhp in the test shop but unfortunately blew up and the experiment was not repeated.

On his return from the Continental Circus. Tyrell Smith joined Ernie Nott at Brooklands with one of the new 250 two valve machines, in at attempt to set new long distance records, but the engine blew up after five hours, after lapping at about 89mph. They also had a 250 four valve machine, running on alcohol fuel, and Ernie attempted the 100mph lap on it. After several laps at over 99mph, the con rod broke and as there were no 250 spares available, the attempts were abandoned. One rider who was successful at Brooklands was J. H. Greenwood, who obtained the Gold Star on a Rudge.

In March 1935, experiments were started to try and improve the steering which, although satisfactory on the road-going machines, gave cause for alarm at high speeds, when racing. First of all attention was paid to the front spring and a version was produced with compressed air damping. Although this development had useful possibilities, it did not go into production. A more interesting development lay in the cross section of the tubing. Up to 1935 this had been 'D' section and it was possible for the fork legs to whip sideways, when under pressure during fast cornering. A new, more rigid, front fork was developed during 1935, with round section front fork blades, made in one piece with a forged fork bridge in place of the bolted up unit used previously. This modified design was prepared for use on the 1936 models, but the Company was now in very serious financial trouble. Production during the year had again failed to reach more than 2000 machines and the Company was therefore put into liquidation. Here the story might have ended but one of the creditors was The Gramaphone Company, part of Electrical & Musical Industries of Hayes, Middlesex. This Company purchased the assets from the Liquidator thus allowing him to declare and first and final payment to the creditors of 10s 0d in the £ with nothing for the shareholders. It was the tragic story repeated many times in the motorcycle industry in that period. It could cost a company £10,000 in research and development to produce the extra one or two brake horsepower to remain competitive in the sporting field but very little of this could be recovered when the general public could not afford the road going machines. Under the new management, the 1936 models were announced and again in many respects it was the mixture as before. The Special continued exactly as the previous year's model, apart from the new front fork, on all black petrol tank with gold lining, plus a new transfer, and a fishtail on the silencer tail pipes. The Ulster too continued much as before, apart from the improved front forks, although the exhaust pipes were now downswept again, the upswept version being an optional extra which could now also be specified for the Special. Again, however, the cylinder head had been redesigned to give a more rigid mounting for the valve gear. The price of the Special had remained at £63 10s 0d and the Ulster at £73 10s 0d, although there had been a subtle economy with the eight day clock being replaced by the Rudge regulator. This was a simple dial mounted in a casing similar to that of the speedometer, which related road speeds to engine revolutions. By rotating an indicator by hand, it was possible to find the engine revolutions in any gear. In later years this idea was used by Triumph but the revolution information was printed around the speedometer scale in this latter instance. The 250 Sports model continued with four valves, but acquired the new 500cc type front forks and the cosmetic alterations. The 250 two valve was renamed the Rapid but was, in fact, similar to the Tourist of the previous year. The cylinder barrel acquired more substantial fins but the lighter 'D' section front forks were retained.

With this range the Company moved into 1936, a year that started with tragic news of John Pugh's death.

FEATURES THAT WILL INTEREST EVERY MOTOR CYCLIST
2-VALVE CYLINDER HEAD (Illustration 1)
ULSTER CYLINDER HEAD (Illustration 2)
PETROL TANK (Illustration 3)
KNOCK-OUT SPINDLE AND DETACHABLE MUDGUARD (Illustration 4)
OIL BATH CHAIN CASE (Illustration 5)
CLUTCH (Illustration 6)
REVULATOR (Illustration 7)
LUBRICATION
PROPORTIONAL COUPLED BRAKES
GEARBOX
FRONT FORKS
COMFORT
RUDGE
FINIS
1
2
3
4
5
6
7
RUDGE WHITWORTH LIMITED COVENTRY

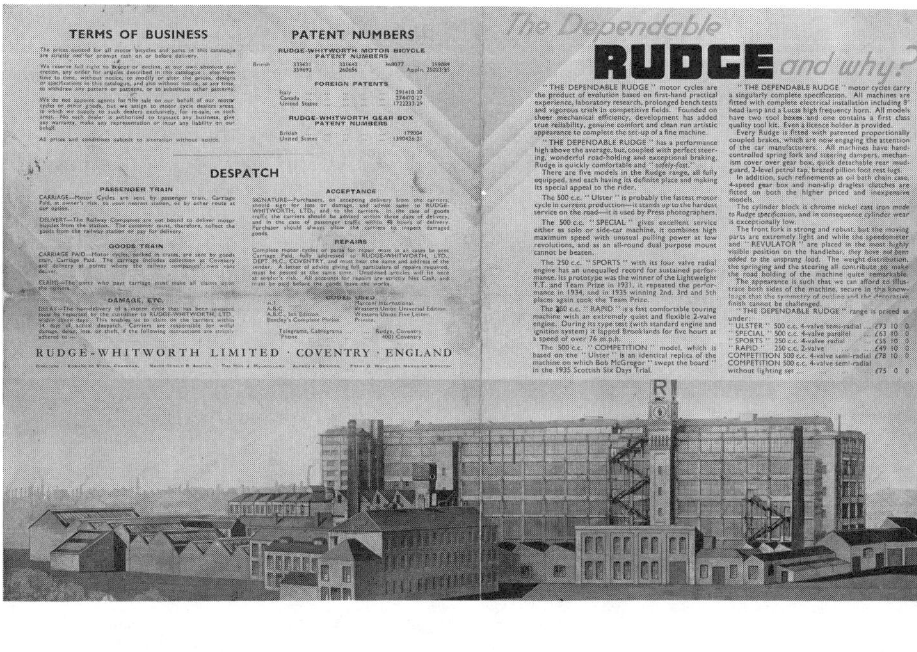
TERMS OF BUSINESS
PATENT NUMBERS
RUDGE-WHITWORTH MOTOR BICYCLE PATENT NUMBERS
FOREIGN PATENTS
RUDGE-WHITWORTH GEAR BOX PATENT NUMBERS
DESPATCH
PASSENGER TRAIN
GOODS TRAIN
DAMAGE, ETC.
ACCEPTANCE
REPAIRS
CODES USED
RUDGE-WHITWORTH LIMITED · COVENTRY · ENGLAND
The Dependable RUDGE and why?
"THE DEPENDABLE RUDGE" motor cycles are the product of evolution based on first-hand practical experience, laboratory research, prolonged bench tests and vigorous trials in competitive fields. Founded on sheer mechanical efficiency, development has added true reliability, genuine comfort and clean run artistic appearance to complete the set-up of a fine machine.
"THE DEPENDABLE RUDGE" has a performance high above the average, but, coupled with perfect steering, wonderful road-holding and exceptional braking, Rudge is quickly comfortable and "safely-fast."
There are five models in the Rudge range, all fully equipped, and each having its definite place and making its special appeal to the rider.
The 500 c.c. "Ulster" is probably the fastest motor cycle in current production—it stands up to the hardest service on the road—it is used by Press photographers.
The 500 c.c. "SPECIAL" gives excellent service either as solo or side-car machine, it combines high maximum speed with unusual pulling power at low revolutions, and as an all-round dual purpose mount cannot be beaten.
The 250 c.c. "SPORTS" with its four valve radial engine has an unequalled record for sustained performance. Its prototype was the winner of the Lightweight T.T. and Team Prize in 1931, it repeated the performance in 1934, and in 1935 winning 2nd, 3rd and 5th places again took the Team Prize.
The 250 c.c. "RAPID" is a fast comfortable touring machine with an extremely quiet and flexible 2-valve engine. During its type test (with standard engine and ignition system) it lapped Brooklands for five hours at a speed of over 76 m.p.h.
The 500 c.c. "COMPETITION" model, which is based on the "Ulster" is an identical replica of the machine on which Bob McGregor "swept the board" in the 1935 Scottish Six Days Trial.
"THE DEPENDABLE RUDGE" motor cycles carry a singularly complete specification. All machines are fitted with complete electrical installation including 8" head lamp and a Lucas high frequency horn. All models have two tool boxes and one contains a first class quality tool kit. Even a licence holder is provided.
Every Rudge is fitted with patented proportionally coupled brakes, which are now engaging the attention of the car manufacturers. All machines have hand-controlled spring fork and steering dampers, mechanism cover over gear box, quick detachable rear mudguard, 2-level petrol tap, brazed pillion foot rest lugs.
In addition, such refinements as oil bath chain case, 4-speed gear box and non-slip dragless clutches are fitted on both the higher priced and inexpensive models.
The cylinder block is chrome nickel cast iron made to Rudge specification, and in consequence cylinder wear is exceptionally low.
The front fork is strong and robust, but the moving parts are extremely light and while the speedometer and "REVULATOR" are placed in the most highly visible position on the handlebar, they have not been added to the unsprung load. The weight distribution, the springing and the steering all contribute to make the road holding of the machine quite remarkable.
The appearance is such that we can afford to illustrate both sides of the machine, secure in the knowledge that the symmetry of outline and the decorative finish cannot be challenged.
"THE DEPENDABLE RUDGE" range is priced as under:
"ULSTER" 500 c.c. 4-valve semi-radial ... £73 10 0
"SPECIAL" 500 c.c. 4-valve parallel ... £63 10 0
"SPORTS" 250 c.c. 4-valve radial ... £55 10 0
"RAPID" 250 c.c. 2-valve ... £49 10 0
COMPETITION 500 c.c. 4-valve semi-radial £78 10 0
COMPETITION 500 c.c. 4-valve semi-radial without lighting set ... £75 0 0
R

Chapter Nineteen A CHANGE OF DIRECTION

BEFORE looking at the progress of the Company in 1936, it is worth diverting for a few moments to a Rudge based experiment which was not directly connected with the factory, yet is bound up in its history. R. C. Cross, an experimental engineer, obtained from the Company a set of engines (250, 350 and 500) of the Replica type, on which he conducted breathing experiments. The experiments mainly consisted of replacing the normal poppet valves with a rotor. The biggest problem was maintaining an efficient gas seal when the working parts expanded and also lubrication of the rotor itself. These problems were resolved sufficiently well for a 500cc version of the Cross engine to be raced in the 1935 TT, but unfortunately the machine was forced to retire on the second lap, with sparking plug trouble. Experiments continued through 1936 with all three capacities of engine and quite remarkable results were achieved. No further attempts were made to produce a racing engine, but experiments continued, using Rudge bottom ends with both Rudge and Vincent HRD cycle parts. The most interesting of these was a Rudge Ulster, to which was fitted a 350cc engine with a rotary top end. With a 10 to 1 compression ratio, the engine achieved 25bhp at 6000rpm, using 65 octane petrol. Another interesting feature was a fuel consumption figure of 99mpg, with the machine cruising at between 60 and 65mph.

Although the Cross Rudge rotary did not go into production, its fuel economy did not go unnoticed. Following the steep increases in the price of petrol in the 1970s, the Esso experimental team developed an engine which performed with remarkable fuel economy and which was based on the experiments first tried, using Rudge engines.

During 1936 very little attention was given to racing machinery. One or two machines of each capacity were produced with racing specifications but these were virtually standard Ulsters or 250 Sports models, which were more highly tuned than standard. Private owners still continued to race these machines or earlier Replicas and racing machines. H. Hartley, for example, achieved seventh place in the 250 TT but in general the machines were now being outclassed in International events. Yet it was the

A 1936 Special and sidecar with the optional upswept exhaust pipes. The forward mounted horn is a more recent modification to this machine, which was exported to Austria

international situation that was opening up new prospects, which were taking up the time of the design team. With the rise of Nazi Germany, rearmament was very much in the air and there were Government contracts for dispatch riders' machines for which the Company could compete. By June 1936, the WD Rudge was well under way. Fortunately the Company had established its name for cross-country machines in the ISDT and it was this latter model that formed the basis of the new model. It was produced in both 250 and 500cc versions, the latter having the Ulster cylinder head. The ISDT quickly detachable rear hub was used but it was necessary to make a number of modifications to comply with the War Department specification, so a rear stand was reintroduced. The Rudge system of using uncaged needle rollers in the gearbox did not find favour with the military authorities, so one or two experimental machines were produced using Burman gearboxes. One of the problems faced by the Company was publicising these machines, apart from the usual procedure of handing over samples to the War Office, to evaluate and compare with other manufacturers' products.

In 1935, the London division of the TA Signals Regiment had formed a display team. The riders wore service dress but rode their own machines and had given four very competent displays. In 1936 the Company donated three of the new machines to the regiment, which were used at the fourteen displays given throughout 1936. This move was well rewarded, as in 1937 twenty machines were purchased from the Company by the TA and fifty displays were given, including one at the Royal Tournament. An interesting sequel to this event occurred in 1967, during the Display Team's reunion at Eastbourne, which was held exactly thirty years after they had appeared at the Royal Tournament. One of the members had obtained and restored a 1936 Rudge Ulster, which was hidden in a toilet next to the hotel dining room before the formal dinner. At the end of the meal (after the table had been cleared), the machine was ridden up a ramp onto the top table, to the applause of old comrades and the consternation of the hotel staff!

In addition to preparing the WD model, the design team had been looking at the whole range of Rudge motorcycles. The gearbox had already received attention at the end of 1935, when the needle rollers around the outside of the 4th speed pinion had been shortened, to make room for a pig-skin washer to reduce the loss of oil from the gearbox. This was followed in 1936 by the replacement of the needle rollers inside the 4-speed pinion by two Oilite bushes.

The 500cc engine received attention next and this was given an entirely new shape. One of the major problems on the Rudge engine up to 1936 was the amount of wear in the rocker gear. This was partly due to the number of separate moving parts and partly to road grit, which became a grinding paste when it worked its way into the rocker grease. The number of moving parts remained unchanged, but the grinding paste aspect was eliminated by totally enclosing the valves. The Special and the Ulster therefore received new cylinder heads with aluminium covers over the valves. The oil was taken through a pipe from the oil pump to the cylinder head, where it was fed through the rocker spindles, over the valves, and back down the push-rod tunnel onto the cam followers. This achieved a secondary object of reducing wear on the cam followers and the camshaft. The opportunity was also taken to eliminate a previous design weakness. The solid push-rods had a tendency to wear inside the first rocker and penetrate the case hardening to eventually emerge through the top of the rocker. The new push-rods were of tubular steel with cup and ball contacts at each end. Finally, the oil pump was enlarged to give an increased capacity, to cope with the extra supply of oil to the head. Of all the engines produced by the Company during its existence, these engines are probably the most symmetrical and pleasing to the eye, particularly the Special.

Up to 1936, the two wheels had been interchangeable, although this was of limited value on the Ulster, where the front wheel was 21in and the rear 20in! Although the mudguard could be quickly removed, the chain had to be detached before the rear wheel could be taken out. In July 1936 a new rear wheel was designed, which was quickly detachable but included a number of new features. In place of the previous cups and cones, the wheel ran on Timken taper roller bearings. The sprocket and the brake drum were integral, the drum having been moved from the right to the left-hand side of the machine. By making this move, the Company came into line with the majority of English manufacturers by having the brake pedal on the left and the gearchange on the right. This removed the necessity for the gearchange crossover shaft, which had been used on production machines since 1932. It was now possible to remove the rear wheel by undoing the rear spindle nut, pulling out the spindle, knocking out the wheel spacer and undoing the three bolts which attached the wheel to the brake drum. Finally, as a result of the elimination of the crossover shaft, the chaincase was redesigned with only one hole in its centre, this being for the footrest hanger.

Before introducing the new enclosed engine 500cc models at the Motorcycle Show, the open valve models achieved one last success for the factory. In the International Six Days Trial, the Silver Vase B Team were all mounted on Rudges and the Trophy was won without any loss of marks. The Rudge riders were R. MacGregor, J. A. MacLeslie and J. E. Edward. Now the Company could claim that only twice had a one make team been selected by the Auto-Cycle Union, that on each occasion Rudge had been the chosen make, and on both occasions the International Silver Vase had been won.

In spite of this success, only 2000 machines were sold during 1936 and this was still not enough. As a result, for 1937 the four valve 250 was dropped, leaving only the 250 two valve in production. The new Ulster and the new Special replaced the previous year's open valve models and a third 500 was added to the range. This was the Sports Special, which was, in effect, an ordinary Special with upswept exhaust pipes. It is strange that the Special engine should have been selected for this model when the ISDT had been won by machines with open valve Ulster engines. The quickly detachable ISDT rear wheel was optionally available on all three 500cc models, although most were fitted to Ulsters. On these, the three securing bolts which held the wheel to the brake drum were replaced by pegs, so that it was only necessary to undo the spindle nut in order to remove the rear wheel (apart from the removal of the mudguard, of course). The only other major differences between the Special and the Sports Special were the Ulster type handlebars and front mudguard fitted to the Sports Special and its own rather peculiar rear mudguard, which had a straight valance to fill in the space between the top of the upswept silencer and the mudguard. The Sports Special also had two toolboxes, mounted on the valances.

No. 1540.—Repair Outfits, 6d size 1/6 per doz
" " 1/- " 2/6 " "
Ordinary filling

Chapter Twenty
GOODBYE COVENTRY

THE enclosed valves on the 500cc models had proved a major talking point at the 1936 Show. Early in 1937 orders for the new machines improved and by the end of the year 3000 had been sold, a 50% increase on the year before. Nevertheless, this was well below the capacity of a factory the size of the Rudge works at Coventry. In addition, control of the new subsidiary was proving difficult for the Gramophone Company and involved frequent trips between London and Coventry. The obvious answer was to sell the factory at Coventry and combine the operations of the Group at Hayes, in Middlesex. This course of action was agreed and arrangements were made during 1937 to move the manufacturing machinery from Coventry to Hayes. One employee who moved to London ahead of the Company was Graham Walker, who resigned to take up the appointment of Chief Editor of *Motor Cycling*. During the previous years he had contributed to the magazine on many occasions and he transferred to commence yet another career.

Very little new development work was carried out during the year, apart from the 'Royal Tournament' War Department machines mentioned previously. Before he left however, Graham managed to arrange for three or four machines to be built to racing specification, most of which were sold abroad. One was built to this specification for Norman Croft, was raced at Brooklands. At the TT however, it was left to Harold Hartley, riding outdated works machines, to keep the name of the Company on the results sheets. Although he retired in the 250 race, he was 22nd in the Junior and 13th in the Senior races. In fact, he rode Rudge motorcycles every year that the TT was held from 1936 to 1954, except 1953, and was far from outclassed. He was seventh in the 250 and 29th in the 500cc TTs in 1939, and after the war on his 250 he achieved 11th place in 1949, 10th place in 1951 and 17th place in 1952. Not a bad record for a machine which was over fifteen years old when last raced.

Several 250 racing machines were built to special order in 1937 but this was the last year that they were produced.

RUDGE
RECAPTURES THE INTERNATIONAL
SILVER VASE
By the MOST BRILLIANT TEAM PERFORMANCE OF 1936, Rudge machines again won the coveted International Silver Vase. Throughout the arduous 1,350 miles of the International Six Days' Trial the three Rudge Ulsters did not lose a single mark. No spares were fitted and the riders experienced an entirely trouble-free week. In the final speed test, running comfortably within its limit, the Team beat all competition to regain the Vase for Britain.
Despite this gruelling treatment all three machines finished in excellent condition—here's what The Motor Cycle says about them:—
ALSO AWARDED
MANUFACTURERS'
TEAM PRIZE
5 GOLD MEDALS

WINS FOR BRITAIN
The all-Rudge, all-Scots Team: R. MacGregor, J. A. McL. Leslie and J. C. Edward—whose magnificent riding throughout the Six Days' contributed so much to this splendid victory.
217
258
133
BVC533

RUDGE 500c.c.'SPORTS SPECIAL'
— GRACE — SPEED — SILENCE —

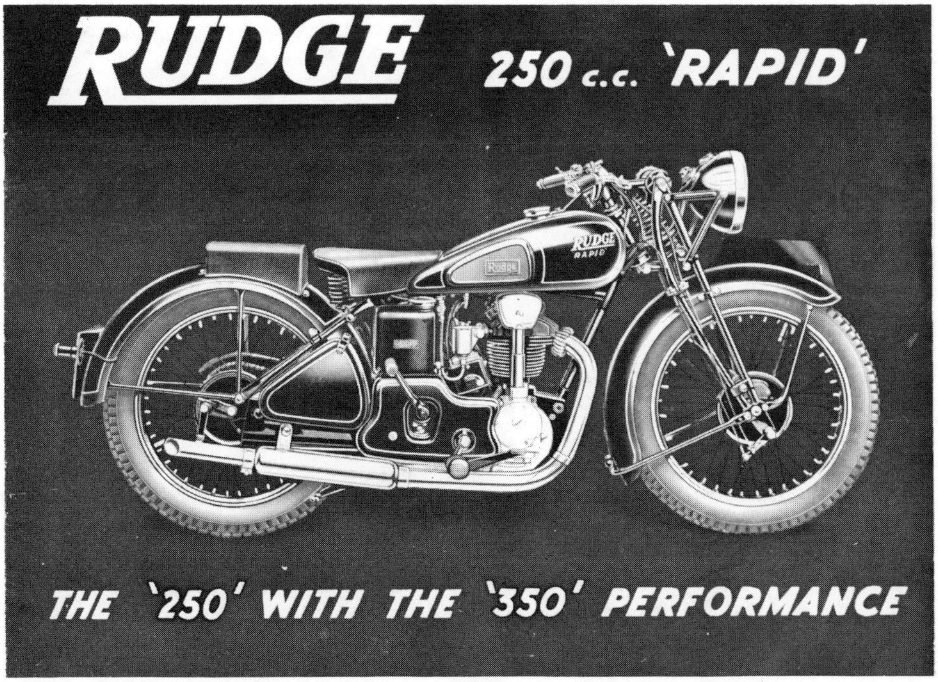
RUDGE 250 c.c. 'RAPID'
THE '250' WITH THE '350' PERFORMANCE

A Special (nearest the camera) keeping company with an Ulster outside the Motor Cycle Museum at Stanford Hall

When the 1938 range was unveiled at Earls Court in September 1937, it was again a matter of the mixture as before. There had been further price increases, the Ulster now costing £82 as compared to £77 the previous year, the Special had risen from £65 to £69 10s 0d and the Sports Special was £72 compared to £67 10s 0d. The Rapid had also increased in price, from £49 10s 0d to £55, but here at least there was an addition to the specification as a speedometer was now listed as a standard fitting, to comply with new legislation, which brought it into line with the 500cc models. An addition to the range was the 250 Sports Model, which was a tuned version of the two valve Rapid. The engine was fitted with a slipper piston in place of the full-skirt type used on the Rapid and this gave a higher compression ratio of 7.7 to 1 compared to the 6.6 to 1 of the Rapid. An interesting variation was introduced into the wheel sizes as the Rapid had 3.25in by 19in wheels, whereas the Sports retained the same size rear wheel, but the front was increased in diameter and reduced in width to 3in by 20in. The main jet size of the Sports model was increased from 120 to 130, and the machine given the cosmetic variation of an upswept exhaust pipe, which brought it into line with the 500cc Sports Special. In addition, the front mudguard was now slightly larger in diameter, to allow for the increase in wheel size.

Of the 500cc range, there were a number of minor improvements and the opportunity was taken to correct a design fault that had occurred the previous year. With the introduction of valve enclosure, it had been anticipated that this would reduce the running temperature of the engine through the circulation of oil over the head. As a result, the oil feed to the rear of the cylinder was discarded. During 1937 a number of complaints of engine seizures were received so for 1938 this oil feed was introduced. It is therefore fairly easy to identify a 1937 cylinder barrel as this is the only round-base type to have no provision for the oil feed.

A later Ulster enjoying the sun at its home in Florida, USA

A 1938 Ulster and box sidecar beside a 1935 Special. The essential difference between the two models is the enclosure of the valves on the Ulster which permits a mechanical oil feed to the rocker gear. The brake and gearchange pedals were also reversed between the two models

Another change which has caused problems with Rudge restorers in subsequent years was the replacement of the rear bottom shackle bolt with one which was slightly longer. This was to take into account the strengthening of the rear of the bottom shackle and the new parts were fitted to all three 500cc models. Very few catalogues list this variation between 1937 and 1938 and as a result the earlier type shackle bolt has on occasions been fitted to the later forks. This causes the thread of the bolt on the inside of the shackle to wear, to the general detriment of the machine's handling.

Immediately prior to the Show, the Company announced that it had again been selected to provide a team for the International Vase in the ISDT, but unfortunately the team failed to retain the Trophy which they had won in the previous year. Nevertheless the Company moved into 1938 with a compact range and the new factory at Hayes, into which production was transferred.

It is probably not appreciated how compact the range was, for although five models were listed, many items were common. For example, virtually all machines from 1925 to 1939 had the same steering cups and top and bottom cones. As a result, a Rudge steering cup will fit any machine made after 1924 whilst the top and bottom cones will fit everything except the speedway machines. In 1938 there were only two types of crankcase, the 250 type and the 500cc type. Having said that, I must admit that there was a slight difference between the models — the prefix stamped in front of the engine number, which indicates the original specification of the engine. The Company was no less interested in standardisation when dealing with the various nuts and bolts which are needed to assemble a motorcycle. Although in many cases these are completely unlike any nuts or bolts used on any other make of motorcycle, this did not prevent a special nut or bolt being used in a number of different places. Such items were given the prefix 'C' to their part numbers, and there were 112. Whereas some, like needle rollers, might only be found in gearboxes and rocker gear, others like nut C20 had no less than twenty-six different functions between 1910 and 1939!

With the removal of the factory from Coventry to Hayes, it might have been expected that the number of machines produced would decline. Although none was made during the course of the move, sales were maintained and by the end of 1938 another 3000 machines had been assembled. It is interesting to note that among the customers in 1938 were the Gramophone Company's associated and subsidiary companies throughout the world, so it cannot be said that the parent did not have faith in its new offspring. George Hack remained in charge of the Company at its new location, even though he continued to live at Coventry. Travelling down to work each day he tended to arrive at about ten am in the morning and leave shortly after four pm in the afternoon. Although this situation was initially accepted by the new management, it could not last for long, and another link with the past was broken when he left the Company in 1939. Before doing so, he completed an investigation into cylinder head material which had started with the bronze skull and finned aluminium head designed at the beginning of the decade. Further bronze and aluminium heads, this time with enclosed valves, were produced in 1938, but the differing rates of expansion of the two metals still created problems which were difficult to solve. The main aim of the change was to save weight as the Ulster bronze head is not the lightest of components. George Hack eventually came up with his RR50 aluminium head, which was used on the 1939 model Ulsters. In these heads, the problem of securing the fixing bolts was solved by bronze inserts, which were threaded to take holding-down studs. The inserts themselves were screwed into position and then locked while the valve seats, which were in austenitic iron, were pressed into the head. The process was fairly original in that the seats were cooled in solid carbon dioxide and then pressed into position in the cylinder head, which had been heated by immersing it in

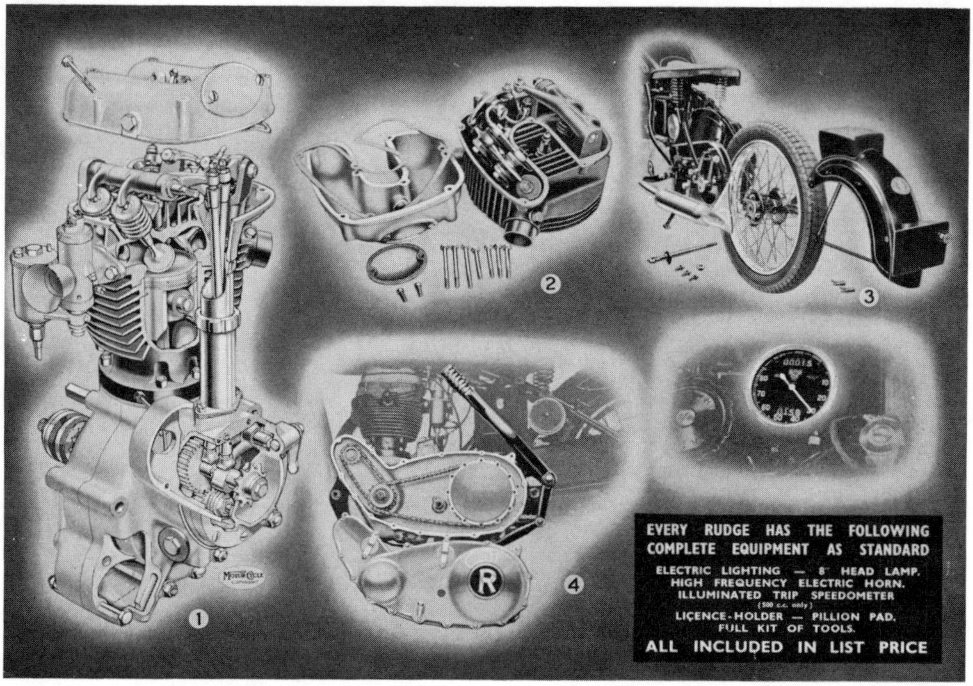

EINIGE DETAILBILDER AUS DER FABRIK

Another 1939 Ulster immaculately restored. This machine is a regular concours winner

The 1939 parallel enclosed valve Special model. The only non-standard part is the battery cover with wing nut fixing. Clearly visible under the saddle is one of the tommy bar bolts securing the rear mudguard which assists in the quick removal of the rear wheel

The timing side of the same machine showing the gearbox apron

A concours winning 1939 Ulster attracting admiring attention

trichlorethylene. The extremes of temperature created the interference fit that was approximately 0.001 of an inch while at atmospheric temperatures the difference was about 0.005 of an inch. For safety's sake however, the outer edge of the seat was very slightly chamfered and the head material rolled over this chamfer.

Another illustration of the care which was taken in matching the materials in the engine was the use of RR56 aluminium for the tubular push-rods. As the engine heated up, the RR56 just about compensated for the expansion of the light alloy head, so that the valve clearances remained very similar, whether the engine was hot or cold.

Although the Ulster engine had been designed primarily for road-going use, its performance was such that it was still competitive in many sporting events, such as the ISDT. It was therefore possible to order a tuned engine, which cost an extra £5. Such engines were fitted with racing camshafts, a carburettor with a larger choke, polished ports and a compression ratio of between 7.25 and 7.5 to 1, according to the results obtained during tuning. This compared to the standard compression ratio of 6.8 to 1 on the standard Ulster. Although the factory was concentrating on the Ulster as the sports machine with a reputation, a number of private owners were finding that the 250 two valve, sports machine was also capable of providing excellent results. Two such riders were the brothers Roland and Stan Pike, who first rode Rudges in the Isle of Man in the 1937 Manx Grand Prix. In 1939 Rex Judd entered them, together with Ginger Wood, as a Rudge team and their beautifully prepared machines fared extremely well against works machinery, with Ginger Wood taking ninth place and Stan Pike eleventh; his brother Roland retiring with engine trouble. As previously mentioned, Harold Hartley led them home in seventh place. The Pike brothers went on to better things after the war, using virtually the same machinery but modified to their 'Pike Rudge' standards. Stan finished fifth in the 1947 Lightweight and seventh in the 1949 Lightweight races. His brother Roland, however, very nearly won the 1948 Lightweight TT, finishing a good second to Maurice Cann's Moto Guzzi and in subsequent Lightweight TTs was second in 1948, third in 1949, fourth in 1950 and thirteenth in 1952.

At the factory attention to the 250 was being given in another direction. Work had been continuing on WD machines since 1936, virtually all of it devoted to various modifications of the 500cc Ulster. In June 1938 work was started on an entirely new WD machine, this time using the 250 two valve Rapid as a basis. By the end of the year a Lightweight 250 was submitted to the War Department for evaluation. It had been appreciated that the standard 250cc gearbox was not really up to the sort of treatment that might be expected in wartime conditions, and so the new WD machine was therefore fitted with a 500cc gearbox although the 250cc type gearbox adjuster was retained. The clutch was also heavier than the standard 250 unit but was not the standard 500 type as it retained the four friction discs in place of the 500cc friction inserts. To meet the Government specification, the gearchange lever was mounted on the right side using 500cc components, which were also used for the left-hand brake drum and bolted on rear sprocket. The standard 250cc brake shoes were however retained. Again, to suit Government specifications, the very sturdy centre stand was discarded and replaced by a rear stand and a prop stand. The electrics were provided by a Lucas Magdyno, which represented a considerable improvement over the previous Maglita.

Another development which commenced when the factory moved to Hayes was the introduction of the Rudge autocycle. It was decided to produce a lightweight runabout so that the Company could move into what is today known as the moped market. As the Company did not have a suitable engine, the 98cc Villiers Junior de luxe engine was used, in an open-type cycle frame, very similar to those produced by other manufacturers such as New Hudson. Although many consider this not to be a real Rudge,

The 998cc 'double Ulster' built by A. L. Bailey, at a Rudge Club Rally held in 1956

The drive side of the 998cc Bailey V-Twin showing the enclosed positive stop mechanism and the two magnetos, one mounted in front and the other behind the timing cover. This machine was also fitted with twin front and rear brakes

Thirty years on. Jimmy Simson *(left)*, Graham Walker *(centre)* and George Hack *(right)* enjoy a smoke and a chat at a Rudge Enthusiasts Club dinner in the early 1960s

it was, in fact, the last of the Rudge machines to remain in production.

Excluding the autocycle, Rudge production during 1939 continued to improve and by the time war was declared, over 2000 had been manufactured. Without this interruption, production might well have reached 4000 by the end of the year. The War Department had accepted the 250cc engined WD machine and the first batch of 200 was delivered by the Company. In later years, when some of these were sold to the general public, the mixture of 500cc and 250cc parts caused many owners to think that the machines were hybrids. Very few survived, as a majority were destroyed in an air raid early in 1940.

The factory was well prepared for a large production run to follow the initial batch, but unfortunately the hand of fate struck again. The main factory was devoted to the production of radar, a defence system which had priority over most other war production. With the demand for radar stations and supporting equipment reaching a peak before the Battle of Britain in 1940, the Gramophone Company needed all possible space to produce this equipment. The Rudge factory immediately adjacent to the electrical buildings was an obvious candidate for the expansion of the electrical side of the organisation. Production of motorcycles finished on 18 December 1939, although the Company had every intention of restarting after hostilities had ceased. A majority of the machine tools which were not required for immediate use were moved into the Regent Cinema, Hanwell, to await the restarting of production. Many dealers in the area were invited to the factory to purchase stocks of spares at knock-down prices and it is unfortunate that many irreplaceable records of the Company were scrapped when the factory was cleared in a hurry.

Motorcycle production ceased quietly and undramatically, although a more colourful story concerning the decision was circulated at the time. It was said that Lord Beaverbrook, Chief of Aircraft Production at that time, was touring the Gramophone Company's works to exhort the management to increase production. Coming to the Rudge factory he asked what was being produced inside. On being told that it was motorcycles for the War Department, he is reported to have ordered the motorcycles out and radar production in. There is no doubt that in 1939 the last Rudge motorcycles were assembled at Hayes, even though the name lived on a little longer.

The Norman Company of Ashford, Kent was given permission to continue production of the autocycle using the Rudge name, and this became the last motorcycle to be produced bearing the name Rudge on its tank.

In fact, the success of the sales side in 1939 had encouraged the Company to design a wider range of machines for 1940.

The 250 machines, the two valve Rapid and the two valve Sports models were to have been continued, having proved fast and reliable. To these was to be added the 250 two valve War Department machine. In the larger capacity class, the Ulster, the Special and the Sports Special were to be retained but an entirely new series of engines had been designed for the 350cc class. Two types of engine were built, both two valve, the first being push-rod operated and second using an overhead camshaft. Although the engines were fairly similar in design to those of the 500cc range, the push-rod version was fitted with a very high camshaft, very similar to that of the Velocette. Unfortunately the war put an end to these most promising designs, which did not progress beyond the prototype stage.

In 1943 it was decided that cycle and motorcycle production would not after all recommence, and the old Rudge Company was sold off. The trademark and right to produce cycles was sold to Raleigh Industries, in 1943. The name was therefore continued on a number of Raleigh-assembled cycles after the war, until the name was phased out. The name and the trademark has now passed into the hands of Tube Investments, who subsequently purchased Raleigh Industries.

On the motorcycle side, the right to produce spares was taken over by Godfreys of Great Portland Street. They in turn obtained spare parts from sub-contractors, to keep the existing machines on the road. The main sub-contractor was A. L. Bailey, of Walthamstow, who had been a Rudge dealer before the outbreak of war. During the war he had turned his showroom into a small machine shop and was therefore able to produce parts when civilian production recommenced.

In addition to producing a majority of the spares, Mr. Bailey had visions of putting a Rudge back into production in an up-to-date form. By 1950 he had produced a new machine which aroused great interest. At a time when the parallel twin was coming into vogue, he had mounted two Ulster heads and barrels on a common crankcase, Vincent style, to produce the 998cc Bailey Twin. The engine was mounted in a frame of his own design, the suspension being provided by Matchless telescopic forks and rear suspension by a Matchless swinging arm, assembly, using 'jam pot' rear suspension units. The vee twin was very much a one off and although two or three crankcases were cast at the same time, no other machines were assembled.

More interesting however, was the machine which he produced in 1953. This was basically a Rudge Ulster, having an engine with an aluminium cylinder barrel and a parallel, pent-roof head. The only other modification to the engine applied to the magneto, which was spigot mounted to the timing cover. The Rudge frame design was retained and the front and rear suspension were the standard Matchless units. The only other major modification was enclosure of the foot-change mechanism.

In addition, Bailey also produced a 250 all-aluminium engine, which had the modifications mentioned above. It was Bailey's aim to put into production a complete range of 250, 350, 500 and 1000cc models under the Rudge name. Unfortunately, lack of finance and a breakdown in negotiations to use the name, put an end to this most interesting project.

It is also interesting to note that a 350 was to be produced, especially as none had left the Rudge factory since 1933.

Godfreys continued the manufacture of Rudge spares until the 1960s, when it was decided to close the Great Portland Street Depot and concentrate motorcycle sales in Croydon.

Earlier, in 1956, the Rudge Enthusiasts Club had been formed, following the disbanding of the Rudge Association which had been formed after the war. By the time Godfreys decided to close, the Club had already realised that it would have to safeguard the spares position if it was to survive. It had already purchased spares from a number of dealers who were clearing their shelves to make room for later products. The remaining stocks were therefore sold to the Club, which has now become the sole supplier of such parts. The 500 members throughout the world are thus able to keep the name Rudge on the road.

Of the factories where Rudge motorcycles were assembled, the Hayes factory still stands and is still part of the Electrical and Musical Industries complex. At Coventry, the main seven-storey building still stands, but the buildings on the other side of Spon Street were demolished to make way for a motorway. This was aptly named Rudge Ringway, after the Company which had brought fame to the City. It is most appropriate that the Company should be commemorated in this way, when it had spent so many years providing quality transport.

Appendix
RUDGE MOTORCYCLE MODELS

Rudge Motorcycle Models, 1910 – 1914

Year	Model	Valves (per cylinder)	Number of cylinders	Bore & stroke	Magneto	Transmission	Starting	Wheelsizes	Last frame numbers in year	Comments
1910		Two, inlet over exhaust	One	85x88 (499cc)	CAV	Fixed	Pedals to rear wheel	26x2¼in	592203	B&B carburettor. Mabon gear or NSU 2-speed optional
1911	Fixed	Two, inlet over exhaust	One	85x88 (499cc)	CAV (model A)	Fixed	Pedals to rear wheel	26x2¼in	635225	
	Free	Two, inlet over exhaust	One	85x88 (499cc)	CAV (model A)	Clutch	Pedals to rear wheel	26x2¼in	635300	
	TT	Two, inlet over exhaust	One	85x88 (499cc)	CAV (model A)	Fixed	Push starting	26x2¼in	635088	
1912	Fixed	Two, inlet over exhaust	One	85x88 (499cc)	Eisemann	Fixed	Pedals to engine	26x2¼in	670451	
	Free	Two, inlet over exhaust	One	85x88 (499cc)	Eisemann	Clutch	Pedals to engine	26x2¼in	670973	
	Multi	Two, inlet over exhaust	One	85x88 (499cc)	Eisemann	Variable pullies	Pedals to engine	26x2¼in	670975	
	TT	Two, inlet over exhaust	One	85x88 (499cc)	Eisemann	Fixed	Push starting	26x2¼in	670970	
	Brooklands	Two, inlet over exhaust	One	85x88 (499cc)	Eisemann	Fixed	Push starting	26x2¼in	669408	
1913	Fixed	Two, inlet over exhaust	One	85x88 (499cc)	Ruthardt	Fixed	Pedals to engine	26x2¼in	705902	
	Free	Two, inlet over exhaust	One	85x88 (499cc)	Ruthardt	Clutch	Pedals to engine	26x2¼in	705943	
	3½hp Multi	Two, inlet over exhaust	One	85x88 (499cc)	Ruthardt	Variable pullies	Pedals to engine	26x2¼in	705942	
	TT	Two, inlet over exhaust	One	85x88 (499cc)	Ruthardt	Fixed	Push starting	26x2¼in	705592	
	Brooklands	Two, inlet over exhaust	One	85x88 (499cc)	Ruthardt	Fixed	Push starting	26x2¼in	703064	
	5/6hp Multi	Two, inlet over exhaust	One	85x132 (750cc)	Ruthardt	Variable pullies	Pedals to engine	26x2¼in	705923	
1914	Fixed	Two, inlet over exhaust	One	85x88 (499cc)	Ruthardt	Fixed	Pedals to engine	650x65mm	731028	All models have foot operated oil pumps
	Free	Two, inlet over exhaust	One	85x88 (499cc)	Ruthardt	Clutch	Pedals to engine	650x65mm	731992	
	3½hp Multi	Two, inlet over exhaust	One	85x88 (499cc)	Ruthardt	Variable pullies	Pedals to engine	650x65mm	732317*	
	TT Roadster	Two, inlet over exhaust	One	85x88 (499cc)	Ruthardt	Fixed	Push starting	650x65mm	732310	
	TT Multi	Two, inlet over exhaust	One	85x88 (499cc)	Ruthardt	Variable pullies	Push starting	650x65mm	732311	
	Brooklands	Two, inlet over exhaust	One	85x88 (499cc)	Ruthardt	Fixed	Push starting	650x65mm	727696	
	3½hp 3-Speed	Two, inlet over exhaust	One	85x88 (499cc)	Ruthardt	3-speed hub ϕ	Pedals to engine	650x65mm	732193	
	5/6hp Multi	Two, inlet over exhaust	One	85x132 (750cc)	Ruthardt	Variable pullies	Pedals to engine	650x65mm	732086	

** The last 'veteran' frame number*
ϕ Sturmey Archer

Rudge Motorcycle Models, 1915 – 1921

Year	Model	Valves (per cylinder)	Number of cylinders	Bore & stroke	Magneto	Transmission	Starting	Wheelsizes	Last frame numbers in year	Comments
1915	3½hp Multi	Two, inlet over exhaust	One	85x88 (499cc)	CAV	Variable pullies	Pedals to engine	650x65mm	742695	Also Army version
	TT Multi	Two, inlet over exhaust	One	85x88 (499cc)	CAV	Variable pullies	Push starting	650x65mm	742658	
	Brooklands	Two, inlet over exhaust	One	85x88 (499cc)	CAV	Fixed	Push starting	650x65mm	740937	
	3½hp 3-Speed	Two, inlet over exhaust	One	85x88 (499cc)	CAV	3-speed hub	Pedals to engine	650x65mm	738126	
	TT 3-Speed	Two, inlet over exhaust	One	85x88 (499cc)	CAV	3-speed hub	Push starting	650x65mm	738424	
	5/6hp Multi	Two, inlet over exhaust	One	85x132 (750cc)	CAV	Variable pullies	Pedals to engine	650x65mm	741645	
	5/6hp 3-Speed	Two, inlet over exhaust	One	85x132 (750cc)	CAV	3-speed hub	Pedals to engine	650x65mm	None made	
	7/9hp Multwin	Two, inlet over exhaust	Two	85x88 (998cc)	CAV	Variable pullies	Pedals to engine	650x65mm	738742	
	7/9hp 4-speed	Two, inlet over exhaust	Two	85x88 (998cc)	CAV	3-speed hub	Pedals to engine	650x65mm	None made	
	Twin	Two, inlet over exhaust	Two	85x88 (998cc)	CAV	4-speed gearbox	Kickstarter	650x65mm	739200	

1916	3½hp Multi	Two, inlet over exhaust	One	85x88 (499cc)	CAV	Variable pullies	Pedals to engine	650x65mm	751301	Mainly Army version
1918	TT Multi	Two, inlet over exhaust	One	85x88 (499cc)	CAV	Variable pullies	Pedals to engine	650x65mm	751325	
	5/6hp Multi	Two, inlet over exhaust	One	85x132 (750cc)	CAV	Variable pullies	Pedals to engine	650x65mm	746577	
	7/9hp Multwin	Two, inlet over exhaust	Two	85x88 (998cc)	CAV	Variable pullies	Pedals to engine	650x65mm	745476	
1919	3½hp Multi	Two, inlet over exhaust	One	85x88 (499cc)	Splitdorf	Variable pullies	Pedals to engine	650x65mm	759966	
	TT Multi	Two, inlet over exhaust	One	85x88 (499cc)	Splitdorf	Variable pullies	Push starting	650x65mm	760306	Pedal starter optional
	5/6hp Multi	Two, inlet over exhaust	One	85x132 (750cc)	Splitdorf	Variable pullies	Pedals to engine	650x65mm	760270	
	7/9hp Multwin	Two, inlet over exhaust	Two	85x88 (998cc)	Splitdorf	Variable pullies	Pedals to engine	650x65mm	760649	
1920	3½hp Roadster Multi	Two, inlet over exhaust	One	85x88 (499cc)	CAV	Variable pullies	Pedals to engine	650x65mm	774899	ML magnetos after June
	TT Multi	Two, inlet over exhaust	One	85x88 (499cc)	CAV	Variable pullies	Push starting	650x65mm	776004	Pedal starter optional
	3½hp 3-Speed	Two, inlet over exhaust	One	85x88 (499cc)	CAV	3-speed gearbox	Pedals to engine	650x65mm	1 prototype only made	
	5/6hp Multi	Two, inlet over exhaust	One	85x132 (750cc)	CAV	Variable pullies	Pedals to engine	650x65mm	775478	
	7/9hp Multwin	Two, inlet over exhaust	Two	85x88 (998cc)	Splitdorf	Variable pullies	Pedals to engine	650x65mm	775479	
	7/9hp 3-Speed	Two, inlet over exhaust	Two	85x88 (998cc)	Splitdorf	3-speed gearbox	Pedals to engine	650x65mm	775702	
1921	3½hp Roadster Multi	Two, inlet over exhaust	One	85x88 (499cc)	ML	Variable pullies	Pedals to engine	650x65mm	790121	
	TT Multi	Two, inlet over exhaust	One	85x88 (499cc)	ML	Variable pullies	Push starting	650x65mm	794428	
	3½hp 3-Speed	Two, inlet over exhaust	One	85x88 (499cc)	ML	3-speed gearbox	Kickstarter	650x65mm	794209	
	5/6hp Multi	Two, inlet over exhaust	One	85x132 (750cc)	ML	Variable pullies	Pedals to engine	650x65mm	787831	
	5/6hp 3-Speed	Two, inlet over exhaust	One	85x132 (750cc)	ML	3-speed gearbox	Kickstarter	650x65mm	None made	
	7/9hp Multwin	Two, inlet over exhaust	Two	85x88 (998cc)	ML	Variable pullies	Pedals to engine	700x80mm	788351	
	7/9hp 3-Speed	Two, inlet over exhaust	Two	85x88 (998cc)	ML	3-speed gearbox	Kickstarter	700x80mm	794208	

Rudge Motorcycle Models, 1922 – 1929

Year	Model	Valves (per cylinder)	Number of cylinders	Bore & stroke	Magneto	Transmission	Starting	Wheelsizes	Last frame numbers in year	Comments
1922	3½hp Roadster Multi	Two, inlet over exhaust	One	85x88 (499cc)	ML	Variable pullies	Pedals to engine	650x65mm	813255	
	3½hp TT Multi	Two, inlet over exhaust	One	85x88 (499cc)	ML	Variable pullies	Push starting	650x65mm	814937	
	3½hp 3-Speed	Two, inlet over exhaust	One	85x88 (499cc)	ML	3-speed gearbox	Kickstarter	650x65mm	814683	
	7/9hp 3-Speed	Two, inlet over exhaust	Two	85x88 (998cc)	ML	3-speed gearbox	Kickstarter	700x80mm	813481	
1923	3½hp Roadster Multi	Two, inlet over exhaust	One	85x88 (499cc)	ML	Variable pullies	Pedals to engine	650x65mm	829812	
	3½hp TT Multi	Two, inlet over exhaust	One	85x88 (499cc)	ML	Variable pullies	Push starting	650x65mm	833273	
	3½hp 4-Speed	Two, inlet over exhaust	One	85x88 (499cc)	ML	4-speed gearbox	Kickstarter	650x65mm	837398	
	7/9hp 4-Speed	Two, inlet over exhaust	Two	85x88 (998cc)	ML	4-speed gearbox	Kickstarter	700x80mm	833476	
1924	350 4-Speed	Four, parallel overhead	One	70x90 (349cc)	ML	4-speed gearbox	Kickstarter	650x65mm	2800 ⊠	Maglita optional
	3½hp 4-Speed	Two, inlet over exhaust	One	85x88 (499cc)	ML	4-speed gearbox	Kickstarter	650x65mm	839288	
	500 4-Speed	Four, parallel overhead	One	85x88 (499cc)	ML	4-speed gearbox	Kickstarter	700x80mm	2800 ⊠	Maglita optional
1925	350 4-Speed	Four, parallel overhead	One	70x90 (349cc)	ML	4-speed gearbox	Kickstarter	650x65mm	12000 ⊠	
	500 4-Speed	Four, parallel overhead	One	85x88 (499cc)	ML	4-speed gearbox	Kickstarter	700x80mm	12000 ⊠	
	500 Sports	Four, parallel overhead	One	85x88 (499cc)	ML	4-speed gearbox	Kickstarter	700x80mm	12000 ⊠	
1926	500 Standard	Four, parallel overhead	One	85x88 (499cc)	ML Maglita	4-speed gearbox	Kickstarter	700x80mm	20000	
	500 Sports	Four, parallel overhead	One	85x88 (499cc)	ML	4-speed gearbox	Kickstarter	700x80mm	20000	
1927	500 Standard	Four, parallel overhead	One	85x88 (499cc)	Maglita	4-speed gearbox	Kickstarter	700x80mm	24605	Amac carburettor
	500 Sports	Four, parallel overhead	One	85x88 (499cc)	ML	4-speed gearbox	Kickstarter	700x80mm		
1928	500 Roadster	Four, parallel overhead	One	85x88 (499cc)	Maglita	4-speed gearbox	Kickstarter	26x3.25in		
	500 Special	Four, parallel overhead	One	85x88 (499cc)	Maglita	4-speed gearbox	Kickstarter	26x3.25in	31120	
	500 Sports	Four, parallel overhead	One	85x88 (499cc)	Maglita	4-speed gearbox	Kickstarter	26x3.25in		
	500 DT	Four, parallel overhead	One	85x88 (499cc)	ML	Single speed	Kickstarter	27x2.75in		
1929	250 5V JAP	Two, side valve	One	64.5x76 (249cc)	Maglita	4-speed gearbox	Kickstarter	25x2.75in		
	250 OHV JAP	Two, overhead	One	62.5x80 (245cc)	Maglita	4-speed gearbox	Kickstarter	25x2.75in		

Year	Model	Valves (per cylinder)	Number of cylinders	Bore & stroke	Magneto	Transmission	Starting	Wheelsizes	Last frame number in year	Comments
	350	Four, parallel overhead	One	70x88 (340cc)	Maglita	4-speed gearbox	Kickstarter	25x2.75in	38418	
	Special	Four, parallel overhead	One	85x88 (499cc)	Maglita	4-speed gearbox	Kickstarter	26x3.25in		
	Ulster	Four, parallel overhead	One	85x88 (499cc)	Maglita	4-speed gearbox	Kickstarter	27x2.75in		
	DT	Four, parallel overhead	One	85x88 (499cc)	ML	Single speed	Push starting	27x2.75in		

Ø *Approximate numbers — records destroyed*

Rudge Motorcycle Models, 1930 – 1934

Year	Model	Valves (per cylinder)	Number of cylinders	Bore & stroke	Magneto	Transmission	Starting	Wheelsizes	Last frame number in year	Comments
1930	250 SV JAP	Two, side valve	One	64.5x76 (249cc)	Maglita	4-speed gearbox	Kickstarter	19x2¼in xWM1		All dry sump vertical oil pump
	250 OHV JAP	Two, overhead	One	62.5x80 (245cc)	Maglita	4-speed gearbox	Kickstarter	19x2¼in xWM1		
	350	Four, parallel overhead	One	70x88 (340cc)	Maglita	4-speed gearbox	Kickstarter	21inxWM1		
	Special	Four, parallel overhead	One	85x88 (499cc)	Maglita	4-speed gearbox	Kickstarter	19inxWM2	45200	
	Ulster	Four, parallel overhead	One	85x88 (499cc)	Maglita	4-speed gearbox	Kickstarter	21inxWM1		
	DT	Four, parallel overhead	One	85x88 (499cc)	ML	Single speed	Push starting	21inxWM1		
1931	250	Four, radial overhead	One	62.5x81.0 (249cc)	Miller coil	4-speed gearbox	Kickstarter	19inxWM1		
	350	Four, radial overhead	One	70x90.5 (349cc)	ML	4-speed gearbox	Kickstarter	21inxWM1		Rear mounted magneto
	350 Replica	Four, radial overhead	One	70x90.5 (349cc)	ML	4-speed gearbox	Push starting	21inxWM1 (f) 20inxWM2 (r)		Front mounted magneto Rear mounted magneto
	Special	Four, parallel overhead	One	85x88 (499cc)	ML	4-speed gearbox	Kickstarter	19inxWM2	47214	Rear mounted magneto
	Ulster	Four, parallel overhead	One	85x88 (499cc)	ML	4-speed gearbox	Kickstarter	20inxWM2		Rear mounted magneto
	500 Replica	Four, parallel overhead	One	85x88 (499cc)	ML	4-speed gearbox	Push starting	21inxWM1 (f) 20inxWM2 (r)		Front mounted magneto Rear mounted magneto
	DT	Four, parallel overhead	One	85x88 (499cc)	ML	Single speed	Push starting	20inxWM2		Front mounted magneto
1932	250	Four, radial overhead	One	62.5x81.0 (249cc)	Miller coil	4-speed gearbox	Kickstarter	19inxWM1		Aluminium oil bath chaincase
	250 Replica	Four, radial overhead	One	62.5x81.0 (249cc)	ML	4-speed gearbox	Push starting	19inxWM2		
	350	Four, radial overhead	One	70x90.5 (349cc)	ML	4-speed gearbox	Kickstarter	21inxWM1		
	350 Replica	Four, radial overhead	One	70x90.5 (349cc)	ML	4-speed gearbox	Push starting	21inxWM1 (f) 21inxWM2 (r)		
	Ulster	Four, radial overhead	One	85x88 (499cc)	ML	4-speed gearbox	Kickstarter	20inxWM2	50422	
	500 Replica	Four, radial overhead	One	85x88 (499cc)	ML	4-speed gearbox	Push starting	21inxWM1 (f) 20inxWM2 (r)		
	Special	Four, parallel overhead	One	85x88 (499cc)	ML	4-speed gearbox	Kickstarter	19inxWM2		
1933	250	Four, radial overhead	One	62.5x81 (249cc)	Lucas Maglita	4-speed gearbox	Kickstarter	19inxWM1		Rear Maglita
	250 Replica	Four, radial overhead	One	62.5x81 (249cc)	BTH	4-speed gearbox	Push starting	21inxWM1		Rear magneto
	350	Four, radial overhead	One	70x90.5 (349cc)	BTH	4-speed gearbox	Kickstarter	21inxWM1		Rear magneto
	350 Replica	Four, radial overhead	One	70x90.5 (349cc)	BTH mag. generator	4-speed gearbox	Push starting	21inxWM1 (f) 20inxWM2 (r)		Front magneto Rear magneto
	Special	Four, parallel overhead	One	85x88 (499cc)	BTH	4-speed gearbox	Kickstarter	19inxWM2	52369	Rear magneto
	Ulster	Four, semi radial overhead	One	85x88 (499cc)	BTH mag. generator	4-speed gearbox	Kickstarter	21inxWM1 (f) 20inxWM2 (r)		Front mag. generator Rear mag. generator
	500 Replica	Four, semi radial overhead	One	85x88 (499cc)	BTH mag. generator	4-speed gearbox	Push starting	20inxWM2		Front magneto
1934	250 Standard	Four, radial overhead	One	62.5x81 (249cc)	Lucas Maglita	4-speed gearbox	Kickstarter	19inxWM1		Upswept exhaust pipes
	250 Sports	Four, radial overhead	One	62.5x81 (249cc)	Lucas Maglita	4-speed gearbox	Kickstarter	20inxWM1	54604	All rear magneto
	Special	Four, parallel overhead	One	85x88 (499cc)	BTH	4-speed gearbox	Kickstarter	19inxWM2		
	Ulster	Four, semi radial overhead	One	85x88 (499cc)	BTH	4-speed gearbox	Kickstarter	21inxWM1 (f) 20inxWM2 (r)		Upswept exhaust pipes

Rudge Motorcycle Models, 1935 – 1939

Year	Model	Valves (per cylinder)	Number of cylinders	Bore & stroke	Magneto	Transmission	Starting	Wheelsizes	Last frame number in year	Comments
1935	250 Tourist	Two, overhead	One	62.5x81 (249cc)	Lucas Maglita	4-speed gearbox	Kickstarter	19inxWM1	56264	Upswept exhaust pipes
	250 Sports	Four, radial overhead	One	62.5x81 (249cc)	Lucas Maglita	4-speed gearbox	Kickstarter	20inxWM1		
	Special	Four, parallel overhead	One	85x88 (499cc)	BTH	4-speed gearbox	Kickstarter	19inxWM2		
	Ulster	Four, semi radial overhead	One	85x88 (499cc)	BTH	4-speed gearbox	Kickstarter	21inxWM1 (f) 20inxWM2 (r)		
1936	250 Rapid	Two, overhead	One	62.1x81 (245cc)	Lucas Maglita	4-speed gearbox	Kickstarter	19inxWM2	58980	
	250 Sports	Four, radial overhead	One	62.5x81 (249cc)	Lucas Maglita	4-speed gearbox	Kickstarter	19inxWM2		

	Special	Four, parallel overhead	One	84.5x88 (495cc) BTH	4-speed gearbox	Kickstarter	19inxWM2		
	Ulster	Four, semi radial over-head	One	85x88 (499cc) BTH	4-speed gearbox	Kickstarter	21inxWM1 (f) 20inxWM2 (r)		
1937	Rapid	Two, overhead	One	62.1x81 (245cc) Maglita	4-speed gearbox	Kickstarter	19inxWM2	62861	Upswept exhaust pipes
	Special	Four, parallel overhead	One	84.5x88 (495cc) BTH	4-speed gearbox	Kickstarter	19inxWM2		
	Sports Special	Four, parallel overhead	One	84.5x88 (495cc) BTH	4-speed gearbox	Kickstarter	19inxWM2		
	Ulster	Four, semi radial over-head	One	85x88 (499cc) BTH	4-speed gearbox	Kickstarter	21inxWM1 (f) 20inxWM2 (r)		
1938	Rapid	Two, overhead	One	62.1x81 (245cc) Maglita	4-speed gearbox	Kickstarter	19inxWM2	64752	Upswept exhaust pipes
	Sports	Two, overhead	One	62.1x81 (245cc) Maglita	4-speed gearbox	Kickstarter	20inxWM1 (f) 19inxWM2 (r)		
	Special	Four, parallel overhead	One	84.5x88 (495cc) BTH	4-speed gearbox	Kickstarter	19inxWM2		
	Sports Special	Four, parallel overhead	One	84.5x88 (495cc) BTH	4-speed gearbox	Kickstarter	19inxWM2		
	Ulster	Four, semi radial over-head	One	85x88 (499cc)	4-speed gearbox	Kickstarter	21inxWM1 (f) 20inxWM2 (r)		

1939 Data as for 1938 – last frame number 65720.
Some later frame numbers issued after production ceased as replacements for damaged frames.

Rudge Enthusiasts' Club

DURING the years that the Rudge motorcycle was in production, various groups of enthusiasts, who appreciated the engineering skill and design, formed Clubs for Rudge owners. Motorcyclists of the 'between the wars' era may well remember the Rudge Night Riders who had the Owl insignia. After the last war, when it was clear that the Marque would not be going back into production, the Rudge Association was formed and prospered during the late forties. Unfortunately, the Association did not last and by 1952 Rudge owners were without a Club. The need for a body to organise the activities of owners was great, so the present Rudge Enthusiasts Club was formed after an informal gathering at Eltham. Then followed the publication of the Club magazine and this set a high standard which has been maintained throughout. Back issues are always in great demand, and it is a lucky member who has a complete set. Membership has grown steadily and is now approximately 550.

Although the Club Headquarters is in London, there are regions with their own programmes, with the result that meetings, runs and activities are held all over the country. Each year the Club joins with the London Douglas Club for a gymkhana and concours at Bicester and has its own rally at Stanford Hall in May. The Annual Dinner and Dance is held each year in October and the Club puts on a display at the BMF Rally and other motorcycle gatherings.

The 1960s have proved even more testing for the Club organisation as more and more dealers gave up stocking Rudge spares. The final blow came when Godfreys Ltd. closed their Great Portland Street showroom and also gave up the production of spares. Through their good offices, however, the Club was able to take over the supply of parts for the benefit of members. This service has been extended with the manufacture of many parts previously not available and prices compare favourably with parts for machines in current production. Although the comprehensive range of parts is mainly for machines manufactured in the 1930s, it has been possible to provide spares for many of the vintage models. With growing successes in the field of sprinting, the production of 'hotter than standard' parts is also receiving attention.

The Club is truly international, with members in many overseas countries and the supply of spares to them is the Club's contribution to the Export Drive. The banking of Dollars, Robles, Marks, Francs, Rupees, Lire, Dinars and other currencies give the treasurer problems not normally met by other Clubs. Parts have been supplied this year to countries as far apart as Sweden and New Zealand, U.S.A. and U.S.S.R. The Spares Secretary is, in fact, getting more and more conversant with Eastern European Customs requirements.

INDEX

FINIS